CATHOLICISM

CATHOLICISM

A Journey to the Heart of the Faith

ROBERT BARRON

IMAGE BOOKS

New York   London   Toronto
Melbourne   Sydney

Published in the United States by Image Books, an imprint of the
Crown Publishing Group, a division of Random House, Inc., New York.
www.crownpublishing.com

IMAGE and the Image colophon are registered trademarks of Random House, Inc.

Library of Congress Cataloging-in-Publication Data
Barron, Robert E., 1959–
Catholicism : a journey to the heart of the faith / Robert Barron. — 1st ed.
Includes index.
1. Catholic Church—Doctrines. I. Title.
BX1751.3.B36 2011
230'.2—dc22
2011003540

ISBN 978-0-307-72051-1
eISBN 978-0-307-72053-5

PRINTED IN THE UNITED STATES OF AMERICA

Book design by Jennifer Daddio / Bookmark Design and Media Inc.
Jacket photograph: Word on Fire
Author photograph: © Word on Fire

5 7 9 10 8 6

First Edition

This book is dedicated to the community of the

Pontifical North American College in Rome,

in whose gracious company it was written.

Contents

Acknowledgments

T his book emerged out of the scripts that I composed for the ten-part documentary film *Catholicism*. The three years of planning, writing, traveling, filming, and editing that went into the production of that series constitute an unforgettable moment in my life. The many, many people who contributed to the film have helped, obviously, to shape the book that you are about to read. I am, from the bottom of my heart, grateful to Father Stephen Grunow, Mike Leonard, Matt Leonard, Nancy Ross, Diane Archibald, Peggy Pandaleon, Robert Mixa, Megan Fleischel, Patrick Thornton, Steve Mullen, Nanette Noffsinger, Brooks Crowell, Rozann Carter, Father Paul Murray, Dr. Denis McNamara, and John Cummings. I am also deeply indebted to my editor, Gary Jansen, who read the manuscript with great care and whose suggestions have resulted in a better book.

CATHOLICISM

THE

CATHOLIC THING

What is the Catholic thing? What makes Catholicism, among all of the competing philosophies, ideologies, and religions of the world, distinctive? I stand with Blessed John Henry Newman who said that *the* great principle of Catholicism is the Incarnation, the enfleshment of God. What do I mean by this? I mean, *the Word of God*—the mind by which the whole universe came to be—did not remain sequestered in heaven but rather entered into this ordinary world of bodies, this grubby arena of history, this compromised and tear-stained human condition of ours. "The Word became flesh and made his dwelling among us" (Jn 1:14): that is the Catholic thing.

The Incarnation tells central truths concerning both God and us. If God became human without ceasing to be God and without compromising the integrity of the creature that he became, God must not be a competitor with his creation. In many of the ancient myths and legends, divine figures such as Zeus or Dionysus enter into human affairs only through aggression, destroying or wounding that which they invade. And in many of the philosophies of modernity God is construed as a threat to human well-being. In their own ways, Marx, Freud, Feuerbach, and Sartre all maintain that God must be eliminated if humans are to be fully themselves. But there is none of this in the Christian doctrine of the Incarnation. The Word does indeed become human, but nothing of the human is destroyed in the process; God does indeed enter into his creation, but the world is thereby enhanced and elevated. The God capable of incarnation is not a competitive supreme being but rather, in the words of Saint Thomas Aquinas, the sheer act of being itself, that which grounds and sustains all of creation, the way a singer sustains a song.

And the Incarnation tells us the most important truth about ourselves: we are destined for divinization. The church fathers never tired of repeating this phrase as a sort of summary of Christian belief: *Deus fit homo ut homo fieret Deus* (God became human so that humans might become God). God condescended to enter into flesh so that our flesh might partake of the divine life, that we might participate in the love that holds the Father, Son, and Holy Spirit in communion. And this is why Christianity is the greatest humanism that has ever appeared, indeed

Christ Pantocrator, Hagia Sophia, Istanbul. WORD ON FIRE

that *could* ever appear. No philosophical or political or religious program in history—neither Greek nor Renaissance nor Marxist humanism—has ever made a claim about human destiny as extravagant as Christianity's. We are called not simply to moral perfection or artistic self-expression or economic liberation but to what the Eastern fathers called *theiosis,* transformation into God.

I realize that an objection might be forming in your mind. Certainly the doctrine of the Incarnation separates Christianity from the other great world religions, but how does it distinguish Catholicism from the other Christian churches? Don't Protestants and the Orthodox hold just as firmly to the conviction that the Word became flesh? They do indeed, but they don't, I would argue, embrace the doctrine in its fullness. They don't see all the way to the bottom of it or draw out all of its implications. Essential to the Catholic mind is what I would characterize as a keen sense of the prolongation of the Incarnation throughout space and time, an extension that is made possible through the mystery of the church. Catholics see God's continued enfleshment in the oil, water, bread, imposed hands, wine, and salt of the sacraments; they appreciate it in the gestures, movements, incensations, and songs of the Liturgy; they savor it in the texts, arguments, and debates of the theologians; they sense it in the graced governance of popes and bishops; they love it in the struggles and missions of the saints; they know it in the writings of Catholic poets and in the cathedrals crafted by Catholic architects, artists, and workers. In short, all of this discloses to the Catholic eye and mind the ongoing presence of the Word made flesh, namely Christ.

Newman said that a complex idea is equivalent to the sum total of its possible aspects. This means, he saw, that ideas are only really known across great stretches of space and time, with the gradual unfolding of their many dimensions and profiles. The Incarnation is one of the richest and most complex ideas ever proposed to the mind, and hence it demands the space and time of the church in order fully to disclose itself. This is why, in order to grasp it fully, we have to read the Gospels, the Epistles of Paul, the *Confessions* of Saint Augustine, the *Summa theo-*

Church of the Holy Sepulchre, detail, Jerusalem.
DENIS R. MCNAMARA

logiae of Thomas Aquinas, *The Divine Comedy* of Dante, Saint John of
the Cross's *Ascent of Mount Carmel, The Story of a Soul* of Thérèse of
Lisieux, among many other master texts. But we also have to *look and
listen.* We must consult the Cathedral of Chartres, the Sainte-Chapelle,
the Arena Chapel, the Sistine Chapel ceiling, Bernini's *Ecstasy of Saint
Teresa,* the Church of the Holy Sepulchre, Grünewald's Crucifixion in
the *Isenheim Altarpiece,* the soaring melodies of Gregorian chant, the
Masses of Mozart, and the motets of Palestrina. Catholicism is a matter
of the body and the senses as much as it is a matter of the mind and the
soul, precisely because the Word became *flesh.*

What I propose to do in this book is to take you on a guided exploration of the Catholic world, but not in the manner of a docent, for I am
not interested in showing you the artifacts of Catholicism as though they
were dusty objets d'art in a museum of culture. I want to function rather
as a mystagogue, conducting you ever deeper into the mystery of the In-

carnation in the hopes that you might be transformed by its power. I stand with the theologian Hans Urs von Balthasar, who held that the truth of Catholicism is best appreciated from within the confines of the church, just as the windows of a cathedral, drab enough when seen from the outside, shine in all of their splendor when viewed from the inside. I want to take you deep within the cathedral of Catholicism, because I'm convinced that the experience will change and enhance your life.

Catholicism is a celebration, in words and imagery, of the God who takes infinite delight in bringing human beings to fullness of life.

I shall commence with Jesus, for he is the constant point of reference, the beginning and the end of the Catholic faith. I will try to show the uniqueness of Jesus, how his claim to speak and act in the very person of God sets him apart from all other philosophers, mystics, and religious founders. And I will demonstrate how his resurrection from the dead not only ratifies his divine identity but also establishes him as the

St. Joseph Cathedral, detail, Wheeling, West Virginia. DENIS R. MCNAMARA

Lord of the nations, the one to whom final allegiance is due. Next I shall explore the extraordinary teachings of Jesus, words at once simple and textured, that have, quite literally, changed the world. I will try to show how they constitute *the* path to joy.

Saint Paul referred to Jesus as "the icon of the invisible God." By this he meant that Jesus is the sacramental sign of God, the privileged way of *seeing* what God looks like. And thus we will look at God—his existence, his creativity, his providence, his Triune nature—through the lens of the Word made flesh. Next I will turn to Mary, the vessel through whom God came into the world. I will stress that Mary is the summation of Israel, the one who gives full voice to the longing of her people for God, the one who is, hence, the prototype of the church, the new Israel. Jesus's closing words to his disciples were an exhortation to go out to all the nations and tell the good news. Peter and Paul were the indispensable players in the early church, for they embodied this missionary spirit. I will show that these very particular first-century men are also determining archetypes in the life of the missionary church to the present day.

Paul consistently proclaimed that the church of Jesus Christ is not so much an organization as an organism, a mystical body. I will present the church accordingly as a living thing, whose purpose is to gather the whole world into the praise of God. And the central act of the church, its "source and summit" in the words of Vatican II, is the Liturgy, the ritualized praise of God. I will therefore walk through the gestures, songs, movements, and theology of the Liturgy. The entire purpose of the Liturgy and the church is to make saints, to make people holy. This is why Catholicism takes the saints, in all their wild diversity, with such seriousness and why it presents them to us with such enthusiasm. And so I will devote a chapter to painting small portraits of four friends of God in order to show what life in Christ concretely looks like. Holy people raise their minds and hearts to God; they seek passionate communion with their Creator; they pray. I will turn next, therefore, to prayer, and I will focus on certain very definite persons—Thomas Merton, Saint John of the Cross, and Saint Teresa of Avila—who give concrete expression to the mystical path. Finally, I shall consider the last things: hell, purgatory, and heaven. God wants intimate friendship with us, but friendship is always a function of freedom. How we ultimately respond to the divine love—the sun that shines on the good and the bad alike—makes all the difference.

I trust you will find that I have not written a plodding theological study, for this book is chockablock with stories, biographies, and images: Cardinal Francis George musing on the loggia of St. Peter's after the election of Benedict XVI, Saint Thérèse of Lisieux's "little way," the candlelit procession at Lourdes, Edith Stein's journey to Auschwitz, Irish penitents at Lough Derg, pilgrims proceeding on their knees to venerate the Virgin of Guadalupe, Mother Teresa picking up the dying off the squalid streets of Calcutta, Karol Wojtyla hunkering down in the underground seminary during the Nazi occupation, the prodigal son gathered into his father's embrace, Paul imprisoned in Philippi, Peter crucified on the Vatican Hill, Angelo Roncalli's "flourishing garden of life," and many more. But since the Catholic tradition is smart, this book also contains theological arguments, sometimes of a technical nature. Again, I hear almost every day from atheists who write off religion as primitive, premodern nonsense.

Sainte-Chapelle, interior, Paris. WORD ON FIRE

Epiphany of the Lord, Chora Church, Istanbul. WORD ON FIRE

even the most skeptical person is changed simply for having heard this message. Christian believers up and down the years are those who have laughed with delight at this sacred joke and have never tired of hearing it repeated, whether it is told in the sermons of Augustine, the arguments of Aquinas, the frescoes of Michelangelo, the stained glass of Chartres, the mystical poetry of Teresa of Avila, or the little way of Thérèse of Lisieux. It has been suggested that the heart of sin is taking oneself too seriously. Perhaps this is why God chose to save us by making us laugh.

One of the most important things to understand about Christianity is that it is not primarily a philosophy or a system of ethics or a religious ideology. It is a relationship to the unsettling person of Jesus Christ, to the God-man. Some*one* stands at the center of Christian concern. Though Christian thinkers have used philosophical ideas and cultural constructs to articulate the meaning of the faith—sometimes in marvelously elaborate ways—they never, at their best, wander far from the very particular and unnerving first-century rabbi from Nazareth. But who precisely was he? We know next to nothing about the first thirty years of Jesus's life. Though people have speculated wildly about these hidden years—that he traveled to India to learn the wisdom of the Buddha, that he sojourned in Egypt where he became adept at healing, and so forth—no reliable information concerning Jesus's youth and young manhood exists, except perhaps the tantalizing story in Luke's Gospel about the finding of Jesus in the temple. Since Joseph, the husband of Mary, Jesus's mother, is described as a carpenter, we can safely assume that Jesus apprenticed to the carpentry trade while growing up. As far as we can determine, Jesus was not formally trained in a rabbinic school, nor was he educated to be a temple priest or a scribe, nor was he a devotee of the Pharisees, the Sadducees, or the Essenes—all recognized religious parties with particular convictions, practices, and doctrinal proclivities. He was, if I can use a somewhat anachronistic term, a layman.

And this made his arrival on the public scene all the more astounding. For this Nazarene carpenter, with no formal religious education or affiliation, began to speak and act with an unprecedented authority. To the crowds who listened to him preach, he blithely declared, "You have heard that it was said . . . but I say . . ." (Mt 5:21–48). He was referring, of course, to the Torah, the teaching of Moses, the court of final appeal to any faithful rabbi; therefore he was claiming for himself an authority greater than that of Israel's most significant teacher and lawgiver. To a

Caesarea-Philippi, modern-day Banias, Israel. WORD ON FIRE

paralyzed man, he says, "Courage, child, your sins are forgiven" (Mt 9:2). Grasping the outrageousness of this assertion, the bystanders remark to themselves, "This man is blaspheming" (Mt 2:3). Moreover, Jesus demonstrated a mastery over the very forces of nature. He tamed the storm that threatened to swamp his disciples' boat; he rebuked the dark powers; he opened deaf ears and brought vision back to sightless eyes; he not only pardoned the paralyzed man's sins—he took away his paralysis; he even raised the daughter of Jairus back to life. All of this made Jesus a figure of utter fascination. Again and again we hear in the Gospels how word of him spread throughout the country and how the crowds kept coming at him from all sides: "and on finding him [the disciples] said, 'Everyone is looking for you'" (Mk 1:37). Why were they drawn to him? Some undoubtedly wanted to witness or benefit from his supernatural power; others wanted to hear the words of an unsurpassably charismatic rabbi; still others simply wanted to commune with a celebrity. But I think it's fair to assume that all of them were wondering just who this man was.

Midway through his public ministry, Jesus ventured with his disciples to the northern reaches of the Promised Land, to the region of Caesarea-Philippi, near the present-day Golan Heights, and there he posed just that question: "Who do people say that I am?" (Mk 8:27). We're so accustomed to hearing this question in the Gospels that we've lost a sense of its peculiarity. He didn't ask them what people thought about his teaching or what impression he was making or how the crowds were interpreting his actions—reasonable enough questions. He wanted to know what they thought about his identity, his being. And this question—reiterated by Christian theologians through the centuries—sets Jesus off from all of the other great religious founders. The Buddha actively discouraged his followers from focusing on his person, urging them instead to walk the spiritual way from which he himself had benefited. Mohammed was an ordinary man who claimed to have received Allah's definitive revelation. He would never have dreamed of drawing attention to his own person; rather he wanted the world to read and abide by the Koran, which had been given to him. Confucius was a moral philosopher who, with particular acuity, formulated a series of ethical recommendations that constituted a balanced way of being in the world. The structure of his being was never a matter of concern either to him or to his followers.

And then there is Jesus. Though he did indeed formulate moral instructions and though he certainly taught with enormous enthusiasm, Jesus did not draw his followers' attention primarily to his words. He drew it to himself. John the Baptist instructed two of his disciples to follow after Jesus. They asked the Lord, "Where are you staying?" (Jn 1:38) and he said, "Come, and you will see" (Jn 1:39). That simple exchange is enormously instructive, for it shows that intimacy with Jesus—staying with him—is what Christian discipleship is fundamentally about. This preoccupation with Jesus himself followed, as I've been hinting, from the startling fact that he consistently spoke and acted in the very person of God. "Heaven and earth will pass away, but my words will not pass away" (Mt 24:35). Sane philosophers and scholars invariably emphasize the provisional nature of what they write, but Jesus claims that his words will last longer than creation itself. Who could reasonably make this assertion except the one who is the Word through which all things came to be? "Whoever loves father or mother more than me is not worthy of me" (Mt 10:37). We could easily imagine a prophet, teacher, or religious founder saying, "You should love God more than your very life," or at the limit, "You ought to love my teaching more than your mother and father," but "unless you love *me*"? It has been said that the healthiest spiritual people are those who have the strongest sense of the difference between themselves and God. Therefore who could sanely and responsibly make the claim that Jesus made except the one who is, in his own person, the highest good?

Now, the possibility remains that Jesus might have been a madman, a deluded fanatic. After all, mental health facilities are filled with people who think they are God. And this is precisely what some of Jesus's contemporaries thought: "For this reason the Jews tried all the more to kill him; because . . . he . . . called God his own father, making himself equal to God" (Jn 5:18). What is ruled out—and C. S. Lewis saw this with particular clarity—is the bland middle position taken by many theologians and religious seekers today, namely that Jesus wasn't divine but was indeed an inspiring ethical teacher, a great religious philosopher. Yet a close reading of the Gospel witness does not bear such an interpretation. Given that he repeatedly spoke and acted in the person of God, either he was who he said he was and purported to be, or he was a bad man. And this is precisely why Jesus compels a choice the way no other religious founder does. As he himself said, "Whoever is not with me is against me" (Lk 11:23), and "Whoever does not gather with me scatters" (Lk 11:23). I realize how dramatically this runs counter to our sensibilities, but Christian evangelization consists in the forcing of that choice.

There is a strange passage in the tenth chapter of Mark's Gospel that is rarely commented upon but that is, in its peculiarity, very telling. Jesus is in the company of his disciples, and they are making their way from Galilee in the north to Judea in the south. Mark reports: "They were on the way, going up to Jerusalem, and Jesus went ahead of them. They were

Sea of Galilee. WORD ON FIRE

amazed, and those who followed were afraid" (Mk 10:32). They were simply walking along the road with Jesus, and they found him overwhelming
and frightening. Why they should have had such a response remains in-
explicable until we remember that awe and fear are, in the Old Testament
tradition, two standard reactions to God. The twentieth-century philosopher of religion Rudolf Otto famously characterized the transcendent
God as the *mysterium tremendum et fascinans,* the mystery that fascinates
us even as it causes us to tremble with fear—in whose presence we are
amazed and afraid. In his sly, understated way, Mark is telling us that this
Jesus is also the God of Israel.

Once we grasp that Jesus was no ordinary teacher and healer but Yahweh moving among his people, we can begin to understand his words and
actions more clearly. If we survey the texts of the Old Testament—and
the first Christians relentlessly read Jesus in light of these writings—we
see that Yahweh was expected to do four great things. He would gather
the scattered tribes of Israel; he would cleanse the Temple of Jerusalem;
he would definitively deal with the enemies of the nation; and, finally,
he would reign as Lord of heaven and earth. The eschatological hope
expressed especially in the prophets and the Psalms was that through
these actions, Yahweh would purify Israel and through the purified Israel
bring salvation to all. What startled the first followers of Jesus was that he
accomplished these four tasks but in the most unexpected way.

When Jesus first emerged, preaching in the villages surrounding the
Sea of Galilee, he had a simple message: "The kingdom of God is at
hand. Repent, and believe in the Gospel" (Mk 1:15). Oceans of ink have
been spilled over the centuries in an attempt to explain the meaning of
"Kingdom of God," but it might be useful to inquire what Jesus's first
audience understood by that term. N. T. Wright argues that they would
have heard, "the tribes are being gathered." According to the basic narrative of the Old Testament, God's answer to human dysfunction was the
formation of a people after his own heart. Yahweh chose Abraham and
his descendants to be "peculiarly his own," and he shaped them by the
divine law to be a priestly nation. God's intention was that a unified and

spiritually vibrant Israel would function as a magnet for the rest of humanity, drawing everyone to God by the sheer attractive quality of their way of being. The prophet Isaiah expressed this hope when he imagined Mount Zion, raised high above all of the mountains of the world, as the gathering point for "all the tribes of the earth." But the tragedy was that more often than not Israel was unfaithful to its calling and became therefore a scattered nation. One of the typical biblical names for the devil is *ho diabalos,* derived from the term *diabalein* (to throw apart). If God is a great gathering force, then sin is a scattering power. This dividing of Israel came to fullest expression in the eighth century BC, when many of the northern tribes were carried off by the invading Assyrians, and even more so in the devastating exile of the sixth century BC when the Babylonians destroyed Jerusalem and carried many of the southern tribes away. A scattered, divided Israel could never live up to its vocation, but the prophets continued to dream and hope. Ezekiel spoke of Israel as sheep wandering aimlessly on the hillside, but then he prophesied that one day Yahweh himself would come and gather in his people.

Now we can begin to understand the behavior of the one who called himself "the good shepherd" (Jn 10:11). As so many contemporary scholars have emphasized, Jesus practiced open table fellowship, serving as host for many who would normally be excluded from polite society: the public sinner, the prostitute, the handicapped, the tax collector. At the very place where, in his time as well as ours, the stratifications and divisions of society were often on clearest display, he was making possible a new kind of social space, one marked by compassion and forgiveness. It is important to note that he was not simply exemplifying the generic virtue of "inclusivity" so valued today; he was acting in the very person of Yahweh gathering in his scattered children. This helps to explain why he healed so many. In the society of Jesus's time, physical illness was typically construed as a curse, and in many cases sickness or deformity prevented one from participating fully in the life of the community, especially in common worship. Curing the blind, the deaf, the lame, and the leprous, Jesus was Yahweh binding up the wounds of his people and restoring them to communion. A particularly good example of this work is Jesus's healing of a woman who had for many years been bent over at the waist. Jesus restored her to health in the physical sense, but he also thereby permitted her to assume once more the correct attitude of praise.

Jesus turned upside down many of the social conventions of his time and place precisely because he was so concerned to place the instantiation of the Kingdom of God first in the minds of his followers. Among first-century Jews, the family was of paramount social and cultural importance. One's existence was largely defined by one's tribal affiliations and familial obligations. An enthusiastic disciple of Jesus took this for granted when she shouted out, "Blessed is the womb that carried you and the breasts at which you nursed" (Lk 11:27). But Jesus dramatically relativized the family in responding, "Rather, blessed are those who hear the word of God and observe it" (Lk 11:28). Another time, a prospective disciple said that he was willing to follow Jesus but first begged permission to bury his father. In that time, as in ours, it would be hard to imagine a more pressing familial duty than attending the funeral of one's own father. Surely such an obligation would justify a slight delay in giving oneself to the work of the Kingdom. But Jesus, having none of it, responded in a manner that undoubtedly scandalized him: "Let the dead bury their dead" (Lk 9:60). Once again, he was not being gratuitously insensitive to a grieving son; he was insisting that the in-gathering of the tribes into God's family is of paramount importance. He makes much the same point in one of the most puzzling scenes recorded in the Gospel. "Do you think that I have come to bring peace upon the earth? I have come to bring not peace but the sword. For I have come to set a man 'against his father, a daughter against her mother, and a daughter-in-law against her mother-in-law'" (Mt 10:34–36). He would break up even the most revered social and religious system if it took precedence over the new community of the Kingdom. Indeed, when we give the family a disproportionate importance it becomes in short order dysfunctional, as is evidenced in the fact that much violent crime, even to this day, takes place within families.

In first-century Palestine men did not speak to women publicly, Jews didn't associate with Samaritans, and righteous people had nothing to do with sinners. But Jesus spoke openly and respectfully to the woman at the well, who, as a woman, a Samaritan, and a public sinner, was triply objectionable. Even if we delight in fashioning structures of domination and exclusion, the in-gathering Yahweh plays by an entirely different set of rules. Jesus asked the Samaritan woman to give him something to drink. Saint Augustine's magnificent commentary: he was thirsting for her faith. A pious Jew of that time would have been rendered ritually unclean by touching a dead body, but Jesus readily touched the dead body of the daughter of Jairus in order to raise her back to life. All of the rituals, liturgies, and practices of the Jews, he was insinuating, are subordinate to and in service of the great task of bringing Israel back to life. How wonderful that the Gospel writers preserve Jesus's Aramaic in their account of this episode: "*Talitha koum,*'" which means, "'Little girl, I say to you, arise!'" (Mk 5:41). It is Yahweh speaking these intimate words to his people who had fallen into spiritual death. Again and again

Apostles, Notre Dame, Paris. DENIS R. MCNAMARA

Jesus is portrayed as violating the sacred command to rest on the seventh day. His disciples pick grain on the Sabbath, and many times he cures on the Sabbath, much to the dismay of the protectors of the Jewish law. When challenged he declared himself Lord of the Sabbath (still another breathtaking claim for a Jew to make, since Yahweh himself held that title), and he clarified that the Sabbath was made for man and not man for the Sabbath. In short, he claimed the properly divine prerogative of relativizing the significance of perhaps the defining practice of pious Jews and placing it in subordination to the Kingdom of God.

One of the facts that even the most skeptical of New Testament scholars affirm is that Jesus chose twelve men as his intimate disciples. The number was hardly accidental. He was forming around his own person a kind of microcosm of the gathered Israel, all twelve tribes joined in prayer and common purpose. And this core group he sent out to proclaim and further instantiate the Kingdom: "As you go, make this proclamation: 'The kingdom of heaven is at hand.' Cure the sick, raise the dead, cleanse lepers, drive out demons" (Mt 10:7–8). Upon returning from their mission, they exulted, "Lord, even the evil spirits are subject to us because of your name" (Lk 10:17). In time, he commissioned a further seventy-two (six times twelve) to preach, heal, and gather in. He encouraged this group to travel light and to do their work while relying utterly on God's providence. These first apostles and missionaries were the new Israel and hence constituted the core of what would become the church, which still has the mission of drawing the tribes into the community of Jesus.

According to the Synoptic Gospels, Jesus came, at the climax of his ministry, to Jerusalem and entered the Temple precincts. Taking a "whip of cords," he drove the money changers out and turned over their tables, announcing, "Is it not written: 'My house shall be called a house of prayer for all peoples'? But you have made it a den of thieves" (Mk 11:17). By Saint John's telling, Jesus, upon being asked for a sign to justify this outrageous act, calmly stated, "Destroy this temple and in three days I will raise it up" (Jn 2:19). To perform such an act and to say such things in the Jerusalem Temple was to be massively, even unsurpassably, offensive to

Herod's Temple, model. DENIS R. MCNAMARA

Jews of that time. The Temple was everything to a first-century Israelite. It was the center of his political, cultural, and religious life; even more, it was appreciated literally as the dwelling place of God on earth. To get a sense of what Jesus's provocative action might mean in an American context, we'd have to imagine the violation of some combination of the National Cathedral, the Lincoln Center, and the White House. Or perhaps we could evoke the texture of it more adequately if we compared it, in a Catholic context, to the desecration of St. Peter's Basilica in Rome. Jesus's cleansing of the Temple most likely led directly to his crucifixion, for this action not only offended Jews but also alarmed the Romans, who were acutely sensitive to civil disturbances in and around the Temple. What in the world was Jesus doing, and what precisely did he mean when he spoke of tearing down the Temple and raising it up again? In order to answer these questions, we have to step back from this scene and examine the mystery of the Temple.

We have to go back to the very beginning, to the Genesis account of Adam and the garden. The ancient rabbinic interpreters appreciated the first human being as the prototypical priest and the Garden of Eden as the primordial temple. In fact, the same Hebrew term is used to designate Adam's cultivation of the soil and, much later in the biblical narrative, the priest's activity within the Jerusalem Temple. Adam, we hear, walked in easy fellowship with God in the cool of the evening and spoke to him as to a friend. This ordering of Adam to God meant that our first parent was effortlessly caught up in adoration. The term "adoration" comes from the Latin *adoratio,* which in turn is derived from "ad ora" (to the mouth). To adore, therefore, is to be mouth to mouth with God, properly aligned to the divine source, breathing in God's life. When one is in the stance of adoration, the whole of one's life—mind, will, emotions, imagination, sexuality—becomes ordered and harmonized, much as the elements of a rose window arrange themselves musically around a central point. The beautiful garden in which the first priest lived is symbolic of the personal, and, indeed, cosmic order that follows from adoration. This is why, by the biblical telling, orthodoxy, literally "right praise," is consistently defended as the key to flourishing and why idolatry, incorrect worship, is always characterized as the prime source of mischief and disharmony. The worship of false gods—putting something other than the true God at the center of one's concern—conduces to the disintegration of the self and the society. Another way to formulate this idea is to say that we become what we worship. When the true God is our ultimate concern, we become conformed to him; we become his sons and daughters. When we worship money, we become money men; when we worship power, we become power brokers; when we worship popularity, we become popular men, and so on. How trenchantly the psalmist, speaking of carved idols and idolators, spoke this truth: "They have mouths but do not speak, eyes but do not see. They have ears but do not hear, noses but do not smell. They have hands but do not feel, feet but do not walk, and no sound rises from their throats. Their makers shall be like them, all who trust in them" (Ps 115:5–8).

I mentioned previously that God's rescue operation required the formation of a people, and now we see why that people was marked, according to the book of Exodus, as "priestly." The people Israel were shaped primarily according to the laws of right worship and derivatively by the laws of right behavior so that they could model to the nations how to praise and how to act. Some readers of Exodus and Leviticus appreciate the ethical teachings found in those books but puzzle over the lengthy excurses into the arcana of ritual and Temple practice that they find there. This is to get things backward from a biblical perspective, for right belief is the necessary condition for right action, not the other way round. Once we know whom to worship, we then know what to do. At the heart of Jewish right praise was the formal and explicit worship of God, first in the desert tabernacle during the Exodus, then in provisional centers of worship in Hebron and Shiloh as the Israelites established themselves in the Promised Land, and finally in the great Jerusalem Temple constructed by David's son Solomon. When Isaiah dreamed of all the tribes of the world streaming to Mount Zion, he was thinking primarily of Mount Zion as the locale of the Temple. His hope was that the orthodoxy of Israel would prove compelling to the rest of the nations so that, in time, all the people of the world would come to the Temple, the proper place of praise. The Jerusalem Temple was constructed so as to be evocative of the Garden of Eden. It was covered inside and out with symbols of the cosmos—planets, stars, plants, animals, and so forth—because, as we have seen, the ultimate purpose of right praise was to order the universe itself. Furthermore, the curtain that shielded the holy of holies was woven of fabrics dyed in four colors—purple for the sea, blue for the sky, green for the earth, and red for fire—for it represented the totality of the material realm that the immaterial God had made. In its temple worship, Israel saw itself as carrying forward Adam's priestly vocation to "Eden-ize" the whole of culture and the whole of nature.

Now all of this was true in principle, but throughout its history Israel fell into the worship of false gods, sometimes the deities of the surrounding nations, but other times the gods of wealth, power, nationalism, and pleasure. When we read the great prophets, from Hosea and Amos through Isaiah, Jeremiah, and Ezekiel, we hear, again and again, the summons back to righteousness and away from idols and wicked deeds: "How has she turned adulteress, the faithful city, so upright! Justice used to lodge within her, but now, murderers. . . . Your princes are rebels and comrades of thieves. . . . The fatherless they defend not, and the widow's plea does not reach them" (Is 1:21–23); "But my people have changed their glory for useless things . . . Two evils have my people done: they have forsaken me, the source of living waters; They have dug themselves cisterns, broken cisterns, that hold no water" (Jer 2:11–13); and "[My people] consult their piece of wood, and their [divining rod] makes pronouncements for them . . . they commit harlotry, forsaking their God" (Hos 4:12). For the prophets, the symbolic focus for this wickedness was the corruption of the Jerusalem Temple, the devolution of the place of right praise into a place of idol worship. Isaiah expresses this by imagining God himself as disgusted with the sacrifices of the Temple: "I have had enough of whole-burnt rams and fat of fatlings; In the blood of calves, lambs and goats, I find no pleasure . . . When you spread out your hands, I close my eyes to you" (Is 1:11–15). But Ezekiel envisions it even more dramatically, imagining that, because of Israel's corrupt worship, the glory of Yahweh has abandoned the Temple, forsaking its customary earthly dwelling place. However, he prophesies that one day Yahweh himself will return to the Temple and cleanse it of its impurities, and on

Crucifix, Church of the Gesù, Rome. WORD ON FIRE

that day water will flow forth from the side of the Temple for the renewal of the earth. This is, once again, the Edenic vocation of Israel.

Against this complex background of Temple theology and prophetic expectation, we can understand many of Jesus's words and actions much more clearly. On one occasion Jesus said in reference to himself, "I say to you, something greater than the temple is here" (Mt 12:6). This was, of course, still another example of Jesus's outrageousness, for the only reality that could possibly be construed by a first-century Jewish audience as greater than the Temple would be Yahweh himself. But this statement also serves as a particularly helpful interpretive lens for Jesus's ministry. One would have come to the Temple for instruction in the Torah, for the healing of disease, and for the forgiveness of sin through sacrifice. If Jesus is, in his own person, the true Temple, then he should be the definitive source of teaching, healing, and forgiveness, and this is just what the Gospels tell us. The enormous crowds gather on a Galilean hillside or on the seashore or even in the Temple precincts, but not to listen to the official scholars of the law. Rather they soak in Jesus's teaching. The woman with the hemorrhage, the man born blind, the man with the shriveled hand, blind Bartimaeus—all find healing, not from the Temple priests, but from Jesus, the one greater than the Temple. And the woman caught in adultery, the woman at the well, Mary Madgalene, and Matthew the tax collector all find the divine forgiveness, but not through Temple sacrifice. They experience it through Jesus. He was not so much eliminating the Temple as redefining it, indeed relocating it, in relation to his own person.

It is fascinating in this context to consider the baptizing ministry of Jesus's forerunner, John the Baptist. When a worshiper entered the Jerusalem Temple to offer sacrifice or to pray, he would cleanse himself in a ritual bath called a "mikvah." John, who was the son of a Temple priest and hence knew this ritual well, was offering a new mikvah, a cleansing in the Jordan, in preparation for a new priest, a new temple, a new sacrifice. When he spied Jesus, John said, "Behold, the Lamb of God, who takes away the sin of the world" (Jn 1:29). That, of course, was Temple language, designating the lamb that would be ritually sacrificed so as to affect forgiveness. John was telling those who had received his cleansing bath that the true Lamb had arrived.

Now we are ready to understand more adequately what Jesus was doing on the Temple Mount as he turned over the tables and announced the destruction of the Temple. He was not simply a 1960s-style radical, protesting against the political and religious establishment. He was re-iterating the prophetic judgments of Isaiah and Ezekiel against the corruption of Israelite worship; but even more than this, he was acting in the very person of Yahweh who had come to cleanse his temple and to make it a place of true *adoratio*. Even the most vociferous of the prophets wanted only to reform the Temple, but Jesus declared that he would tear it down—and then re-establish it in his own body: "in three days I will

Church of the Nativity, interior, Bethlehem.
DENIS R. MCNAMARA

raise it up" (Jn 2:19). In these words he was drawing out the logical implication of his earlier statement "something greater than the temple is here"
(Mt 12:6), telling the people that the entire purpose of the earlier temple
would be transfigured in him, transposed, as it were, into a new key. He
himself would be the place where faithful Israel and faithful Yahweh
would come together. This outrageous claim would be ratified, of course,
in the resurrection of Jesus from the dead, but also, more indirectly, in a
curious event just after the death of Jesus. We are told in John's Gospel
that a Roman soldier, in order to verify that Jesus was dead, thrust a
lance into the side of the crucified Christ, "and immediately blood and
water flowed out" (Jn 19:34). Physicians tell us that this is a credible account, given that the lance would have pierced the pericardium, the sac
around the heart, which contains a watery substance; theologians have
speculated that the blood and water have a symbolic valence, evoking the
sacraments of Eucharist and Baptism. But which first-century Jew would
have missed the most obvious interpretation: this was the fulfillment of
Ezekiel's prophecy that when Yahweh cleansed his temple, water would
flow forth for the renewal of the world?

Therefore Jesus gathered the tribes and he cleansed the Temple. But
if Jesus truly is Yahweh moving among his people, we should also expect
him to fight. As we have seen, one of the eschatological hopes of ancient
Israel was that God would definitively deal with the enemies of the nation. That in the course of its history Israel had been enslaved by the
Egyptians, harassed by the Philistines and Amalekites, overrun by the
Assyrians, exiled by the Babylonians, and dominated by the Greeks and
Romans was not simply a political or military problem; it was a profoundly theological problem. If Israel was God's chosen people, meant
magnetically to attract all the peoples of the world to true worship, then
its subjugation was anomalous, puzzling, and frustrating. Had the people
of Israel misunderstood the divine promise? Was God not truly faithful? Therefore the prophets longed for the day when Israel's God, who
had fought mightily for his people against Pharaoh and upon their entry
into the Promised Land, would finally settle accounts with the Gentiles.

Isaiah expressed the hope this way: "The Lord has bared his holy arm in the sight of all the nations; All the ends of the earth will behold the salvation of our God" (Is 52:10). The uncovering of the arm of the Lord means the full display of his conquering power. A clear teaching of the Gospels is that Jesus was this divine fighter, but what a strange and surprising warrior he was.

The first glimpse of Jesus the warrior is at Bethlehem of Judea, the little town outside of Jerusalem, where Israel's greatest fighter, King David, was born. The Christmas stories in the Gospels are not charming children's tales, for they are full of the motifs of opposition and confrontation. C. S. Lewis, who saw these themes very clearly, asked, "Why did God enter into our human condition so quietly, as a baby born in obscurity?" His answer: "because he had to slip clandestinely, behind enemy lines."

Angels, Orvieto Cathedral, Umbria, Italy. WORD ON FIRE

Let us turn to Luke's familiar telling of the story. The narrative commences as one would expect poems and histories in the ancient world to commence, namely with the invocation of powerful and important people: "In those days a decree went out from Caesar Augustus that the whole world should be enrolled. This was . . . when Quirinius was governor of Syria" (Lk 2:1–2). And these two mighty figures are doing something paradigmatically powerful, for by counting one's people one could tax them more efficiently, draft them into the army more easily, and order them about more completely. But then Luke pulls the rug out from under us, for we promptly learn that the story isn't about Augustus and Quirinius but rather about two nobodies making their way from one forgotten outpost of Augustus's empire to another. And the narrative will unfold as the tale of two emperors—rival claimants to power—the one in Rome and the one born to Mary in Bethlehem. When Mary and Joseph arrived in David's city, there was no room, even at the crude travelers' hostel, and so the child is born in a cave, or as some scholars have recently suggested, the lower level of a dwelling, the humble part of the house where the animals spent the night. Who was the best protected person in the ancient world? It was undoubtedly Caesar Augustus in his palace on the Palatine Hill in Rome. But the true emperor, Luke is telling us, arrives vulnerable and exposed, because the good life is not about the protection of the ego, but rather about the willingness to become open to the other in love. And we hear that the baby king was wrapped up in swaddling clothes. Imagine a newborn infant, too weak even to raise his head, and now picture that child wrapped up from head to toe in swaddling bands. It is an image of consummate weakness. Who was the rangiest and freest person in the ancient world? It was certainly Caesar Augustus, able to exert his will to the farthest reaches of the Mediterranean basin and to the wilds of Britain and Germany. Luke is telling us that true kingship hasn't a thing to do with this sort of worldly dominion, but rather with the willingness to be bound for the sake of the other. The child was then placed in a manger, where the animals eat. Who was the best-fed person in the ancient world? It was Caesar in Rome, who could snap his fingers and taste of any sensual pleasure. But the true emperor, Luke insists, is not the one who feeds himself but who is willing to offer his life as food for the other. At the climax of his life, this child, come of age, would say to his friends, "This is my body, which will be given for you; do this in memory of me" (Lk 22:19).

There is one more telling detail from Luke's infancy narrative to which I would draw attention. We hear that an angel appeared to shepherds keeping night watch over their flocks in the hills around Bethlehem. We shouldn't get romantic or sentimental about angels, for in the biblical accounts the typical reaction to the appearance of an angel is fear. If a reality from a higher dimension suddenly broke into your world, fear would be your immediate and appropriate response. The angel announced the good news of the birth of Jesus and then, Luke informs us, there appeared with the angel an entire *stratias* of angels. That Greek term is often rendered in English as "host," but its most basic sense is "army." Our words "strategy" and "strategic" come from it. Luke is informing us that an army of overwhelmingly frightening realities from heaven

Golgotha Shrine, Church of the Holy Sepulchre, Jerusalem. WORD ON FIRE

have appeared to signal their solidarity with the baby king. Who had the biggest army in the ancient world? Caesar Augustus in Rome, and that is precisely how he was able to dominate that world. Nevertheless, his army is nothing compared to this angelic *stratias* that has lined up behind the new emperor. Remember Isaiah's prophecy that Yahweh would one day bare his mighty arm before all the nations. N. T. Wright has magnificently observed that the prophecy finds its fulfillment in the tiny arm of the baby Jesus coming out of his manger-crib.

The battle that began in Bethlehem, this lining up of two very different personifications of power, would play itself out in the life and ministry of Jesus. John Courtney Murray said that as the Gospels unfold we witness the ever increasing *agon*, or struggle, between Jesus and the powers that oppose him. From the moment of his arrival on the public scene, the demons screamed and the scribes and Pharisees schemed. Many of the major sections of the Gospels end with ominous phrases such as "[the devil] departed from him for a time" (Lk 4:13); and "the chief priests and the Pharisees had given orders that if anyone knew where [Jesus] was, he should inform them, so that they might arrest him" (Jn 11:57); and "So they picked up stones to throw at him" (Jn 8:59). This shouldn't surprise us, for Jesus, God made flesh, entered a world that was distorted by sin, by deep-seated opposition to God. In fact, the very intensity of the divine presence in Jesus disclosed the powers of darkness most completely, just as a particularly intense light casts the deepest shadows. The fight would reach its culmination in Jerusalem, on the top of Mount Zion, where the Davidic warrior would confront definitively the enemies of Israel. The battle would be joined, not on an open field, but on a terrible instrument of torture.

On what we call Palm Sunday, Jesus entered the holy city, hailed as the Son of David, and almost immediately after his arrival he went into the Temple and picked a fight. As we have seen, his provocative action in the Temple was practically guaranteed to arouse the opposition of both the Jewish and the Roman establishment. But as the last week of his life unfolded, Jesus did not contrive to confront these powers in the conventional manner. Rather he allowed them to spend themselves on him; he permitted the darkness of the world to envelop him. In the densely textured passion narratives of the Gospels we see all forms of human dysfunction on display. Jesus was met by betrayal, denial, institutional corruption, violence, stupidity, deep injustice, and incomparable cruelty, but he did not respond in kind. Rather, like the scapegoat, upon whom all the sins of Israel were symbolically placed on the Day of Atonement, Jesus took upon himself the sins of the world. As he hung from the cross, he *became* sin, as Saint Paul would later put it, and bearing the full weight of that disorder he said, "Father, forgive them, they know not what they do" (Lk 23:34). Jesus on the cross drowned all the sins of the world in the infinite ocean of the divine mercy, and that is how he fought. We can see here how important it is to affirm the divinity of Jesus, for if he were only a human being, his death on the cross would be, at best, an inspiring example of dedication and courage. But as the Son of God, Jesus died a death that transfigured the world. The theological tradition has said that God the Father was pleased with this sacrifice of his Son, but we should never interpret this along sadistic lines, as though the Father needed to see the suffering of his Son in order to assuage his infinite anger. The Father loved the willingness of the Son to go to the very limits of godforsakenness—all the way to the bottom of sin—in order to manifest the divine mercy. The Father loved the courage of his Son, the nonviolent warrior.

Jesus claimed divinity, and I've been defending his divine status throughout this chapter, but what finally prevents us from saying that the crucified Jesus wasn't simply a failed revolutionary, an admirable idealist who was, sadly enough, ground under by the wheel of history? What prevents us from taking that route of interpretation is the stubborn and unnerving fact upon which Christian faith is grounded: the resurrection of Jesus from the dead. N. T. Wright has reminded us that from a strictly historical standpoint it is practically impossible to explain the emergence of Christianity as a *messianic* movement apart from the resurrection. In the context of first-century Judaism, the clearest indication possible that someone was not the Messiah would be his death at the hands of Israel's enemies, for, as we have seen, one of the tasks of the Messiah was to battle those enemies successfully and unite the nation. In the year 132, a Jew named Bar Kochba led a revolution against the Romans. Many of his followers proclaimed him the Messiah; they even minted coins stamped with the motto Year One of Bar Kochba. His rebellion was put down, he was executed by the Romans, and precisely no one further entertained the thought that he was the Messiah. Yet the first Christians stubbornly and consistently proclaimed the crucified Jesus as Messiah. Paul refers time and again in his letters to Iesous Christos, which is his Greek rendition of Ieshoua Maschiach (Jesus the Messiah). The first disciples went to the ends of the world and to their deaths declaring the messiahship of Jesus. How can we realistically account for this apart from the actual resurrection of Jesus from the dead?

Far too many contemporary scholars attempt to explain away the resurrection, turning it into a myth, a legend, a symbol, a sign that the cause of Jesus goes on. But this kind of speculation is born in faculty lounges, for few in the first century would have found that kind of talk the least bit convincing. Can you imagine Paul tearing into Corinth or Athens or Philippi with the message that there was an inspiring dead man who symbolized the presence of God? No one would have taken him seriously. Instead what Paul declared in all of those cities was *anastasis* (resurrection). What sent him and his colleagues all over the Mediterranean world (and their energy can be sensed on every page of the New Testament) was the shocking novelty of the resurrection of a dead man through the power of the Holy Spirit.

According to the Gospel accounts, the risen Jesus typically did two things: he showed his wounds and he pronounced a word of peace. The wounds of Jesus are a continual and salutary reminder of our sin. The author of life appeared in our midst and we killed him, and this gives the lie to any attempt at self-justification or exculpation. But the risen Lord never leaves us in guilt; instead, he says, "Peace be with you," the Jewish greeting, Shalom (Jn 20:19). This is the peace that the world cannot give, for it is the shalom that comes from the heart of God. In his letter to the Romans, Paul said, "For I am convinced that neither death, nor life, nor angels, nor principalities, nor present things, nor future things, nor powers, nor height, nor depth, nor any other creature will be able to separate us from the love of God in Christ Jesus our Lord" (Rom 8:38–39). How does Paul know this? He knows it because we killed God, and God returned with forgiving love. He knows it because the enemies of Israel have been defeated.

As we saw, the Old Testament writers anticipated that Yahweh would gather the tribes, cleanse the Temple, fight the final battle, and finally would reign as Lord of all the nations. In the light of the resurrection, the first Christians understood that this great work had been accomplished and that Yahweh would reign precisely in the person of Jesus. And they saw their task as announcing this new state of affairs to the world. That is why Paul darted all over Asia Minor, Cyprus, and Greece, and why he longed to go to Spain, which for a first-century Jew would have meant

Arch of Titus, Rome. WORD ON FIRE

the ends of the earth. If someone today wanted to get a message out far and wide, he would go to New York or Los Angeles or London—centers of culture and communication. Many of the first believers in Jesus—including Peter and Paul—went forth with a similar hope to Rome.

In the Roman Forum stands the Arch of Titus, which was built to commemorate the destruction of Jerusalem by the Romans in AD 70. On the inside of the arch is a depiction of the conquering soldiers carrying the Menorah from the Temple. I believe it is fair to say that the soldiers involved in that conquest, as well as those men who designed the Arch of Titus, undoubtedly thought that this humiliating defeat signaled the end of the Jewish religion and the disappearance of the God of Israel. The supreme irony is that just before the destruction of the Temple, Peter, Paul, and their Christian colleagues arrived in Rome, and in proclaiming the risen Jesus they brought the God of Israel to Rome, and through Rome, to the world. In the letters he wrote to the tiny Christian communities that he had founded Paul often spoke of Iesous Kyrios (Jesus the Lord). This can sound blandly "spiritual" to us, but in Paul's time and place those were fighting words, for a watchword of the era was Kaiser Kyrios (Caesar the Lord). This was the way that one signaled one's uncompromised loyalty to the Roman emperor, one's conviction that Caesar was the one to whom final allegiance was due. The revolutionary message of Paul was that Jesus, the crucified Messiah, was Lord, and not Caesar. Having unpacked that simple phrase, it is easy enough to see now why Paul spent so much time in jail! On the slopes of the Capitoline Hill in Rome, in the second half of the first century, a Christian named Mark had a residence. Mark had been a secretary, translator, and companion to Saint Peter, and around the year 70 Mark composed the first of what came to be called the "Gospels." Here is the opening line of the text: "The beginning of the gospel of Jesus Christ [the Son of God]" (Mk 1:1). Again, this can sound anodyne and harmlessly pious to us, but those too were fighting words. Mark's Greek term, *euanggelion,* which we render as "good news," was a word that was typically used to describe an imperial victory. When the emperor won a battle or quelled a rebellion, he sent evangelists ahead with the good news. Do you see how subversive Mark's words were? He was writing from Rome, from the belly of the beast, from the heart of the empire whose leaders had killed his friends Peter and Paul just a few years before, and he was declaring that the true victory didn't have a thing to do with Caesar, but rather with someone whom Caesar had put to death and whom God raised up.

In April of 2005 the newly elected pope Benedict XVI came onto the front loggia of St. Peter's Basilica to bless the crowds. Gathered around him on the adjoining balconies there appeared all of the cardinals who had just chosen him. The news cameras caught the remarkably pensive expression on the face of Cardinal Francis George of Chicago. When the cardinal returned home, reporters asked him what he was thinking about at that moment. Here is what he said: "I was gazing over toward the Circus Maximus, toward the Palatine Hill where the Roman Emperors once resided and reigned and looked down upon the persecution of Christians, and I thought, 'Where are their successors? Where is the successor of Caesar Augustus? Where is the successor of Marcus Aurelius? And finally, who cares? But if you want to see the successor of Peter, he is right next to me, smiling and waving at the crowds.'"

Jesus Christ is Lord. That means that neither Caesar nor any of his descendants is Lord. Jesus Christ, the God-man risen from the dead, the one who gathered the tribes, cleansed the Temple, and fought with the enemies of the human race—he is the one to whom final allegiance is due. Christians are those who submit to this Lordship.

Chapter 2

HAPPY ARE WE:
THE TEACHINGS OF JESUS

I was at great pains in the first chapter to emphasize the centrality of Jesus's person. Christian faith centers on who Jesus is and not what he said. The great creeds, for example, never mention the words of Jesus, but they are desperately interested in articulating his identity with exactness. Having said this, I would be loath to give the impression that the teachings of Jesus are a matter of indifference to Christians, for nothing could be further from the truth. Once they clearly understood that Jesus was Yahweh moving among his people, that he was, in the language of Saint John, the very Word of God made flesh, the first Christians were keenly interested in remembering, understanding, and propagating Jesus's teaching. And, in fact, wherever they've been heard, the words of Jesus have proved fascinating, disorienting, sometimes confounding, deeply transformative, and always unforgettable. Would the end of slavery have happened without Jesus's command to love one's neighbor as oneself? Would the civil rights movement in the United States have gotten under way without Jesus's teaching about loving one's enemy? Would Gandhi's liberation of India or the collapse of Communism have been possible without Jesus's summons to nonviolence? How many prospective perse-cutors have been brought up short by Jesus's word: "Let the one among you who is without sin be the first to throw a stone at her" (Jn 8:7)? How many, locked in a stance of resentment and wounded pride, have been changed by Jesus's story of the prodigal son? How many social reforms have been prompted by Jesus's devastating line, "whatever you did for one of these least brothers of mine, you did for me" (Mt 25:40)? How many anxious hearts have been calmed by the reminder to "Learn from the way the wild flowers grow. They do not work or spin" (Mt 6:28)?

Jesus himself, though he was consistently reluctant to claim the title

Christ as Teacher, Notre Dame, Paris.
DENIS R. MCNAMARA

of Messiah, readily enough assumed the mantle of prophet, a teacher of the divine truth. The throngs followed him because of his miracles, to be sure; but they also were captivated by the sweet discourse that came from his mouth. That preaching was a paramount aspect of his work is disclosed in one of the commonest refrains in the Gospels: "and Jesus taught the crowds." Scholars speculate today that even during Jesus's lifetime his disciples were memorizing and passing on his sayings. At a particularly difficult point in his ministry, most of Jesus's disciples left him. He turned to his inner circle and plaintively asked, "Do you also want to leave?" (Jn 6:67). Peter, speaking for the whole apostolic company replied, "Master, to whom shall we go? You have the words of eternal life" (Jn 6:68). I cannot imagine a clearer witness to the power of Jesus's speech.

THE BEATITUDES

Certainly the best place to begin in order to understand Jesus's teachings is the Sermon on the Mount, which fills the fifth, sixth, and seventh chapters of Matthew's Gospel, and which most likely summarizes the typical instruction that Jesus gave to his followers. Matthew tells us that Jesus, seeing a large crowd gathering around him, went up a mountain, sat down, and commenced to teach. Within a Jewish context, the reference to a mountain would immediately call to mind Moses, who went up Mount Sinai to receive the Ten Commandments and the Torah from God. Therefore, Jesus is being presented here as the new Moses who will promulgate from this Galilean mountain the definitive law. This interpretation is reinforced by Matthew's description of Jesus's physical attitude, for sitting was the customary posture of the teacher and the lawgiver in the ancient world. I realize that this immediately poses a problem for contemporary readers, who are instinctually put off by a religion that leads with laws, rules, and prohibitions. An Irish wag once summed up the Catholicism that he was taught with this phrase: "In the beginning was the word, and the word was no!" Since the Ten Commandments have been honored mostly in the breach, why should anyone think it a good idea to introduce new and even more stringent laws? But then we attend to the first word out of the mouth of the lawgiver: "Blessed." The Greek term in Matthew's Gospel is *makarios,* which is probably best rendered with the simple word "happy." The law that the new Moses offers is a pattern of life that promises, quite simply, to make us happy. In John's Gospel, Jesus says to his disciples on the eve of his death, as a sort of summation of his preaching, "I have told you this so that my joy might be in you and your joy might be complete" (Jn 15:11). And in Matthew's Gospel, Jesus speaks winsomely of his "yoke" which is, in point of fact, light and easy to bear, precisely because it brings fullness of life.

How can we think together joy and the law, two realities that seem, at first blush, mutually exclusive? We might begin by analyzing the famously slippery idea of freedom. On the more modern reading, freedom is primarily choice and self-determination, the capacity to choose between various options, without any constraint either interior or exterior. That this kind of liberty is reverenced in the modern Western cultures can be seen in the sometimes dismaying range of options available to us

Mount of the Beatitudes Church, Israel. WORD ON FIRE

politically, culturally, and, above all, economically. For those who love freedom as choice, the law is, at best, something grudgingly accepted. For instance, we know that traffic rules are necessary for the relatively good order of our streets, but deep down most of us would prefer not to have them so that we could drive as we please. The same is true in regard to moral restrictions, which are accepted by many as a sort of lesser of two evils: not really desirable in themselves, but necessary for social order. But let us consider another way of construing freedom, one more in line with biblical sensibilities. On this interpretation, freedom is not primarily a choice, but rather the shaping of desire so as to make the achievement of the good first possible and then effortless.

Shakespeare was one of the freest writers in the history of the English language, by which I mean he was able to say anything he wanted to say, to express every shade of thought and nuance of feeling that his wickedly complex dramas called for. He did not achieve this mastery by speaking and writing according to the whim of his choice, but rather through subjecting himself to a whole series of masters, by studying English grammar and syntax, by listening to patterns and rhythms of speech, and by steadily immersing himself in the ocean of English vocabulary. I think it is fair to say that Michael Jordan was the freest person ever to play basketball. Whatever the game demanded—three-point shooting, two-point shooting, defense, driving and dribbling, free throws, dunking the ball—Jordan could do effortlessly. Again, he didn't come to this freedom by choosing to play any way he wanted to play. He listened to an array of coaches, watched hours of film, studied the greatest players, practiced endlessly, learned from his mistakes, and so forth. He mastered the basics. In the cases of both Shakespeare and Jordan, law was not the enemy of freedom but precisely the condition for its possibility. What is joy but the experience of having attained the true good? Therefore in this more biblical way of looking at things joy (beatitude) is the consequence and not the enemy of law. What Jesus gives us in the Sermon on the Mount, therefore, is that new law that would discipline our desires, our minds, and our bodies so as to make real happiness possible.

Cathedral of Segovia, interior, Spain. WORD ON FIRE

I would like to suggest a reading of the eight beatitudes that looks first at the more "positive" formulations and then, in light of those, at the more "negative" prescriptions. Jesus says, "Blessed are the merciful, for they will be shown mercy" (Mt 5:7). This stands at the heart of the matter, for mercy or tender compassion (*Chesed* in the Hebrew of the Old Testament) is God's most distinctive characteristic. Saint John would give this same idea a New Testament expression in saying "God is love" (1 Jn 4:16). Saint Augustine reminded us that we are, by our very nature, ordered to God: "O Lord, you have made us for yourself, and therefore our hearts are restless until they rest in thee." If this is true, then nothing short of God, no substitute for God, will ever finally satisfy us. But since God is tender mercy, "having" God is tantamount to exercising compassion, being merciful ourselves. And attend to the way Jesus articulates this law: those who exercise mercy will themselves receive mercy. According to the "physics" of the spiritual order, the more one draws on the divine life, the more one receives that life, precisely because it *is* a gift and is properly infinite. God's life is had, as it were, on the fly: when one receives it as a gift, he must give it away, since it only exists in gift form, and when he gives it away he will find more of it flooding into his heart. If you want to be happy, Jesus is saying, this divine love, this *Chesed* of God, must be central to your life; it must be your beginning, your middle, and your end, your "work day and Sabbath rest." Everything else that is good will find its place around that central desire, which is why Jesus said, "seek first the kingdom [of God] and his righteousness, and all these things will be given you besides" (Mt 6:33).

We turn now to the closely related beatitude: "Blessed are the clean of heart, for they will see God" (Mt 5:8). This means that you will be happy if there is no ambiguity in your heart (the deepest center of the self) about what is most important. The philosopher Søren Kierkegaard said that the saint is someone whose life is about one thing. He didn't mean that the saint lives a monotonous existence; he meant that a truly holy person has ordered her heart toward pleasing God alone. Again, many interests and passions and actions can cluster around that central longing, but none of them can finally compete with it. And thus, "Blessed are they who hunger and thirst for righteousness, for they will be satisfied" (Mt 5:6). We want many things—food, drink, shelter, fame, financial security, and so on—but what, most fundamentally, do we want? What is the Hunger that defines and orders the attendant and secondary hungers? What, in Paul Tillich's language, is your "ultimate concern"? If it is anything other than the will and purpose of God—righteousness—then you will be unhappy and unfulfilled. The last of the "positive" beatitudes is: "Blessed are the peacemakers, for they will be called children of God" (Mt 5:9). Since God is the Creator, he is that power through which all creatures are connected to one another. As we have seen in the first chapter, God is a gathering force, the unifier of all that he has made. Therefore someone who has ordered himself fundamentally toward God is, ipso facto, a peacemaker, for he will necessarily channel the metaphysical energy that draws things and people together. One of the most readily recognizable marks of sanctity—on clear display in all the saints—is just this radiation of reconciling power. This is why peacemaking will make us children of God and therefore happy.

With these more positive beatitudes in mind we can turn with increased understanding to those beatitudes that can strike us initially as perhaps confounding and counterintuitive. The simple fact of the matter is that on account of the mysterious curvature of the will that we call original sin, we deviate from the very actions and attitudes that will make us happy. In the elegant formulation of Saint Augustine, we have turned from the Creator to creatures, and as a result we are wandering in "the land of unlikeness," which is to say, a place of spiritual aridity. Jesus recommends a series of negative prescriptions, designed to orient us wanderers aright. One of the most fundamental problems in the spiritual order is that we sense within ourselves the hunger for God, but we attempt to satisfy it with some created good that is less than God. Thomas Aquinas said that the four typical substitutes for God are wealth, pleasure, power, and honor. Sensing the void within, we attempt to fill it up with some combination of these four things, but only by emptying out the self in love can we make the space for God to fill us. The classical tradition referred to this errant desire as "concupiscence," but I believe that we could neatly express the same idea with the more contemporary term "addiction." When we try to satisfy the hunger for God with something less than God, we will naturally be frustrated, and then in our frustration, we will convince ourselves that we need more of that finite good, so we will struggle to achieve it, only to find ourselves again, necessarily, dissatisfied. At this point, a sort of spiritual panic sets in, and we can find ourselves turning obsessively around this creaturely good that can never in principle make us happy.

And so Jesus says: "Blessed are the poor in spirit, for theirs is the kingdom of heaven" (Mt 5:3). This is neither a romanticizing of economic poverty nor a demonization of wealth, but rather a formula for detachment. Might I suggest a somewhat variant rendition: how blessed are you if you are not attached to material things, if you have not placed the goods that wealth can buy at the center of your concern? When the Kingdom of God is your ultimate concern, not only will you not become addicted to material things; you will, in fact, be able to use them with great effectiveness for God's purposes. Under this same rubric of detachment consider the beatitude "Blessed are they who mourn, for they will be comforted" (Mt 5:4). Again, this can sound like the worst sort of masochism, but we have to dig deeper. We could render this adage as how blessed, how "lucky" (a legitimate rendering of *makarios,* according to some scholars) you are if you are not addicted to good feelings. Pleasant sensations—physical, emotional, psychological—are wonderful, but since they are only a finite good, they can easily drive an addiction, as can clearly be seen in the prevalence of psychotropic drugs, gluttonous habits of consumption, and pornography in our culture. Again, Jesus's saying hasn't a thing to do with puritanism; it has to do with detachment and hence with spiritual freedom. Unaddicted to sensual pleasure, one can unreservedly follow the will of God, even when such a path involves psychological or physical suffering.

Jesus says, "Blessed are the meek, for they will inherit the land" (Mt 5:5). I don't know of any culture at any time that would be tempted to embrace this beatitude as a practical program of world conquest! Meek people don't come to positions of political or institutional influence. But once more, Jesus is not so much passing judgment on institutions of power as he is showing a path of detachment. How lucky you are if you are not attached to the finite good of worldly power. Many people up and down the centuries have felt that the acquisition of power is the key to beatitude. In the temptation scene in the Gospel of Matthew, the devil, after luring Christ with the relatively low-level temptations toward sensual pleasure and pride, brings Jesus to the top of a tall mountain and reveals to him all of the kingdoms of the world in their glory and offers them to Jesus. Matthew's implication is that the drive to power is perhaps the strongest, most irresistible temptation of all. In the twentieth century, J. R. R. Tolkien, who had tasted at first hand the horrors of the First World War and had witnessed those of the Second, conceived a ring of power as the most tempting talisman in his *Lord of the Rings* trilogy. But if you are detached from worldly power, you can follow the will of God, even when that path involves extreme powerlessness. Meek—free from the addiction to ordinary power—you can become a conduit of true divine power to the world.

The last of the "negative" beatitudes is "Blessed are they who are persecuted for the sake of righteousness, for theirs is the kingdom of heaven" (Mt 5:10). We must read this, once again, in light of Thomas Aquinas's analysis. If the call to poverty holds off the addiction to material things, and the summons to mourn counters the addiction to good feelings, and the valorization of meekness blocks the addiction to power, this last beatitude gets in the way of the addictive attachment to honor. Honor is a good thing in the measure that it is a "flag of virtue," signaling to others the presence of some excellence, but when love of honor becomes the center of one's concern, it, like any other finite good, becomes a source of suffering. Many people who are not terribly attracted to wealth, pleasure, or power are held captive by their desire for the approval of others, and they will, accordingly, order their lives, arrange their work, and plot their careers with the single value in mind of being noticed, honored, and endowed with titles. But this again involves the attempt to fill up the infinite longing with a finite good, and it produces, by the laws of spiritual physics, addiction. Therefore, how lucky are you if you are not attached to honor and hence are able to follow the will of God even when that path involves being ignored, dishonored, and, at the limit, persecuted.

Thomas Aquinas said that if you want to see the perfect exemplification of the beatitudes, you should look to Christ crucified. The saint specified this observation as follows: if you want beatitude (happiness), despise what Jesus despised on the cross and love what he loved on the cross. What did he despise on the cross but the four classical addictions? The crucified Jesus was utterly detached from wealth and worldly goods. He was stripped naked, and his hands, fixed to the wood of the cross, could grasp at nothing. More to it, he was detached from pleasure. On the cross, Jesus underwent the most agonizing kind of physical torment, a pain that was literally excruciating (*ex cruce,* from the cross), but he also experienced the extreme of psychological and even spiritual suffering ("My God, my God, why have you forsaken me?"). And he was bereft of power, even to the point of being unable to move or defend himself in any way. Finally on that terrible cross he was completely detached from the esteem of others. In a public place not far from the gate of Jerusalem, he hung from an instrument of torture, exposed to the mockery of the crowd, displayed as a common criminal. In this, he endured the ultimate of dishonor. In the most dramatic way possible, therefore, the crucified Jesus demonstrates a liberation from the four principal temptations that lead us away from God. Saint Paul expressed this accomplishment in typically vivid language: "[13] And even when you were dead [in] transgressions and the uncircumcision of your flesh, he brought you to life along with him, having forgiven us all our transgressions; [14] obliterating the bond against us, with its legal claims, which was opposed to us, he also removed it from our midst, nailing it to the cross; [15] despoiling the principalities and the powers, he made a public spectacle of them, leading them away in triumph by it" (Col 2:15).

But what did Jesus love on the cross? He loved the will of his Father. His Father had sent him, as we saw, into the farthest reaches of godforsakenness in order to bring the divine love even to that darkest place, and Jesus loved that mission to the very end. And it was precisely his detachment from the four great temptations that enabled him to walk that walk. What he loved and what he despised were in a strange balance on the cross. Poor in spirit, meek, mourning, and persecuted, he was able to be pure of heart, to seek righteousness utterly, to become the ultimate peacemaker, and to be the perfect conduit of the divine mercy to the world. Though it is supremely paradoxical to say so, the crucified Jesus is the man of beatitude, a truly happy man. And if we recall our discussion of freedom, we can say that Jesus nailed to the cross is the very icon of liberty, for he is free from those attachments that would prevent him from attaining the true good, which is doing the will of his Father.

One of the most brutally realistic and spiritually powerful depictions of the crucifixion is the central panel of the *Isenheim Altarpiece* painted in the late fifteenth century by the German artist Matthias Grünewald. Jesus's body is covered with sores and wounds, his head is surrounded by a

Isenheim Altarpiece *by Matthias Grünewald (Unterlinden Museum, Colmar, France).* WORD ON FIRE

particularly brutal crown of thorns, his hands and feet are pierced, not with tiny nails, but with enormous spikes, and, perhaps most terribly, his mouth is agape in wordless agony. The viewer is spared none of the horror of this most horrible of deaths. To the right of the figure of Jesus, Grünewald has painted, in an eloquent anachronism, John the Baptist, the herald and forerunner of the Messiah. John is indicating Jesus as the Lamb of God, but he does so in the most peculiar way. Instead of pointing directly at the Lord, John's arm and hand are oddly twisted, as though he had to contort himself in order to perform his task. One wonders whether Grünewald was suggesting that our distorted expectations of what constitutes a joyful and free life have to be twisted out of shape (and hence back into proper shape) in order for us to grasp the strange truth revealed in the crucified Christ.

THE PATH OF NONVIOLENCE

I have spent a good deal of time interpreting the opening verses of the Sermon on the Mount, for it is most important to be clear on the priority of joy in the teaching of Jesus. However, the beatitudes are perhaps best thought of as a kind of overture to the entire sermon, as a preparation for what is in fact the rhetorical and spiritual highpoint of Jesus's programmatic speech, namely, the teaching on nonviolence and loving one's enemies. In words that still take our breath away, Jesus says, "You have heard that it was said, 'You shall love your neighbor and hate your enemy.' But I say to you, love your enemies and pray for those who persecute you" (Mt 5:43–44). In order to understand this radical teaching, we have to be clear on what Jesus means by "love" (*agape* in Matthew's Greek). Love is not a sentiment or feeling, not merely a tribal loyalty or family devotion. Love is actively willing the good of the other as other. Often we are good or kind or just to others so that they might be good, kind, or just to us in return. But this is indirect egotism, not love. And this is why loving one's enemies is the surest test of love. If I am good to someone who is sure to repay me, then I might simply be engaging in an act of disguised or implicit self-interest. But if I am generous to someone who is my enemy, who is not the least bit interested in responding to me in kind, then I can be sure that I have truly willed his good and not my own. And this is why Jesus says, "For if you love those who love you, what recompense will you have? . . . And if you greet your brothers only, what is unusual about that? Do not the pagans do the same?" (Mt 5:46–47). Jesus wants his followers to rise above the imperfect forms of benevolence that obtain among the general run of human beings and to aspire to love the way that God loves: "for he makes his sun rise on the bad and the good, and causes rain to fall on the just and the unjust" (Mt 5:45). God loves those who love him and those who hate him; he loves his friends and his enemies; he gives good things to those who deserve them and also to those who don't deserve them. If we are truly free from our attachments, especially from the attachment to approval, then we can become "sons and daughters" of this God and hence conduits of his peculiar grace. We will explore what this looks like concretely when we look, later, at the saints.

The already radical teaching on loving one's enemies becomes even more intensely focused as Jesus turns his attention to the practice of nonviolence. Giving voice to the common consensus among law-abiding Jews, Jesus declares, "You have heard that it was said, 'An eye for an eye and a tooth for a tooth.' But I say to you, offer no resistance to one who is evil. When someone strikes you on [your] right cheek, turn the other one to him as well. If anyone wants to go to law with you over your tunic, hand him your cloak as well" (Mt 5:38–40). It is most important not to overlook the fact that this was, for its time, quite an enlightened, compassionate rule, for many individuals and nations would have felt justified in answering a violent affront with a devastating and disproportionate counterviolence. The seemingly brutal "eye for an eye" rule was in fact an attempt to delimit the retaliatory instinct. But, as we can see, Jesus is uneasy even with this relatively benign recommendation. I fully realize that Jesus's instruction can sound like simple acquiescence to the power of violence, but we have to probe further. There are two classical responses to evil: fight or flight. When confronted with injustice or violence, we can answer in kind—and sometimes in our sinful world that is all that we can reasonably do. But as every playground bully and every geopolitical aggressor knows, this usually leads to an act of counterviolence, and then still another retaliation until the opponents are locked in an endless round of fighting. Gandhi expressed it this way: "an eye for an eye makes the whole world blind." The other typical responses to aggression are running away or submitting—and sometimes, given our finite, sinful situation, that is all we can do. But, finally, we all know that ceding to violence tends only to justify the aggressor and encourage even more injustice. And therefore it appears as though, in regard to solving the problem of violence, we are locked in a no-win situation, compelled to oscillate back and forth between two deeply unsatisfactory strategies.

In his instruction on nonviolence Jesus is giving us a way out, and we will grasp this if we attend carefully to the famous example he uses:

"To the person who strikes you on one cheek, offer the other one as well" (Lk 6:29). In the society of the time, one would never have used one's left hand for any form of social interaction, since it was considered unclean. Thus, if someone strikes you on the right cheek, he is hitting you with the back of his hand, and this was the manner in which one would strike a slave or a child or a social inferior. In the face of this kind of violence, Jesus is recommending neither fighting back nor fleeing, but rather standing one's ground. To turn the *other* cheek is to prevent him from hitting you the same way again. It is not to run or to acquiesce, but rather to signal to the aggressor that you refuse to accept the set of assumptions that have made his aggression possible. It is to show that you are occupying a different moral space. It is also, consequently, a manner of mirroring back to the violent person the deep injustice of what he is doing. The great

Blessed Teresa of Calcutta, 1987.
MICHAEL COLLOPY

promise of this approach is that it might not only stop the violence but also transform the perpetrator of it.

Some contemporary examples might illumine these dynamics more clearly. A story is told of Mother Teresa, the saint of the Calcutta slums. She went with a small child to a local baker and begged some bread for the hungry lad. The baker spat full in Mother Teresa's face. Undaunted, she calmly replied, "Thank you for that gift to me. Do you have anything for the child?" Desmond Tutu, when he was a young priest in Johannesburg, was making his way along a wooden sidewalk, raised above the muddy street. He came to a narrow section of the sidewalk and was met by a white man coming from the other direction. The man said to Tutu: "Get off the sidewalk; I don't make way for gorillas." Tutu stepped aside, gestured broadly, and responded, "I do!" The third example I offer is by far the most powerful, at least if we measure power in terms of practical consequences. On June 2, 1979, Pope John Paul II came to Victory Square in the heart of Warsaw and celebrated Mass in the presence of hundreds of thousands of people and the entire Polish Communist government. During his homily the pope spoke of God, of freedom, and of human rights—all topics frowned upon by the Communist regime. As the pope preached, the people began to chant, "We want God; we want God; we want God." The pope continued, and the chant went on, "We want God; we want God," and did not stop for an astonishing fifteen minutes. It is said that during this demonstration of the people's will, John Paul turned toward the Polish government officials and gestured, as if to say, "Do you hear?" Prescient commentators of the time, including Zbigniew Brzezinski, President Carter's national security advisor, saw that Communism, at least in Poland, was, from that moment, moribund. In point of fact, that government did fall and a few years later the entire Soviet Communist empire disintegrated with barely a shot fired. If someone had laid out that scenario to me when I was coming of age in the 1970s, I would never have believed it. In all three cases, an offended person responded, neither with counterviolence nor with flight, but rather with a provocative gesture meant to draw the aggressor into a new spiritual consciousness.

*Pope John Paul II's Pilgrimage to Poland, June
2–10, 1979.* EAST NEWS/FOT. LESEZK LOZYNSKI

And certainly in the case of John Paul and his Polish people, this move
unleashed extraordinary transformative energy.

THE PRODIGAL SON

So far we have been considering the teaching of Jesus as it is articulated
in the Sermon on the Mount. But we would be greatly remiss if we did
not attend to the instruction that emerges from those startling, funny,
off-putting, and strangely enlightening stories that Jesus loved to tell. I'm
speaking, of course, about the parables. There are dozens of such stories
sprinkled throughout the Gospels, but since space permits us to look at
only one, I would like to examine what most think the greatest, the story
of the father and his two sons, better known as the parable of the prodigal son. The story is about the nature of God and the manner in which we

should properly relate to God, but since it is a parable, it does its work by turning our ordinary conception of the spiritual world upside down.

Jesus begins by telling us of a man and his two sons. The younger of the two approached his father with a request that was breathtaking in its rudeness and presumption: "Father, give me the share of your estate that should come to me" (Lk 15:12). Because one does not receive an inheritance before one's father has passed away, what the child was saying to his father was, essentially, "I can't wait for you to die!" And he was asking, with a double emphasis, for something to have as his own: "give *me* the share of the *property* that will belong to *me*." If we picture ourselves acting in this way in relation to God, we have a problem. The God whom Jesus consistently proclaimed is, as we have seen, a God of tender mercy and superabundantly generous love, the one whose very nature is to give. And the right relation to this God of grace is to receive what is freely offered and then to give it away as a grace to others, thereby allowing more of the divine life to flow into oneself. The younger son has all of this backward, since he is both insulting his father's generosity and trying to keep as a possession what can only be received as a gift and only "kept" by being given away.

Having taken his inheritance, the son wanders off into what is usually translated as "a distant country," but the original Greek (*chora makra*) is instructive, for it means, literally, "the big emptiness." Cut off from the source of grace, clinging desperately to what we think we are owed, we necessarily lose the little that we have. In very short order, the prodigal son finds himself destitute, starving, and alone, in fact so desperate that he hires himself out to keep and feed the pigs, a task of unsurpassable indignity for a Jew. Coming to his senses at last, the young man reasons, "How many of my father's hired workers have more than enough food to eat, but here am I, dying from hunger" (Lk 15:17). He resolves to return home and confess his sin to his father. What we are meant to grasp is that closeness to the One Who Gives leads to sufficiency and even abundance, for the infinite life of God never runs out. As the son nears home, the father sees him from a long way off (he had obviously been looking for him) and then, throwing caution and respectability to the winds, the father comes running out to meet him. This detail would have caught the particular attention of Jesus's listeners, since it would have been considered unconscionably unseemly for an older man, a patriarch, to run to anyone. People were expected to present themselves to him. The father embraces his son and orders his servants to "put a ring on his finger," a kind of ring of marriage, symbolizing their restored union, and shoes on his feet (in order to restore him to dignity). When the son commences his carefully rehearsed speech of confession, the father cuts him off and declares a general celebration, because "this son of mine was dead, and has come to life again; he was lost, and has been found" (Lk 15:23). This is Jesus's brilliant and deeply moving portrait of his heavenly Father, who does not play games of calculation and recompense, but "makes his sun rise on the bad and the good" (Mt 5:45), the Father who doesn't know how to do anything but love.

Meanwhile the older brother is "in the field," which is to say, in his own kind of exile. Though he has remained relatively close to his father in a physical sense, we promptly see how far he is psychologically and spiritually from him. This son hears the sounds of celebration and, discovering that it is a feast for his long-lost brother, he smolders with resentment and refuses to come in. Never easily put off, his father moves to meet him, as he had moved to greet his other son. But the older son refuses the entreaties of his father: "Look," he says, "all these years I served you and not once did I disobey your orders; yet you never gave me even a young goat to feast on with my friends. But when your son returns who swallowed up your property with prostitutes, for him you slaughter the fatted calf" (Lk 15:29–30). The older son's language gives him away as surely as his brother's language had betrayed him. For all these years this son has been "*working* like a *slave*" for his father and "*obeying* all of his *commands*." There is nothing of giving and receiving, nothing of the joy of reciprocal love, in that language. It is thoroughly marked by mercantile calculation. The father tries to lure him back into the circle of celebration with words that are among the most important in the New

Testament: "My son, you are here with me always; everything I have is yours" (Lk 15:31). I don't know a pithier description of how God relates to us anywhere in the spiritual literature of the world. We are always with God, since God is the very ground of our being, closer to us than we are to ourselves. We could not exist even for a moment without the loving press of God. And God gives all that he has to us. His whole being is for giving. Both sons, in different ways, fall out of relationship with that divine manner of existence and hence fall into deep sadness. When, on the contrary, we enter with abandon into the loop of grace—giving away in love what was given to us through love—then the celebration begins.

MATTHEW 25

Once a rabbi inquired of Jesus which of the many laws (there were well over six hundred) that governed Jewish life was the most important. With disarming simplicity and directness Jesus responded: "You shall love the Lord, your God, with all your heart, with all your soul, and with all your mind. This is the greatest and the first commandment. The second is like it: You shall love your neighbor as yourself." The mutuality of these two loves is implicit in the entire teaching of Jesus. In the next chapter we shall see in more metaphysical detail why this is the case, but for now suffice it to say that the absolute love for God is not in competition with a radical commitment to love our fellow human beings, precisely because God is not one being among many, but the very ground of the existence of the finite world. Thomas Aquinas would state it this way: to love God is to love, necessarily, whatever participates in God, and this is to say the entire world. In his magnificent first letter Saint John expresses the same idea as follows: "If anyone says, 'I love God,' but hates his brother, he is a liar; for whoever does not love a brother whom he has seen cannot love God whom he has not seen" (1 Jn 4:20).

Perhaps the most powerful evocation of this principle in the teaching of Jesus is the haunting parable of the sheep and the goats contained in chapter 25 of Matthew's Gospel. Jesus tells the crowd that when the Son of Man comes in his glory to judge the living and the dead "he will separate them one from another, as a shepherd separates the sheep from the goats" (Mt 25:31–32). To those on his right, he will say, "Come, you who are blessed by my Father. Inherit the kingdom prepared for you from the foundation of the world. For I was hungry and you gave me food, I was thirsty and you gave me drink, a stranger and you welcomed me, naked and you clothed me, ill and you cared for me, in prison and you visited me" (Mt 25:34–36). In their puzzlement, the righteous will ask when they performed all of these acts of love for the Lord, and he will reply, "Amen, I say to you, whatever you did for one of these least brothers of mine, you did for me" (Mt 25:40). Then comes the reversal. To those on his left, the Lord will say, "Depart from me, you accursed, into the eternal fire prepared for the devil and his angels. For I was hungry and you gave me no food, I was thirsty and you gave me no drink, a stranger and you gave me no welcome, naked and you gave me no clothing, ill and in prison, and you did not care for me" (Mt 25:41–43). Puzzled, the people will wonder when they neglected the Lord so thoroughly. Here comes the answer: "Amen, I say to you, what you did not do for one of these least ones, you did not do for me" (Mt 25:45). To love Christ *is* to love the ones whom Christ loves. The very drama of the parable is intended to stir us out of any complacency and beguile us out of any confusion on this score.

A man who understood the theology and ethics of Matthew 25 in his bones was Peter Maurin, the cofounder of the Catholic Worker Movement. Maurin was born in France in 1877, one of twenty-three children. In the course of his early education, which was supervised by the Christian Brothers, he became deeply inspired by the example of Saint Francis of Assisi. In 1909, when the French government turned aggressively against the church, Peter left his native country and settled in Canada, where for almost twenty years he lived a radical sort of Franciscan life, embracing poverty out of love for the Gospel, working as a simple laborer during the day and sleeping in skid-row shelters at night. During those vagabond years, he was struggling to develop a coherent Catholic social philosophy, a theory of economics and politics thoroughly informed by Matthew 25. He knew that the church had codified that section of Matthew as "the corporal and spiritual works of mercy," among which were feeding the hungry, clothing the naked, visiting the imprisoned, burying the dead, counseling the doubtful, and praying for the living and the dead. He wondered what society would look like if those ideals were the foundation of the political and social order. He also read with great care the social teaching of the church, especially as articulated in Pope Leo XIII's *Rerum novarum* of 1891 and Pope Pius XI's *Quadragesimo anno* of 1931. In Pope Leo's text Maurin found the line, "once the demands of necessity and propriety have been met, the rest that one owns belongs to the poor," and he discovered a principle that the pope had borrowed from Thomas Aquinas, namely, that while the ownership of private property is allowed, the use of private property should always be for the common good. In Pope Pius's encyclical Maurin discovered what has been characterized as the structuring element of all of Catholic social teaching: the principle of subsidiarity, which stipulates that in matters political and economic there ought always to be a preferential option for the most local level of authority and operation. The unambiguous application of this principle, Maurin saw, would prevent individuals and communities from abdicating their direct responsibility for practicing the corporal works of mercy. He wanted to build a society in which, in his words, "it would be easier for men to be good."

Maurin recognized Matthew 25 as "dynamite," from the Greek *dynamus* (power), a favorite word of Saint Paul, by the way. But Maurin worried that "we have taken the dynamite of the church, placed it in hermetically sealed containers and sat on the lids." We have tended, in other words, to see the Gospel commands as a matter of private spirituality and not as society-transforming power. It is time, he concluded, "to blow up the dynamite of the church!" As a nonnative speaker of English, he was sensitive to peculiar turns of phrase that Anglophones would take for granted. He delighted in the term "go-getter," but he wanted at the same time to undermine it: "We should turn a nation of go-getters into a nation of go-givers!"

Dorothy Day and Peter Maurin. MARQUETTE
UNIVERSITY ARCHIVES

In 1932, just as the Great Depression was getting under way, Peter
Maurin arrived in New York City. There he met a young social activist
and spiritual seeker who had recently converted to Catholicism. Her name
was Dorothy Day. Dorothy had been a radical and a friend to some of the
leaders in the cultural and political avant-garde of the 1920s, including
the playwright Eugene O'Neill and the political agitator John Reed. But
she had become fascinated with the Catholic Church, especially after
the birth of her first child, when she said that she felt a gratitude so great
that it corresponded to nothing in this world. When she met Peter Maurin she was looking for a way to combine her radical political commitment with her newfound Catholic faith. The vagabond philosopher was
the answer to her prayers. When they met, Peter spoke, uninterrupted,
for seven hours! Despite this overwhelming loquaciousness, Dorothy
was entranced by Peter's vision of a renewal of American society and his
recommendation that the revolution should start with the founding of a

newspaper that would present Catholic social teaching, and the establishment of "houses of hospitality" where the poor would be welcomed and where the corporal and spiritual works of mercy would be practiced. On May 1, 1933, Dorothy Day went to Washington Square Park in Greenwich Village and distributed the first edition of the *Catholic Worker* newspaper, selling it for one penny a copy (still the price today). Not long afterward she and Maurin set up the first Catholic Worker House of Hospitality on the Lower East Side of Manhattan and commenced to take care of the poor. Today there are such houses all over the country and indeed around the world. It is most important to see that neither of these figures could be blandly described as a "social worker." Throughout their lives they attended Mass, assisted at Benediction, participated in retreats, prayed the Rosary, and so forth, for they saw in their radical devotion to the poor an inescapable correlation to their even more radical love of Christ.

Someone who operated very much in the spirit of Dorothy Day was

Dorothy Day, 1934. MARQUETTE UNIVERSITY ARCHIVES

a figure to whom we have already alluded and whom we will consider in detail later in the book, Mother Teresa of Calcutta. Much of Mother's day was taken up with prayer, meditation, Mass, Eucharistic Adoration, and the Rosary, but the rest of her time, as we well know, was spent doing the grittiest work among the poorest of the poor, practicing the corporal and spiritual works of mercy, blowing up the dynamite of the church. Father Paul Murray, the Irish Dominican spiritual writer and sometime advisor to Mother Teresa, relates the following story. He was one day in deep conversation with Mother, searching out the sources of her spirituality and mission. At the end of their long talk she asked him to spread his hand out on the table and, touching his fingers one by one as she spoke, said, "You did it to me."

GO BEYOND THE MIND YOU HAVE

In his inaugural speech, as reported in the Gospel of Mark, Jesus announced the arrival of the Kingdom of God and thereupon he immediately called people to change: "Repent, and believe in the gospel" (Mk 1:15). The word that we typically render as "repent" is *metanoiete*, a term that is based on the two Greek words *meta* (beyond) and *nous* (mind). With the inbreaking of the Kingdom of God, we must change our attitude, our way of thinking, our perspective on things, the manner in which we see. We have to *see* the world differently and in light of that new vision; we have to change the way we act. Once we envision our own existence—and indeed the being of the entire universe—as the gift of a gracious God, we gladly resolve to give our lives away as a gift in love. And when we do that, we find ourselves increased thirty-, sixty-, and a hundredfold, the divine life continuing to flood into us. Once we see that God *is* love, we are no longer afraid to risk the path of love. The teaching of Jesus is all about this new vision and this summons to change.

Chapter 3

"THAT THAN WHICH NOTHING GREATER CAN BE THOUGHT": THE INEFFABLE MYSTERY OF GOD

After many years of exile from the courts of Egypt where he had been raised, a Hebrew man named Moses, while tending the flock of his father-in-law on the slopes of Mount Sinai, saw an extraordinary sight: a bush that was on fire but was not being consumed. He resolved to take a closer look. As he approached, he heard a voice: "Moses! Moses! . . . Come no nearer! Remove the sandals from your feet, for the place where you stand is holy ground" (Ex 3:5). Then the speaker identified himself as "the God of your father . . . the God of Abraham, the God of Isaac, the God of Jacob" (Ex 3:6), and he gave Moses a mission to liberate his people enslaved in Egypt. When Moses asked for the name of this mysterious speaker, he received the following answer: "I am who am" (Ex 3:14). Moses was asking a reasonable enough question. He was wondering which of the many gods—deities of the river, the mountain, the various nations—this was. He was seeking to define and specify the nature of this particular heavenly power. But the answer he received frustrated him, for the divine speaker was implying that he was not one god among many, not this deity rather than that, not a reality that could, even in principle, be captured or delimited by a name. In a certain sense, God's response amounted to the undermining of the very type of question Moses posed. His name was simply "to be," and therefore he could never be mastered. The ancient Israelites honored this essential mysteriousness of God by designating him with the unpronounceable name of YHWH.

Following the prompting of this conversation between Moses and God, the mainstream of the Catholic theological tradition has tended not to refer to God as *a* being, however supreme, among many. Thomas Aquinas, arguably the greatest theologian in the Catholic tradition, rarely designates God as *ens summum* (the highest being); rather he prefers the names *ipsum esse* (to be itself) or *qui est* (the one who is). In fact,

Saint Joseph Cathedral, detail, Wheeling, West Virginia.
DENIS R. MCNAMARA

Aquinas goes so far as to say that God cannot be defined or situated within any genus, even the genus of "being." This means that it is wrong to say that trees, planets, automobiles, computers, and God—despite the obvious differences among them—have at least in common their status as beings. Aquinas expresses the difference that obtains between God and creatures through the technical language of essence and existence. In everything that is not God there is a real distinction between essence (*what* the thing is) and existence (*that* the thing is); but in God no such distinction holds, for God's act of existence is not received, delimited, or defined by anything extraneous to itself. A human being is the act of existence poured, as it were, into the receptacle of humanity, and a podium is the act of existence poured into the form of podium-ness, but God's act of existence is not poured into any receiving element. To be God, therefore, is to be to be.

Saint Anselm of Canterbury, one of the greatest of the early medieval theologians, described God as "that than which nothing greater can be thought." At first blush this seems straightforward enough: God is the highest conceivable thing. But the longer one meditates on Anselm's description, the stranger it becomes. If God were simply the supreme being—the biggest reality among many—then God plus the world would be greater than God alone. But in that case he would not be that than which nothing greater can be thought. Zeus, for example, was, in ancient mythology, the supreme deity, but clearly Zeus plus the other gods, or Zeus plus the world of nature, would be greater than Zeus alone. Thus the God whom Anselm is describing is not like this at all. Though it is a very high paradox, the God whom Anselm describes added to the world as we know it is not greater than God alone.

This means that the true God exceeds all of our concepts, all of our language, all of our loftiest ideas. God (YHWH) is essentially mysterious, a term, by the way, derived from the Greek *muein* (to shut one's mouth). How often the prophets and mystics of the Old Testament rail against idolatry, which is nothing other than reducing the true God to some creaturely object that we can know and hence try to control. The twentieth-century theologian Karl Rahner commented that "God" is the last sound we should make before falling silent, and Saint Augustine, long ago, said, *"si comprehendis, non est Deus"* (if you understand, that isn't God). All of this formal theologizing is but commentary on that elusive and confounding voice from the burning bush: "I am who am."

ARGUMENTS FOR GOD'S EXISTENCE

I have firmly fended off the tendency to turn God into an idol, but have I left us thereby in an intellectual lurch, doomed simply to remain silent about God? If God cannot be in any sense defined, how do we explain the plethora of theological books and arguments? After all, the same Thomas Aquinas who said that God cannot be placed in any genus also wrote millions of words about God. Chapter 33 of Exodus gives us a clue to the resolution of this dilemma. Moses passionately asks God to reveal his glory to him, and Yahweh acquiesces. But the Lord specifies, "I will make all my beauty pass before you . . . But my face you cannot see, for no man sees me and still lives" (Ex 33:19–20). God then tells Moses that

Santa Sabina, Rome. WORD ON FIRE

while the divine glory passes by, God will place his servant in the cleft of a rock and cover Moses's eyes. "Then I will remove my hand, so that you may see my back; but my face is not to be seen" (Ex 33:22–23). God can indeed be seen in this life, but only indirectly, through his creatures and effects. We can understand him to a degree, but only obliquely, glimpsing him, as it were, out of the corners of our eyes. We see his "back" as it is disclosed in the beauty, the intelligibility, and the contingency of the world that he has made.

Following this principle of indirection, Thomas Aquinas formulated five arguments for God's existence, each one of which begins from some feature of the created order. I will develop here the one that I consider the most elemental, the demonstration that commences with the contingency of the world. Though the term is technically philosophical, "contingency" actually names something with which we are all immediately familiar: the fact that things come into being and pass out of being. Consider a majestic summer cloud that billows up and then fades away in the course of a lazy August afternoon, coming into existence and then evanescing. Now think of all of the plants and flowers that have grown up and subsequently withered away, and then of all the animals that have come into being, roamed the face of the earth, and then faded into dust. And ponder the numberless human beings who have come and gone, confirming the Psalmist's intuition that "our years end like a sigh" (Ps 90:9). Even those things that seem most permanent—mountain ranges, the continents themselves, the oceans—have in fact emerged and will in fact fade. Indeed, if a time-lapse camera could record the entire life span of the Rocky Mountains, from the moment they began to emerge to the moment when they finally wear away, and if we could play that film at high speed, those mountains would look for all the world like that summer cloud.

The contingency of earthly things is the starting point of Aquinas's proof, for it indicates something of great moment, namely, that such things do not contain within themselves the reason for their own existence. If they did, they would exist, simply and absolutely; they would not come and go so fleetingly. Therefore, in regard to contingent things, we have to look outside of them, to an extrinsic cause, or set of causes, in order to explain their existence. So let's go back to that summer cloud. Instinctually, we know that it doesn't exist through its own essence, and we therefore look for explanations. We say that it is caused by the moisture in the atmosphere, by the temperature, by the intensity of the winds, and so on, and as far as it goes, that explanation is adequate. But as any meteorologist will tell us, those factors are altogether contingent, coming into being and passing out of being. Thus we go a step further and say that these factors in turn are caused by the jet stream, which is grounded in the movement of the planet. But a moment's reflection reveals that the jet stream comes and goes, ebbs and flows, and that the earth itself is contingent, having emerged into existence four billion years ago and being destined one day to be incinerated by the expanding sun. And so we go further, appealing to the solar system and events within the galaxy and finally perhaps to the very structures inherent in the universe. But contemporary astrophysics has disclosed to us the fundamental contingency of all of those realities, and indeed of the universe itself, which came into existence at the Big Bang some thirteen billion years ago. In our attempt to explain a contingent reality—that evanescent summer cloud—we have appealed simply to a whole series of similarly contingent realities, each one of which requires a further explanation. Thomas Aquinas argues that if we are to avoid an infinite regress of contingent causes, which finally explain nothing at all, we must come finally to some "necessary" reality, something that exists simply through the power of its own essence. This, he concludes, is what people mean when they use the word "God." With Aquinas's demonstration in mind, reconsider that strange answer God gives to Moses's question: "I am who am." The biblical God is not one contingent reality among many; he is that whose very nature it is to exist, that power through which and because of which all other things have being.

Some contemporary theologians have translated Aquinas's abstract metaphysical language into more experiential language. The Protestant theologian Paul Tillich said that "finitude in awareness is anxiety."

He means that when we know in our bones how contingent we are, we become afraid. We exist in time, and this means that we are moving, ineluctably, toward death; we have been "thrown" into being, and this means that one day we will be thrown out of being; and this state of affairs produces fear and trembling. In the grip of this anxiety, Tillich argues, we tend to thrash about, looking for something to reassure us, searching for some firm ground on which to stand. We seek to alleviate our fears through the piling up of pleasure, wealth, power, or honor, but we discover, soon enough, that all of these worldly realities are as contingent as we are and hence cannot finally soothe us. It is at this point that the scriptural word "My soul rests in God alone" (Ps 62:1) is heard in its deepest resonance. Our fear—born of contingency—will be assuaged only by that which is not contingent. Our shaken and fragile existence will be stabilized only when placed in relation to the eternal and necessary existence of God. Tillich is, in many ways, a contemporary disciple of Saint Augustine, who said, "Lord, you have made us for yourself, and our hearts are restless till they rest in Thee."

In 1968 a young theology professor at the University of Tübingen formulated a neat argument for God's existence that owed a good deal to Thomas Aquinas but that also drew on more contemporary sources. The theologian's name was Joseph Ratzinger, now Pope Benedict XVI. Ratzinger commences with the observation that finite being, as we experience it, is marked, through and through, by intelligibility, that is to say, by a formal structure that makes it understandable to an inquiring mind. In point of fact, all of the sciences—physics, chemistry, psychology, astronomy, biology, and so forth—rest on the assumption that at all levels, microscopic and macrocosmic, being can be known. The same principle was acknowledged in ancient times by Pythagoras, who said that all existing things correspond to a numeric value, and in medieval times by the scholastic philosophers who formulated the dictum *omne ens est scibile* (all being is knowable).

Ratzinger argues that the only finally satisfying explanation for this universal objective intelligibility is a great Intelligence who has thought

Hubble image of M101. NASA, ESA, K. KUNTZ (JHU), F. BRESOLIN
(UNIVERSITY OF HAWAII), J. TRAUGER (JET PROPULSION LAB), J. MOULD
(NOAO), Y.-H. CHU (UNIVERSITY OF ILLINOIS, URBANA), AND STSCL

the universe into being. Our language provides an intriguing clue in this
regard, for we speak of our acts of knowledge as moments of "recognition," literally a re-cognition, a thinking again what has already been
thought. Ratzinger cites Einstein in support of this connection: "in the
laws of nature, a mind so superior is revealed that in comparison, our
minds are as something worthless." The prologue to the Gospel of John
states, "In the beginning was the Word," and specifies that all things
came to be through this divine Logos, implying thereby that the being of
the universe is not dumbly there, but rather intelligently there, imbued
by a creative mind with intelligible structure. The argument presented by
Joseph Ratzinger is but a specification of that great revelation. One of the
particular strengths of this argument is that it shows the deep compatibil-

ity between religion and science, two disciplines that so often today are seen as implacable enemies. Ratzinger shows that the physical sciences rest upon the finally mystical intuition that reality has been thought into existence and hence can be known. I say it is mystical because it cannot itself be the product of empirical or experimental investigation, but is instead the very condition for the possibility of analyzing and experimenting in the first place. This is why many theorists have speculated that the emergence of the modern sciences in the context of a Christian intellectual milieu, in which the doctrine of creation through the power of an intelligent Creator is affirmed, is not the least bit accidental.

NAMING GOD

The God whom we have been describing—the sheer power of being itself, the ground of the world's existence and intelligibility—must be characterized as both radically immanent and radically transcendent. Being itself, the One Who Is, cannot be a worldly object, for the world is made up exclusively of particular beings. The Russian cosmonaut who, upon soaring into the heavens, radioed back to earth the news that he had found no trace of God, was simply speaking nonsense. God is neither sequestered in any particular space nor discoverable among a collection of cosmic objects. This is why the prophet Isaiah, conveying the words of Yahweh, can say, "As high as the heavens are above the earth, so high are my ways above your ways and my thoughts above your thoughts" (Is 55:9). At the same time, Being himself, the One Who Is, works his way into every nook and cranny of finite existence, since he is the source of whatever exists in the cosmos. And thus the same Isaiah who spoke of God's radical transcendence can convey these divine words: "Can a mother forget her infant, be without tenderness for the child of her womb? Even should she forget, I will never forget you. See, upon the palms of my hands I have written your name" (Is 49:15–16). And the Psalmist could, with amazement, say to God, "Lord, you have probed me, you know me: you know when I sit and stand . . . before a word is on my tongue, Lord, you know it all" (Ps 139:1–4). Saint Augustine catches this uniquely divine way of being when he says that God is simultaneously *"intimior intimo meo et superior summon meo,"* which might be rendered roughly as "closer to me than I am to myself and higher than anything I could possibly imagine." To be in right relationship with God, therefore, is neither to grasp at him nor to hide from him (for both are finally impossible), but rather to surrender to him in love.

In light of this analysis, the story of Adam and Eve takes on a new resonance, for we discover in that richly symbolic narrative precisely this negative spiritual dynamic of attempting to manipulate Yahweh, and failing that, running from him. According to the author of the book of Genesis, God places our first parents in a garden and walks with them in easy fellowship. This expresses God's desire that his human creatures be fully alive, realizing their powers and finding their joy precisely through their relationship with him. But at the prompting of the serpent, Adam and Eve eat of the tree of the knowledge of good and evil, whose fruit God had forbidden them to eat. This represents the temptation toward grasping at divinity, for the determination of good and evil is a prerogative of God and not a fit object of human choice. It is fascinating to attend to the reasoning of the serpent: "You certainly will not die! No, God knows well that the moment you eat of it your eyes will be opened and you will be like gods who know what is good and what is bad" (Gn 3:4–5). The serpent, later identified as the father of lies, convinces them that God is their rival and that he is, accordingly, trying to keep something from them. In fact, Being itself has nothing whatsoever to gain from creatures and hence is not in any sense in competition with them; what he wants is to prevent them from assuming an impossible and self-defeating spiritual attitude. When this grasping at God fails, as it must, Adam and Eve attempt the other classic sinner's move: they hide from God, concealing themselves in the underbrush of Eden. God discovers them immediately, of course, for as the ground of being, he is inescapably intimate with all his creatures. Much of the subsequent scriptural narrative is the story of

Adam and Eve, *Notre Dame, Paris.* DENIS R. MCNAMARA

human beings repeating the errant moves of our first parents, grasping and hiding, trying to manipulate God or trying to run from him. Both tactics are impossible and hence morally, psychologically, and spiritually frustrating. God wants, throughout the Bible, to lure us out of these hopeless attitudes and into the stance of friendship.

The theological language of the tradition exists not simply to clarify our minds in regard to God but to order our spirits appropriately. Part of the genius of Catholic theology is that it uses a bevy of words to designate the transcendence of God and thus to hold off the grasping tendency, *and* it uses a bevy of words to designate the immanence of God and thus to hold off the hiding tendency. Let us look first at some of the anti-grasping names of God. The great theologians speak of God's infinity, and they mean thereby that God is not definable, not like any of the particular things in the world; similarly, they speak of God's immensity, which simply means God's immeasurability. They affirm that God has eternity, and by this they mean not that God endures endlessly but that God does not exist in time at all. Also they assert that God is immutable, which is to say he is not characterized by the changeability that marks creatures. It is most important to note that there is really very little positive content to these attributions. I can affirm that God is indefinable, but that just means that he's unlike anything in my experience; I can affirm that God is outside of time, but that means I have no idea what he's like positively, for everything in my experience is temporal; I can affirm that God doesn't change, but if I try to imagine what that is like, I'm tripped up, for I've never experienced anything that is not capable of change. I would like to dwell just a moment on this last example, for it has been the source of quite a bit of controversy in recent years. Some thinkers objected to the claim that God is immutable on the grounds that this attribute would render him cold and unresponsive, so unlike the God described in the Bible. In point of fact, we can draw no such conclusion from the assertion of God's immutability, since it simply tells us that God does not change in the creaturely manner, moving from potentiality to actuality. But it does not really tell us anything about the manner of the divine being in itself. All of the qualities that we have considered so far are in service of the anti-grasping principle. Thomas Aquinas observed that, in this life, we don't really know what God is, only what God is not.

On the other hand, if we one-sidedly emphasize the transcendence of God, we can fall into the spiritual trap of hiding from God, joining Adam and Eve in the underbrush of the garden. Much of modern secularism, by the way, can be interpreted under this rubric: for the first time in history, a culture is developing in which indifference to God is normative. And so the theologians use another set of names to designate the unavoidable quality of God. They speak, for instance, of God's omnipotence. By this they don't mean that God is the strongest being around; they mean that God, as the very ground of existence, presses on all things with an un-conditioned power. Similarly, they assert that God is omniscient. Again, this doesn't mean so much that God is the smartest being in existence; it means that God knows the entirety of the universe into existence and hence is inescapably and personally present to every aspect of it. Whereas for us, existence precedes knowledge (we know things because they are), for God knowledge precedes existence (things are because he knows them). Theologians speak as well of God's omnipresence, but this should never be taken to mean that God is the vague "force" or "energy" described by devotees of the New Age. Instead it means that God transcends any particular space and hence can be construed as being present to every space. These sacred attributes hold off the tendency to avoid God by asserting one's own power (he is more powerful), by retreating into privacy (he knows us better than we know ourselves), or by running away (there is no place that he is not).

The Gothic cathedrals of the Middle Ages expressed in stone and glass this eloquent ambiguity in the assigning of attributes to God. I

Cologne Cathedral, Germany.
DENIS R. MCNAMARA

would draw your attention—to give just one example—to the mountain-
ous cathedral that looms over the Rhine River in Cologne, Germany, and
dominates, even today, the skyline of the city. Every line on the exterior
of the building points dramatically upward; the logic of the structure
compels the viewer's gaze skyward; the sheer immensity of the structure
makes it hard to take in. I can personally witness to the fact that vertigo
sets in as one tries to comprehend its dimensions. All of this speaks of
the transcendence, strangeness, and radical otherness of God. The building is telling us that whatever idea we have of God has to be abandoned
as inadequate; the cathedral is summoning us always to look higher.
But the same Cologne Cathedral, which speaks so compellingly of the
divine transcendence, preaches just as convincingly the immanence of
God. All over the surface of the structure—but especially around the
portals—one spies plants, animals, trees, planets, the sun and moon,
angels, devils, and saints—the whole panoply of creation, both natural
and supernatural, vividly portrayed. All of these creatures have to do
with God, and God has to do with all of them. "The heavens proclaim the
glory of God," as do the things that crawl upon the earth, and as do the

Cologne Cathedral, detail, Germany. DENIS R. MCNAMARA

unseen spirits. God is sacramentally represented in all the complexity of creation. The cathedral, in a word, is simultaneously telling us, in regard to God, "not here!" and "right here!" To grasp that tension is to have the most adequate understanding of the One Who Is.

THE PROVIDENT CREATOR

One of the most basic of biblical ideas is that God is the maker of all things. The opening lines of the book of Genesis speak, not so much of God's nature, but of God's creative action: "In the beginning, when God created the heavens and the earth . . ." (Gn 1:1). Now there is a puzzle in regard to this primordial action of God; namely, why did he do it? If God is God, which is to say, the perfect act of being itself, utterly happy in his own nature, why would he bother to make things at all? To answer this question is to move very close, spiritually speaking, to the heart of the matter. Precisely because God doesn't need the world, the very existence of the world is a sign that it has been loved into being. We recall that to love is to will the good of the other as other. Since he has no needs in himself, all of God's intention and activity in regard to what is other is therefore utterly for the sake of the other. The perfect God *cannot be* self-interested, and hence in regard to the universe he has made he can only be loving. Drawing on Plato, the ancient Christian theologian Dionysius the Areopagite said that since the good is diffusive of itself, the infinitely good God naturally and exuberantly expresses his goodness to the world. The fathers of the First Vatican Council echoed Dionysius in saying that God made the world not out of need but in order to "manifest his glory" and to share his life and perfection. What we see in the lives of the saints is an iconic representation of this completely generous divine manner of relating to the other.

If God is the sheer act of *to be* itself, then God's creation must be *ex nihilo,* from nothing. To understand this idea, it might be helpful to propose a contrast. When an artist produces a sculpture, he begins with marble or clay and then shapes that substance into something aesthetically pleasing. When a chef makes a meal, she blends water, meats, vegetables, spices, and sauces into a palatable conglomeration. Both agents are making something *from* something; they are reordering in a creative manner a pre-existing substrate. But God, the very fullness of being itself, does not operate this way; he doesn't shape some alien substance or matter into form; rather he brings whatever exists outside of himself into being in its entirety from nothing. Several important insights cluster around this truth. First, creatures do not so much *have* a relationship to God; they *are* a relationship to God. Nothing in a creature exists independently of, or prior to, God's creative act, and hence no creature stands, as it were, over and against God, simply *in* a relationship to God. Instead every aspect of a creature's being is already constituted by God's creative will. This is why Meister Eckhart, the great medieval mystic, could say that the best metaphor for the spiritual life is not so much the climbing of a holy mountain in order to get to a distant God, but rather the "sinking into" God.

Second, all creatures are connected to one another by the deepest bonds precisely because every creature is coming forth, here and now, from God's creative act. When I find my deepest center in God, I necessarily find your deepest center and that of every other creature, even of "brother sun and sister moon," to use the language of Saint Francis.

Third, creation from nothing is a nonviolent act. In so much of the mythological tradition, the creation of the world takes place through a primal act of violence, one god defeating another, or a set of gods doing battle with their rivals. Often the physical universe is pictured as the remains of the conquered enemy. Even in the more refined philosophical accounts of Plato and Aristotle, the universe is formed through the imposition of form on recalcitrant matter. But there is none of this in the Christian conception. God does not wrestle a rival into submission, for he has no rival; nor does he intervene to shape matter according to his aggressive will, for there is no matter that confronts him. Rather, through a sheerly nonviolent, nonintrusive, non-interruptive act of speech, God gives rise to the whole of finite reality: "Let there be light, and there was light . . . Let the water under the sky be gathered into a single basin, so that the dry land may appear . . . Let the earth bring forth vegetation: every kind of plant that bears seed and every kind of fruit tree . . . And so it happened" (Gn 1:3, 9, 11). We can see now the deepest roots of Jesus's ethic of nonviolent love articulated in the Sermon on the Mount. Though it seems ludicrous to our sinful minds, the recommendation to love one's enemies and to resist evil through nonviolence is actually to dance in step with the most fundamental metaphysical rhythm of the world.

This God who continually creates the universe from nothing must also be described as provident. The Deist view—on display in both classical and modern times and especially prevalent today—is that God is the orderer of the universe, but only in a distant way, as the source of the laws and basic structures of the universe. But Christian theology has no truck with Deism. It stands, instead, with the book of Wisdom, which speaks of God's power "stretching from end to end mightily and ordering all things sweetly" (Wis 8:1). God is not a celestial CEO, managing earthly affairs from an antiseptic distance; he holds the world in the palm of his hand, involving himself in things both great and small. Thomas Aquinas summed up this biblical perspective when he said that God's providence "extends to particulars." Now to give the Deists their due, all of this stress on the particularity of God's providence does seem to pose a threat to the independence and integrity of the created order. If God is hovering fussily over the whole of reality in every detail, how could we speak, for instance, of freedom or chance? A full treatment of the thorniest of theological issues would require an entire book, but for our purposes I would draw the reader's attention, once again, to the noncompetitive relationship that God has to the world. God's creativity and providence are necessarily expressions of the divine love and hence of the "letting be" of the other. The providential God is not one great cause among many, interfering with the nexus of conditioned causes. We recall the language of the book of Wisdom, how "sweetly" God exercises his power, operating precisely *through* the realm of secondary causes. Perhaps I could illustrate this with a simple example. If asked, "How do you make a cherry pie," one would say, presumably, "you bring together cherries, sugar, flour, water, fat, and the skill of the baker, and the heat of the oven." Even the religious believer would not say, "You bring together cherries, sugar, flour, God, water, fat, and the skill of the baker, and the heat of the oven." God is not one cause among many, but rather the reason there are cherries, flour, water, fat, the baker, and so on, at all. Hence, it is precisely through those causes and not in competition with them that the providential God works out his purposes.

THE PROBLEM OF EVIL

I fully realize that even those who have been following the logic of my argument so far with sympathy, even those who are predisposed to believe in God and his providence, balk when they consider the overwhelming presence of evil. To state the problem simply: if God really exists, how could there possibly be so much wickedness, corruption, and suffering in the world? In the nineteenth century, the British philosopher John Stuart Mill formulated the objection this way: if an omniscient, omnipotent, and omnibenevolent God exists, there would be no evil, for in his omniscience he would know about it, in his omnipotence he could do something about it, and in his omnibenevolence he would want to do something about it. Therefore if there is evil (and there surely is), then such a God does not exist. In the thirteenth century, Thomas Aquinas stated the dilemma even more pithily. If one of two contraries be infinite, Thomas argued, the other would be altogether destroyed; yet God is called the infinite good. Therefore if God exists there would be no evil. To make the force of these abstract observations felt, all we have to do is allow the specter of Hiroshima, the killing fields of Cambodia, the hundreds of thousands murdered in the Rwanda massacres, a child dying of leukemia, and the horrors of Auschwitz-Bierkenau to come before the mind's eye. How can all of that suffering—which is, of course, only a tiny sampling of the full agony suffered by members the human race over time—ever be reconciled

Auschwitz. WORD ON FIRE

with the existence of a loving, providential God? These are extremely powerful arguments, and they constitute, to my mind, the only really serious challenges to the proposition that there is a God.

There are three ways not so much to solve the problem as to "dissolve" it. The first is atheism: if there is no God, then the dilemma of evil simply disappears, and there is nothing to explain. The second is a mitigated theism, which says that God is not really God. Following the prompts of some popularizing theologians, many today say that God is indeed good and all-knowing, but he's not all-powerful. Therefore, though he knows about our pain and deeply sympathizes with us over it, he cannot finally do much to stop it. And a third way of dissolving the issue is to argue that evil is not really evil, and this we find, for example, in the Buddhist assertion that suffering is an illusion born of our clinging egotism. All of these "dissolutions" are, in my judgment, too easy, for they don't take with requisite seriousness the two horns of the dilemma: the existence of a God worthy of the name, and the objective presence of evil. We have to dig for a deeper answer.

To be sure, any "answer" that a theologian might offer to this most fundamental of existential questions will necessarily be inadequate, but I believe it is possible at least to gesture in the direction of a resolution. The first observation to make is that evil, strictly speaking, does not exist, since evil is always some sort of privation of the good, a lack of a perfection that ought to be present. Thus we speak of a cavity in a tooth, or a cancer that compromises the right functioning of an organ, or a twisting of the will as evil. Therefore it is inappropriate ever to think of God as "causing" or "creating" evil or ever to imagine evil in the Manichaean manner as an opponent standing athwart God's purposes. We must speak, instead, of God permitting or allowing certain evils to emerge. But this affirmation seems to postpone the question rather than to answer it. Why would God "allow" such deep corruption in his creation? The classical response, articulated by Augustine, Thomas Aquinas, and an army of their followers, is that God permits evil so as to bring about a greater good. To be sure, we can see this principle verified in many cases. Some great calamity—a grave illness, a failure in business, the loss of a loved one—results, over time, in a good that would never have come about except through and because of the calamity. As the popular adage has it: God can write straight with crooked lines. Yet in the presence of truly profound evil, doesn't this explanation seem a tad facile?

The biblical authors both defend this classical argument and understand the hesitancy about it—and this becomes particularly obvious in the book of Job. We hear of Job, an utterly righteous man, who, in one fell swoop, loses everything that he holds dear: family, profession, wealth, and health. In the wake of the disaster, three of his friends sit in silent solidarity with him for seven days. But then they begin to theologize.

Following the prompts of the biblical tradition, they try to convince Job that he must have sinned in some way so as to warrant such a harsh divine punishment. And, in accordance with the principle we've been defending, they speculate that God is permitting the terrible evil of Job's suffering so as to bring about the greater good of his repentance. But Job knows (and we the readers know) that he is in fact innocent, and thus he rejects the speculations of his theologically minded friends and, with an unprecedented boldness, calls God himself into the dock, challenging the provident Creator to explain himself. Here Job speaks for every believer in God who has ever suffered unjustly.

In one of the most dramatic scenes in the Bible, God speaks out of the desert whirlwind. "Who is this that obscures divine plans with words of ignorance? Gird up your loins now, like a man; I will question you, and you tell me the answers!" (Job 38:2–3). God then proceeds to take Job on a tour of the cosmos, showing his human interlocutor mystery after mystery, wonder after wonder, anomaly after anomaly. "Where were you when I founded the earth? . . . Who determined its size; do you know? . . . And who shut within doors the sea, when it burst forth from the womb . . . Which is the way to the dwelling place of light, and where is the abode of darkness?" (Job 38:4–5, 8, 19). God's oration closes with an evocation of two great beasts, Leviathan and Behemoth—perhaps a whale and a hippopotamus. With an artist's delight, God describes the power and beauty of these animals. In reference to Leviathan, he says, "any hope of capturing it will be disappointed . . . no one is so fierce as to dare to stir it up. Who can stand before it" (Job 41:1–2); and in regard to Behemoth, he exults, "Behold the strength in his loins, and his vigor in the sinews of his belly . . . He came at the beginning of God's ways" (Job 40:16, 19). God made these creatures just as surely as he made Job, and though Job has probably never in his life even considered Behemoth and Leviathan, they are as ingredient in the complex weave of God's providence as is Job. The overall point of God's speech seems to be this: the suffering of any one person must be seen within the context of the infinitely subtle working out of God's purposes throughout the whole of space and time. In a

Sunday Afternoon on the Island of La Grande Jatte *by Georges Seurat* (*Art Institute of Chicago*). WORD ON FIRE

universe of numberless individuals, events, and relations, certain goods can emerge only in balance with certain evils, or to state it perhaps a bit more precisely, good and evil, within this stunningly complicated milieu, are, to a degree, relative terms. As Thomas Aquinas put it, there would be no life in the lion were it not for the deaths of an inordinate number of other animals, and there would be no virtue of the martyr without the cruelty of the tyrant.

One of the most impressive paintings in the collection of the Art Institute of Chicago is Georges Seurat's pointillist masterpiece *Sunday Afternoon on the Island of La Grande Jatte.* The picture is composed of millions of tiny points of color that Seurat applied to the canvas with long brushes while he sat on a high stool. If you look at the painting with your nose pressed up against it, you see only a collection of meaningless blotches, but as you step back the points begin to blend together and figures, groups, and patterns emerge. Only when you view it from the far side of the room does the painting disclose itself as a gorgeously harmonic unity. God is like an artist, and his canvas is the whole of space and time. Most of us look at his masterpiece with our noses pressed up against it, seeing only a tiny swath, and wondering how these few points—some light and many dark—could possibly make sense. God's speech to Job might be construed as an artist's plea to view his work from the proper vantage point. I might propose another analogy along these lines, having to do with William James and his dog. In an essay written toward the end of his life, the great American philosopher told of his dog, who would typically enter his master's office at the end of the work-day to receive a pat on the head. The animal, James explained, would look around the cluttered room and see the thousands of books on the shelves, the many papers covering the desk, and the globe that rested in the corner. He would see them but understand them hardly at all. And if James made bold to expatiate on the meaning of these things—that the books were collections of symbols evocative of ideas, that the papers, by a similar semiotic system, conveyed intelligent messages, that the globe was a representation of the spherical planet that both master and dog inhabited—the animal would have looked at him with utter incomprehension. But then it occurred to James that we are in a similar relation to a higher mind. Is it possible that we, like the dog, see everything there is to see, but actually *understand* it in only the most superficial way? And is it the case that the higher intelligence could not, even in principle, begin to explain the deepest meaning of things to us, due to the limited capacity of our minds?

Still unsatisfied? Good. Though all of these images, perspectives, and insights are illuminating, none finally "solves" the problem of reconciling a loving God and a universe marked by great cruelty. For the Christian faith, the only adequate "resolution" of this dilemma is the one effected by God himself on the cross of Jesus Christ. On that cross, the darkness of the human condition met the fullness of the divine love and found itself transfigured into life. On that cross, God went to the limits of godforsakenness and made even death itself a place of hope. God, in his love, *becomes* the answer to the problem of evil.

THE TRINITY

Thus far almost everything I have said about God in this chapter could be echoed by a faithful Jew or Muslim, believers in the one God. So what is it, precisely, that makes the Christian doctrine of God distinctive? The answer is given every time we make the sign of the cross and invoke the three divine persons, the Father, the Son, and the Holy Spirit. We are signaling that God is one, but not monolithically so; rather in his unity he is a communion, a family of love.

Where does this doctrine come from? As is always the case with Christian teaching, we have to go back to Jesus. Jesus consistently referred to himself as one who had been sent by the Father; and in this regard he would seem little different from, say, Abraham or Moses or Isaiah. But as we have seen in the first chapter, there is something that sets Jesus apart from those figures, namely, that he spoke and acted in the very person of God. Therefore Jesus was sent by another whom he acknowledged as divine, yet he himself is divine also. The Father was clearly other than the Son he sent; nevertheless, the Son could say, "I and the Father are one" (Jn 10:30). And to make things even more complex, Jesus promised his disciples at the Last Supper that he and his Father would send an "advocate," a Spirit who would lead the church into the fullness of Truth. It was this "breath" (*pneuma*) that blew through the church at the first Pentecost, sustained the early Christian community, and brings divinizing life to believers in Jesus: "no one can say, 'Jesus is Lord,' except by the holy Spirit" (1 Cor 12:3). Now, the first believers were all Jews, trained in the strict monotheism of Israel and holding passionately to the great Shema, the Jewish declaration of faith from the sixth chapter of the book of Deuteronomy: "Hear, O Israel! The Lord is our God, the Lord alone!" Yet they knew that the one God had revealed something new about himself in Jesus and the Holy Spirit. None of the pioneers of the Christian faith summed up this novelty more succinctly than did Saint John, who in his first letter said simply, "God is love." He wasn't defending the proposition that God *has* love, or that love is one of

God's attributes; he was saying that love names the very essence of God. And this means that God must be, in his own life, an interplay of lover (the Father), beloved (the Son), and shared love (the Holy Spirit).

What the Bible bequeathed to the great tradition was this tension, this dilemma: how to square the Shema with the claim that God *is* love. For the first several centuries of the church's life, some of the greatest minds in both the east and the the west struggled to work out the right balance between the two. The discussion swung between the poles of tritheism (belief in three gods) and Monarchianism (the belief in the supreme unity of God), and no finally satisfying resolution was achieved until the fourth century when three brilliant theologians from Asia Minor—Basil, Gregory of Nazianzus, and Gregory of Nyssa—and one supreme genius from North Africa—Augustine of Hippo—brought their powers of reflection to bear on the matter. Within the confines of this short chapter, I have space to consider—however inadequately—only Augustine's meditations.

Throughout the course of twenty years, during his intellectual prime,

St. Monica–St. George Church, detail, Cincinnati. DENIS R. MCNAMARA

Augustine composed a text entitled *De Trinitate* (About the Trinity) in which he sought to clarify and explain the church's doctrine of the one God in three persons. In the ninth book of that text Augustine lays out a remarkably illuminating analogy for the Trinity, which has proven over the centuries to be massively influential on other theologians. Taking his cue from the book of Genesis, Augustine speculates that, though all things reflect the Trinity to varying degrees, the best model of the Trinity would be the human person himself, the one made "in the image and likeness of God." When we look within—and Augustine was one of the greatest masters of introspection—we find, he says, a mirror of the Trinity in the very dynamics of human consciousness. The ground of the intellect, the mysterious source from which all intellectual activity surges forth, Augustine called *mens.* It would be wrong to translate this simply as "mind," for that reduces its meaning too drastically. *Mens* is closer to *esprit* in French or *Geist* in German, designating the full range of spiritual energy. *Mens* is capable of a doubling or mirroring activity by which it poses itself as an object for its own contemplation. This Augustine calls *notitia sui,* or self-knowledge. Though this sounds rather abstract, we all acknowledge *notitia sui* whenever we say, "What was I thinking?" or whenever we engage in introspection under the guidance of a therapist or counselor, searching out our motives and bringing to consciousness our often unconscious impulses. And when *mens* comes to self-awareness through *notitia sui,* it falls in love. Again, we sense this whenever, through introspection or counseling, we come to a richer understanding of ourselves and experience, thereby, a deeper level of self-acceptance. What Augustine finds so intriguing about these dynamics is that though their components are separate from one another, though they can be clearly distinguished one from the other, they do not constitute a dividing of the mind into three. For example, when I say, "What was I thinking?" I'm certainly distinguishing *mens* from *notitia sui,* but I'm not falling into schizophrenia.

It was precisely this tensive ambiguity that makes the analogy so apt. The Father, Augustine claimed, is the *mens* of God, the dark, elemental ground of the divine life. The Father is capable of a perfect and utterly interior act of self-othering. The mirror or Word of the Father, his *notitia sui*, is the Son. When Father and Son gaze at each other, they breathe back and forth their mutual love, and this is the *amor sui* of God, or the Holy Spirit. Hence we have three dynamisms but not three Gods; we have a lover, a beloved, and a shared love, within the unity of one substance, not a one plus one plus one adding up to three, but a one times one times one, equaling one.

The one God of Israel—"I am who am"—is a play of subsistent relations—"God *is* love"—and thus we learn the deepest meaning of the verb "to be" is "to love." It was the Son, the Father's beloved, who became incarnate in Jesus, and it was the Holy Spirit, the love breathed back and forth between the Father and the Son, that came to dwell in the church. And the church's mission, therefore, is to make real in the world precisely this love that God is.

Church of the Gesù, detail, Rome. WORD ON FIRE

Chapter 4

OUR TAINTED NATURE'S SOLITARY BOAST: MARY, THE MOTHER OF GOD

One day, early in the first century, in a hovel in the little Galilean town of Nazareth, an angel appeared to a young Israelite girl who was perhaps no more than fourteen or fifteen years old, and they had a rather extraordinary conversation. The angel greeted her: "Hail, favored one! The Lord is with you" (Lk 1:28). As is invariably the case when an angel makes an appearance, the girl was afraid. "Do not be afraid," the angel told her, "for you have found favor with God. Behold, you will conceive in your womb and bear a son, and you shall name him Jesus" (Lk 1:30–31). When she wondered how this would be possible, since she had had no sexual experience, the angel explained, "The holy Spirit will come upon you, and the power of the Most High will overshadow you. Therefore the child to be born will be called holy, the Son of God" (Lk 1:35). And the girl responded to this overwhelming message with utter simplicity: "Behold, I am the handmaid of the Lord. May it be done to me according to your word" (Lk 1:38). With that the angel departed.

The Annunciation *by Fra Angelico (Prado, Madrid)*. WORD ON FIRE

This young Israelite woman has beguiled the finest poets of the West, from Dante to T. S. Eliot; she has been the subject of paintings by the greatest masters, from Fra Angelico and Michelangelo, to Rembrandt and El Greco; over the centuries, millions of people have visited her shrines seeking her aid and calling out to her, their mother. She is referred to as the Queen of all the saints, the Queen of the angels, and the Queen of heaven. And she has been invoked, over and over again, across the centuries, in the words of the simplest and most beautiful prayer in the Catholic tradition: the Hail Mary.

Why has she had this staggering impact? The best answer is found in the angelic encounter, in which the essence of the biblical drama is distilled. We see the nature of God on display in the graceful, nonviolent manner of the invitation. In story after story from the mythological tradition, we note that when the gods intervene in human affairs, they do so violently, interruptively, in the manner of a rape. But in the sweet invitation of the angel at the Annunciation something altogether different is on display. Mary's freedom and dignity are respected and her curiosity is encouraged;

Annunciation *by Leonardo da Vinci (Uffizi Museum, Florence).* WORD ON FIRE

she is, if I can put it this way, courted by the heavenly messenger. We also see a human being in full in the Virgin Mary. The church fathers were eager to contrast Mary, the Mother of God, with Eve, the mother of all the living. At the decisive moment, Eve took the fruit of the tree of the knowledge of good and evil, succumbing to the temptation to seize at godliness and committing, thereby, the fundamental sin. Why had God prohibited the eating of that fruit? The serpent suggests that a competitive God was envious of his human creatures, not wanting them to "be like him, knowing good and evil," but we know that the devil is the father of lies. For God in fact had given to our first parents practically free rein in the garden, inviting them to eat of all of the trees save one. This generous permission is a symbolic expression of God's desire that we exercise our powers to the full. The church fathers saw the Garden of Eden, in all of its beauty, as a sign of the full range of possibilities and opportunities available to us: politics, philosophy, art, science, friendship, and so forth. So why the prohibition? God forbade the eating of that particular tree not because he is our rival but precisely because he wanted us to fall in love with him.

When two people meet and are mutually attracted, they use their reason and their powers of perception and analysis in order to assess each other. To fail to do this would be irresponsible. Yet their relationship will come to life only to the extent that in the end they surrender to each other; they, as the phrase has it, "fall in love" with each other. We witness something similar in the arts. John Coltrane, Eric Clapton, and Daniel Barenboim—all masters of their respective musical instruments—each commented that he plays his best when he lets his instrument "play him," when he surrenders control and lets the music seize him. God has no interest in dominating us. He wants us to use the full range of our intellectual and moral energies when relating to him, but he also wants us, finally, to let go and to fall in love with him. And this is why he prohibited Adam and Eve from grasping at the uniquely divine prerogative of knowing good and evil: not because he wanted them to be less alive but because he wanted them to be fully alive.

With this clarification in mind, let us return to the maiden of Nazareth. None of Mary's integrity, freedom, or intelligence is negated in the course of her conversation with the angel, but at the limit of her striving and knowing, she willingly surrenders to the alluring power of God. Barely grasping the full extent of what this surrender would entail, she nevertheless says, "I am the handmaid of the Lord." And in obediently adding, "May it be done to me according to your word," she reversed the grasping disobedience of Eve. This is why the medieval illustrators and commentators—so in love with the parallels, rhymes, and echoes within the Bible—imagined the Ave ("hail") of the angel reversing Eva (Eve). On the basis of the angel's greeting, "Kecharitomene," Mary has been called "full of grace," (charis is the Greek for "grace"), and this means, basically, that she is someone who is profoundly disposed to receive gifts. In this, she becomes the new Eve, the mother of all those who would be reborn by being receptive to God's life as a gift.

THE TRUE ISRAELITE

Let us move now from the simple hovel of the Annunciation in Nazareth to one of the most sumptuous and beautiful enclosed spaces in the world, the Cathedral of Chartres. Like almost all of the other Gothic

cathedrals that sprang up in France in the twelfth and thirteenth centuries, Chartres is dedicated to *Notre Dame* (Our Lady). In his magisterial
Mount-Saint-Michel and Chartres, Henry Adams argues that the mediev-
als would have seen Chartres not only as dedicated to Mary, but in a very
real sense as Mary's dwelling place, or even as Mary's body. In accord
with this last suggestion, we might imagine the apse of the church as cor-
responding to the Virgin's head, the transept to her breasts and arms, and
the labyrinth to her womb. The Chartres labyrinth is a carefully designed
circular path that lies about one-third of the way up the nave and that
winds, intestine-like, around on itself. It is thought that pilgrims to the
cathedral would walk it on their knees, making their way symbolically to
the heavenly Jerusalem, which was depicted in bronze at the center of the
intricate set of paths. The labyrinth is the exact same circumference as
the rose window that graces the façade of the cathedral, and this means
that when the sun is correctly positioned in the sky the colors of the
rose window gently and perfectly play on the labyrinth. This juxtaposition
speaks, therefore, of the Incarnation, which took place through Mary's
acquiescence: the impregnation of her virginal womb by heavenly light.
Just as the labyrinth is not obliterated by the light of the rose window but
is enhanced and illumined by it, so Mary's humanity is not compromised
by God's proximity but transfigured and made fruitful.

All around this building dedicated to the Blessed Mother are depictions of figures from the Old Testament—Adam, Job, David, Moses,
Aaron—and this is only appropriate, for Mary, the Mother of God, is the
fulfillment of Zion. She recapitulates all of the great figures of the holy
people whom God had prepared, in the course of many centuries, to receive his Word and make it flesh. She is, accordingly, the daughter of Abraham, the first one to listen to God in faith; she is like Sarah, Hannah, and
the mother of Samson, since she gave birth while trusting in God against
all expectations; she is the true Ark of the Covenant and the true temple,
for she bore the divine presence in the most intimate way possible; she
is like the authors of the Psalms and the books of Wisdom and Prov-
erbs, for she becomes the very seat of Wisdom. And she is like Isaiah,

Portal of Chartres Cathedral, France. DENIS R. MCNAMARA

Jeremiah, and Ezekiel—the prophets who longed for the coming of the Messiah. This last connection can be seen very clearly in the account of the wedding feast at Cana in the Gospel of John. In the midst of their celebration (wedding banquets went on for days in first-century Palestine), a young couple runs out of wine, and Mary brings this problem to the attention of Jesus. We can read this story at the literal level and see Mary as graciously acting to spare the young people embarrassment, but we can also read it more symbolically and appreciate Mary as expressing the prophetic longing of Israel. Wine—delicious, refreshing, intoxicating—is a sign, throughout the Old Testament, of the divine life. Running out of wine, therefore, is an incisive description of the spiritual condition of Israel, alienated in its sin from God's grace. In asking Jesus to act, Mary is speaking according to the rhythms and cadences of the great prophets, who continually called upon Yahweh to visit his people, and when she turns to the waiters and says, "Do whatever he asks," she is summing up the instruction of every teacher, every patriarch, and every prophet of Israel. Saint Irenaeus says that throughout the history of salvation God was, as it were, trying on humanity, gradually suiting divinity and humanity to each other—in a word, preparing for the Incarnation. All of that preparation was a prelude to the Israelite girl, full of grace, who would say yes to the invitation to be the mother of God. A telling detail: just after the Annunciation, Mary, we are told, "set out and traveled to the hill country in haste to a town of Judah, where she entered the house of Zechariah and greeted Elizabeth" (Lk 1:39–40). For centuries Israel had heard the word of Yahweh, but more often than not the people were sluggish in responding. The true Israelite, once she had heard the word of the Lord, moved!

THEOTOKOS

As he was dying on the cross, Jesus looked to his mother and to the disciple whom he loved, and he said to Mary, "Woman, behold, your son," and then to John, "Behold, your mother" (Jn 19:26–27). We are told that "from that hour the disciple took her into his own home" (Jn 19:27). This text supports an ancient tradition that the apostle John took Mary with him when he traveled to Ephesus in Asia Minor and that both ended their days in that city. Indeed, on the top of a high hill overlooking the Aegean Sea, just outside Ephesus, there is a modest dwelling that tradition holds to be the house of Mary. In the year 431 a great council of the church met in the cathedral of Ephesus in order to adjudicate a bitter dispute about the identity of Jesus, but the debate became focused on a technical question in regard to Mary, namely, whether she could legitimately be called Theotokos, or Mother of God. The council fathers were trying to understand Jesus more accurately, precisely by teasing out the

Theotokos, Chora Church, Istanbul. WORD ON FIRE

implications of the conversation that took place between the girl of Nazareth and the angel of the Annunciation.

The background for this council meeting at Ephesus is fascinating. We have to begin by returning, once more, to that conversation at Caesarea-Philippi, when Jesus asked the disciples, "Who do people say that I am?" That question, especially in light of the resurrection, haunted the minds of the members of the ancient church, and the best intellects of the time strove to answer it accurately. Important steps were taken at the Council of Nicaea in 325, when Jesus was declared to be *homoousios* (one in being) with the Father, and at the Council of Constantinople in 381, when that teaching was reiterated. But in the 420s a controversy arose over the teaching of Nestorius, who was the patriarch of Constantinople and a much-revered theological figure. Influenced by the school of Antioch, which placed a great stress on the humanity of Jesus, Nestorius said that in Christ two distinct persons—one divine and one human—come together in a kind of moral union. This meant that

Mary, who was responsible only for the human element in Jesus, could be called Christotokos (mother of Christ) but not Theotokos (mother of God). In fact, Nestorius argued, the use of that latter title would be the height of blasphemy, since it would imply that a mere human being had a sort of primacy over God. Cyril, the bishop of Alexandria, and another theological heavyweight, was so outraged by Nestorius's position that he called the bishop of Constantinople a heretic. The ecumenical council of Ephesus was summoned in order to resolve this controversy.

After much deliberation during the summer of 431, the council fathers taught that Jesus ought not to be understood as a human person with a particularly intense relationship to the person of God, for that would make him a kind of supreme saint but not the incarnate Son of God. And if he were not himself divine, he would require a savior as much as anyone else. Rather it was decided that in the unity of his person both divinity and humanity come together. And this meant, they concluded, that Nestorius was wrong to deny Mary the title Theotokos, for if Jesus was divine and Mary was the mother of Jesus, then Mary could and should be called the Mother of God. To Nestorius's point about the blasphemous nature of this description, the council fathers said that Mary is not the mother of Jesus's divinity, but the mother of Jesus, who is, in fact, divine. Historians report that when this resolution was publicly declared, the people of Ephesus responded with a joyful torch-lit parade through the streets of the town. Perhaps these ordinary Christians did not fully grasp the theological subtleties of the conciliar definition, but they understood viscerally that the statement glorified the Virgin Mary whom they loved and who had once lived among them—and so they celebrated.

I would like to spend just a bit more time with those Ephesians who celebrated the Theotokos, for some have suggested that the cause for their celebration was deep in their cultural DNA. For centuries Ephesus had been the center for the lively cult of Artemis, the great mother goddess. In fact, the temple to Artemis, which stood just outside the city, was one of the wonders of the ancient world, more magnificent, Herodotus said, than the pyramids of Egypt or the gardens of Babylon. Statues of

Theotokos. DENIS R. MCNAMARA

Artemis—covered in dozens of breasts, signifying her nurturing motherhood—were produced at Ephesus and distributed all over the Mediterranean world. Therefore some have insinuated that Mary simply replaced Artemis in the imagination of the common people, as one more iteration of the mother goddess archetype. Without denying that there might have been confusion in the minds of some on this score, there in fact yawns a huge gulf between a mother goddess and the Mother of God. The fathers of the council of Ephesus were not declaring the divinity of Mary; they were not turning the humble handmaid of the Lord into a goddess. But in a certain way they were saying that Mary was indeed greater than Artemis, for she had the privilege, through grace, of bringing into the world the God who would save the world. The declaration of Mary as Mother of God is an instance of the general principle that whatever is said about Mary is meant not so much to draw attention to her as to throw light on Christ. To say that Mary is the Mother of God is to insist on the density of the claim that God truly became human, one of us, bone of our bone and flesh of our flesh. As Archbishop Fulton J. Sheen commented, "Mary is like the moon, for her light is always the reflection of a higher light."

Catholic theology has drawn a further implication from Mary's status as Mother of God, namely, her role as mother of the church. If she is the one through whom Christ was born, and if the church is Christ's mystical body, then she must be, in a very real sense, the mother of the church. She is the one through whom Jesus continues to be born in the hearts of those who believe. This is not to confuse her with the Savior, but it is to insist on her mission as mediator and intercessor. At the close of the great prayer the Hail Mary, we Catholics ask Mary to pray for us "now and at the hour of our death," signaling that throughout one's life Mary is the privileged channel through which the grace of Christ flows into the mystical body. Here again, the principle of God's noncompetitive transcendence is apposite. God is not threatened by his creation. On the contrary, he delights in drawing secondary causes into the dense complexity of his providential plan, granting to them the honor of cooperating with him and his designs. The handmaid of the Lord, who is the mother of the church, is the humblest of these humble instruments—and therefore the most effective. Hans Urs von Balthasar has argued that the Marian form is the matrix of all church life and ministry. He means that her *fiat* (be it done to me according to your word) opens up the creaturely space within which God can work. Mary's freedom, surrendered utterly to God, becomes the condition for the possibility of all forms of mission and outreach in the life of the church. The Petrine ministry of office, the Johannine ministry of prayer and contemplation, and the Pauline ministry of theologizing and evangelization—the kingly, priestly, and prophetic offices, if you will—are all finally reducible to the Marian form. This is why in much medieval and early modern Christian art Mary is often depicted gathering all manner of life under her protective mantle. This

Isenheim Altarpiece, *detail, by Matthias Grünewald (Unterlinden Museum, Colmar, France).* WORD ON FIRE

is not sentimental piety, but a robust presentation of Mary, the mother of the church.

THE IMMACULATE CONCEPTION AND THE ASSUMPTION OF MARY

The doctrines of the Immaculate Conception and the Assumption of Mary were formally declared only in recent years (the first in 1854 and the second in 1950), but their provenance is quite ancient. Indications of the doctrine of the Immaculate Conception can be traced to the New Testament in the angel's greeting to Mary, and the roots of the second doctrine go back to the liturgies and theologies of the church fathers. Perhaps what we notice first about these dogmas is how *physical*, even disturbingly so, they are—how they compel us to see God's activity in the functions and destiny of the lowly human body. The English Catholic novelist David Lodge has observed that upon hearing of these and similar doctrines his Protestant school friends were ashamed to tell their parents about them! Here again, the ultimate purpose of these teachings is to speak of Christ and his Incarnation.

In 1854 Pope Pius IX declared the dogma of the Immaculate Conception of Mary, which is to say, the truth that Mary, through a special grace, was preserved free from original sin from the first moment of her conception. Were this not the case, the angel would not have referred to her at the Annunciation as *Kecharitomene* (full of grace). Two questions naturally present themselves when this doctrine is proposed: why would God do such a thing? And wouldn't this imply that Mary does not need to be redeemed? The traditional answer to the first question is that God wanted to prepare a worthy vessel for the reception of his Word. Just as the holy of holies in the Temple was kept pure and inviolate, so the definitive temple, the true Ark of the Covenant, which is Mary herself, should all the more be untrammeled. In this context, the stories concerning the young Mary's close association with the Temple in Jerusalem (found in the Protoevangelium of James, a third-century text) are, if not necessarily historically accurate, nevertheless theologically suggestive. Even some of the finest minds in the church have found the second question difficult to answer. Though liturgies celebrating the Immaculate Conception date from the seventh century, theologians as weighty as Alexander of Hales, Saint Bonaventure, and Saint Thomas Aquinas himself couldn't find a sufficient justification for the teaching. It appeared to them that to declare Mary free of original sin from the moment of her conception would preclude the universality of Christ's redemptive act, which took place many years after Mary was conceived. It was Blessed John Duns Scotus who, in the early fourteenth century, showed a way forward. He argued that Mary is indeed, like the rest of the human race, redeemed by the grace of her Son, but since that grace exists, properly speaking, outside of time, it can be applied in a way that transcends the ordinary rhythms of time. Therefore, Mary was preemptively delivered by Christ's grace from original sin. With typical scholastic laconism, Duns Scotus said with regard to God's effecting of this deliverance: *"potuit, decuit, ergo fecit"* (he could do it; it was fitting that he do it; therefore, he did it).

This teaching of the church received its strangest and most surprising ratification just four years after it was promulgated. The setting was a town in far southern France, in the Pyrenees region quite near the Spanish border, a town that at the time was unknown to practically anyone and that today is renowned across the world. And it happened through the ministrations of an unlettered shepherd girl named Bernadette Soubirous.

In February of 1858 the six members of the Soubirous family were living in a tiny one-room hovel in a poor section of Lourdes. The locals referred to the place as the Cachot because it was a converted prison.

Site of the Apparition, Lourdes, France. WORD ON FIRE

The city officials of Lourdes evidently felt that the conditions there were too harsh and primitive for the prisoners, and they had allowed it to be sold. With its single fireplace, low roof, and tiny window, it was really little more than a cave. On February 11, Bernadette, who was the eldest child in the family, made her way from the Cachot to Massabielle, a garbage dump on the outskirts of Lourdes, a place where trash from the town and detritus from the local hospital were piled up to be burned. She had come there with one of her sisters and a friend to look for scraps of wood with which to heat her family's tiny home. While the other two girls scampered away in search of firewood, Bernadette, due to her asthma, tarried for a time by the Gave, a fast-flowing stream. She felt a puff of wind and heard a sound. When she turned to see what had caused the stir, she spied a beautiful young woman, clothed in white, with a yellow rose on each foot, standing in the niche of massy rock of Massabielle. Afraid, Bernadette instinctually reached for her rosary and made the sign of the cross. The Lady only smiled and began to pray along silently with Bernadette on her own rosary made of pearls. When the girl finished her prayer, the Lady smiled again and vanished.

Bernadette felt compelled to return to Massabielle, so the next day she went to the spot with a handful of her friends. Again she saw the lady, but this time the mysterious visitor spoke: "Would you do me the favor of returning for the next fifteen days?" She also had a message for Bernadette to convey to the local priest: "Build a temple on this site and let processions come." When the girl brought this word to the priest, Father Perymale, he responded with scorn and a stern warning never to return to the place. Yet the young Bernadette continued to visit Massabielle, despite official opposition and the mockery of many. During one encounter the Lady asked Bernadette to dig in the ground to find a spring of water. Bernadette dug and dug but uncovered just a bit of muddy earth. At the Lady's prompting, the girl smeared some of the mud on her face and also ate a few roots and weeds from the site. Those witnessing these strange happenings thought that the girl had lost her mind. But in time water indeed flowed from the spot where Bernadette had dug, and a young crippled boy who bathed in it was cured.

Bernadette kept returning for those fifteen days and communed with the Lady, falling into a kind of trance during which she remained impervious to pain and oblivious to her surroundings. Even the most skeptical of observers came away impressed by the eerie, otherworldly quality of the girl's concentration. But despite the speculations of many, Bernadette never claimed to know who the mysterious visitor was. She referred to her consistently as "the Lady" or, in her local patois, *Aquero* (that one). On March 24, the eve of the feast of the Annunciation, Bernadette felt an inner impulse to go to the grotto. The Lady was there to meet her, and Bernadette this time asked her interlocutor for her name. Three times she petitioned, and finally the Lady looked at her with a serious expression and, her voice trembling with emotion, said, "I am the Immaculate Conception." The uneducated Bernadette had never heard the expression before and had no idea what it meant. She kept repeating it to herself on the way to Father Perymale's residence, making sure that she would remember it. Keep in mind that the apparitions took place only four years after the declaration of the dogma by Pope Pius IX. When she repeated to the priest what the Lady had said, he initially balked, insisting that the Lady should have said "I am the fruit of the Immaculate Conception," not "I am the Immaculate Conception." But Bernadette insisted that she had accurately reported the Lady's communication, and eventually Perymale and the entire town were won over both by the girl's sincerity and by the stunning content of what the Lady had spoken.

Why would the Mother of God have chosen to reveal this particular name to Bernadette at Lourdes? Obviously, chronology had something to do with it, but I also believe that there is an important correlation between the dogma of the Immaculate Conception and the particular gift that was given at Lourdes through Bernadette. To this day people go to Lourdes to bathe in and drink the water that Bernadette uncovered, in the hopes of finding healing for body, soul, and mind, and every single night a magnificent candlelight procession of thousands of pilgrims takes place in front of the "temple" that was built according to the Lady's directive. What is the Immaculate Conception but a great act of healing on the part of Jesus, the preemptive removal of the stain of original sin from the soul of his mother? And therefore how appropriate that Mary's ratification of that title would be forever accompanied by, and associated with, the curing of the sick. And finally, how wonderful and how typical that Mary would appear to such a person in such a place. In her great Magnificat in Luke's Gospel, Mary sings the praises of the God who "has thrown down the rulers from their thrones and lifted up the lowly" (Lk 1:52). Bernadette, who was something of a cave girl, was visited in a garbage dump by the Immaculate Conception, by the Queen of heaven, who herself had received the message of an angel in a hovel and who had given birth to the Son of God in a cave.

Now we turn to the dogma of the Assumption of the Virgin, declared as such by Pope Pius XII in 1950. Before the formal promulgation of the doctrine, Pius sponsored a worldwide survey of the Catholic people, a consultation of the faithful, to see whether they sanctioned this teaching, and the response was overwhelmingly positive. Also, as I have already suggested, the roots of this dogma in the tradition of the church are old and deep. But what precisely does the dogma teach? That Mary, upon leaving this life, was taken, body and soul, into heaven. I fully realize that this assertion can strike the contemporary mind as bizarre, mythological, a holdover from a naïve, prescientific world. First, let us place it within the context of the radically nondualistic perspective of the Bible in regard to the soul and the body. Greek philosophy tends to construe salvation as an escape of the soul from the prison of the body. To see this attitude on full display, consult Plato's dialogue, the *Phaedo*, in which Socrates urges his friends not to mourn over his coming death but to see it as a much longed for liberation. This philosophy is utterly alien to the biblical imagination, which does not envision salvation as the separation of the soul from the body, but rather as the transfiguration of the entire self. To give just two examples of this pervasive attitude, the authors of both the book

Assumption of Mary *by El Greco (Art Institute of Chicago).* WORD ON FIRE

of Revelation and the first letter of Peter dream not of an escape from the world but of "a new heavens and a new earth" (Pet 3:13). The dogma of the Assumption of Mary describes the full salvation of this prime disciple of Jesus—Mary's entry, in the fullness of her person, into the presence of God. At the close of the Apostles' Creed, we speak of our hope for "the resurrection of the body." Mary, assumed body and soul into heaven, has experienced precisely this kind resurrection and hence becomes a sign of hope for the rest of the human race.

If we are to respond adequately to the skeptics, a second observation must be made. When we speak of the Assumption of the Blessed Mother's body, we are not envisioning a journey through space, as though Mary moved up into the sky. The "heavens" are a rich and consistent biblical symbol for the transcendent, for a manner of existence that lies beyond our familiar dimensions of space and time. The Assumption of Mary means that the Blessed Mother was "translated," in the totality of her being, from this dimensional system to the higher one for which we use the symbolically evocative term "heaven." Perhaps a comparison would help here. Think of a square, a circle, and a triangle plotted out on a two-dimensional plane. Now imagine those figures elevated through the introduction of a third dimension into a cube, a sphere, and a pyramid. They have not so much lost their former identities as found them heightened, deepened, and perfected. What if there were a conscious subject who lived exclusively in a two-dimensional world? He would know only squares, circles, triangles, and so on, and if you spoke to him of cubes, spheres, and pyramids, he would find your language utterly impenetrable, so much nonsense. Heaven is a symbol for a higher dimensional system that contains the dimensions with which we are familiar but that also elevates them and situates them in a richer context. Mary, who exists now in this other world, is not so much *somewhere* else as *somehow* else, and this helps to explain why we can speak of her, especially in her heavenly state, interceding, helping us and praying for us. Again, to people who have known only this world, such a concept will necessarily seem opaque, even ridiculous. The doctrine of Mary's As-

Coronation of the Virgin, *detail, by Botticelli (Uffizi Museum, Florence).* WORD ON FIRE

sumption both whets our appetite for this higher world and teases our minds into the consideration of it.

At this point I could offer just a word of reflection on an idea that is related to the dogma of the Assumption but that is not a formal doctrine of the church: the teaching concerning the "dormition" or the "falling asleep" of Mary. According to this notion, at the end of her days Mary did not so much die in the ordinary sense but fell asleep in the Lord. Again, although this can strike us as strange, it actually conveys something of great spiritual importance. Death can be taken in a purely biological or physiological sense to mean the cessation of bodily activity: heartbeat, breathing, brain waves, and so on. Or it can be construed in a wider psychological and spiritual sense to mean the full range of feelings, reactions, and fears that accompany this biological dissolution. At the prospect of death, most of us recoil in terror, either at the mystery of it (the unknown is what frightens us the most) or because of the judgment that awaits us. In either case, our horror is prompted by sin, a lack of confident trust in the love of God. What would it be like for a sinless person to approach death? Wouldn't he or she face it with utter calmness of spirit, the way most of us fall effortlessly into the oblivion of sleep

Statue of Mary and Child, Pantheon, Rome. WORD ON FIRE

each night, convinced that we shall awaken the next morning? That the sinless Mary didn't "die," in the full sense of that term, but merely "fell asleep," confidently expecting a transition into God's dimension, strikes me as a not altogether unreasonable way to speak of the end of Mary's earthly life.

MARY IN THE LIFE OF THE CHURCH

Immaculate Mary, the Mother of God, assumed body and soul into heaven, is not of merely historical or theoretical interest. Nor is she simply a spiritual exemplar. Instead as "Queen of all the saints" (another of her titles) Mary is an ongoing presence, an actor in the life of the church. In entrusting Mary to John ("Behold, your mother"), Jesus was, in a real sense, entrusting Mary to all those who would be friends of Jesus down through the ages. The Blessed Mother's basic task is always to draw people into deeper fellowship with her son. The church's conviction is that the Blessed Mother continues to say yes to God and to "go in haste" on mission around the world. She does so usually in quiet, hidden ways, responding to prayer and interceding for the church, but sometimes she does so in a remarkable manner, breaking into our world strikingly and visibly. There have been literally tens of thousands of reports of apparitions of the Blessed Mother up and down the Catholic centuries. Many, perhaps most, can be traced to the overexcited subjectivities of certain believers, but there are some that are much more difficult to dismiss. We've already considered one of them, the manifestation to Bernadette at Lourdes; I would like to look at another that is similarly marked by simplicity, credibility, and rich efficaciousness. It is the extraordinary encounter between the Queen of heaven and, typically enough, one of her little ones; and it is, without doubt, the manifestation of Mary that has had the most explosive impact on the wider world. I'm speaking of Tepeyac and of Our Lady of Guadalupe.

On December 9, 1531, just about ten years after the Spaniards had first brought the faith to Mexico, an Indian man named Juan Diego, a recent convert to Christianity, was making his way along the hill of Tepeyac, just outside the city of Tenochtitlan, which would later evolve into Mexico City. He was heading to morning Mass. He heard a burst of birdsong and turned to see where it was coming from. What he saw took his breath away, for standing before him was a woman clothed in celestial light. The Lady announced herself as the "Mother of the Most High God," and she had a request for Juan Diego: "Would you ask the bishop to construct a temple here in my honor?" Being a simple man, Juan Diego obeyed. He was ushered into the presence of Bishop Juan Zumárraga, a Franciscan friar and a good man, the builder of the first hospital and university in the Americas, and a protector of the native population. Bishop Zumárraga listened patiently to Juan Diego's story, but, understandably enough, he asked Juan Diego for a confirming sign from the heavenly Lady. On December 12, Juan Diego went once again to Tepeyac and found the Virgin there. She invited him to remove his tilma, the simple, coarse poncho-like garment he was wearing, and then, with her help, he gathered up a bunch of roses that were, despite the lateness of the year, in bloom. This, she said, would be a sign for the bishop. Juan Diego hurried with his bundle to the bishop's office, but he was made to wait. It is said that officious aides of Zumárraga's tried, without success, to find out what the Indian was carrying in his tilma. Finally Juan Diego was brought into the bishop's presence. He opened his cloak and the roses spilled out, but then, to Juan Diego's amazement, the bishop and his assistants were kneeling, for on the inside of the tilma was something extraordinary: an image of the woman clothed in light. On the spot, Zumárraga vowed to build the temple the Lady had asked for, and it still stands near the hill of Tepeyac.

One might be tempted to dismiss this as a charming story from a simpler, more credulous time, but the best contradiction to this kind of skepticism is the tilma itself, which is displayed in the massive basilica of Our Lady of Guadalupe in Mexico City. Careful studies have shown that the tilma is indeed from the sixteenth century and woven from cactus fibers.

Our Lady of Guadalupe. WORD ON FIRE

This juxtaposition is itself puzzling, since that kind of garment, under the best of conditions, usually lasts for at most twenty or twenty-five years. And then there is the image, the strange and beautiful image, which has beguiled millions for the past five hundred years. Scientific analysis has revealed that no known pigmentation was involved and that no under-drawing is discernible. Therefore, just *how* those colors were transferred onto the tilma is mysterious. Moreover, the symbolic power of the image is extraordinary. The Virgin on the tilma is not a European or an Indian, but a mestiza, a blend of the two races. Mexicans today refer to her affec-tionately as La Virgen Morena (the brown-skinned Virgin). It is as though the Blessed Mother was humbly identifying herself with the new people who were emerging in that time and place. The cincture that she wears was an Aztec sign of pregnancy, and therefore it is clear that La Virgen Morena is bringing a new life and a new birth to the people of Mexico. She stands in front of the sun, whose rays can be seen behind her, her feet are on the moon, and her mantle is bedecked with stars. The sun, moon, and stars were all deities for the ancient Aztecs, and thus the Lady is declar-ing herself to be more powerful than the Indian gods. At the same time, she keeps her eyes down and her hands folded in an attitude of prayer, acknowledging that there is one still greater than she. In recent years astronomers have noted that the arrangement of the stars on her cloak corresponds precisely to the position of the constellations on December 12, 1531. And perhaps most astonishingly, through microscopic investigation ophthalmologists have discovered images of human figures in the eye of La Virgen Morena that correspond to the positions such images would have in a functioning eye, and these reflections are credibly of Zumárraga and his confreres at the moment of the unfolding of the tilma. Her name, "Guadalupe," is probably a Spanish deformation of the Nuatl term *coatlaxopeuh,* (pronounced *coat-la-soupay*), which means "the one who crushes the serpent." This name has a double sense, for the serpent was another chief divinity of the Aztecs, and, in the Christian context, the book of Genesis speaks of the serpent (the tempter) that would "strike at the heel" of the offspring of the archetypal woman.

What no one, even the most stubborn skeptic, can dispute is that within ten years of the apparition to Juan Diego almost the entire Mexican nation—nine million people—converted to Christianity. That amounts to approximately three thousand people per day for ten years, a mini-Pentecost every day for a decade. And the image continues to beguile, fascinate, and beckon. The shrine of Our Lady of Guadalupe is the most visited religious site in the Christian world, surpassing Lourdes, the Church of the Holy Sepulchre, and St. Peter's itself. People still go there by the millions every year in order to commune with La Virgen Morena, many journeying to her over many miles on their knees. There is a story told about a charismatic evangelical preacher in California who was trying to draw Hispanics away from what he took to be the heresies of Catholicism. He gathered a huge crowd in central Los Angeles and proceeded to harangue them about the outrages of the papacy, the superstition of the Rosary, and the silliness of invoking the saints. After each of these sections of his speech, the people cheered lustily. Then the preacher took out a large reproduction of the image of Our Lady of Guadalupe and proceeded to tear it in two. There was a moment of shocked silence. Then the people rushed the stage, and the poor preacher had to be removed by the police!

The total capturing of the hearts of the Mexican people—across five hundred years—is but one dimension of La Virgen Morena's impact. Because of her, another major cultural shift was effected, namely, the ending of human sacrifice in the New World. The Aztec divinities—the gods of the stars, the moon, and the sun, as well as the great serpent god—were regularly appeased through human sacrifice, the offering of the heads and hearts of innocent victims. The cultural anthropologist and philosopher René Girard helps us to understand the pervasiveness of this practice in the ancient world as well as the presence of it, in mitigated forms, today. When tensions arise within a society, Girard argues, a scapegoating mechanism is triggered. Following this largely unconscious impulse, we find someone or some group to blame and then, together, we discharge our anxiety onto him or them. In doing so we feel, however fleetingly, a rush of relief and a sense of common purpose. This is why we tend to feel that the gods are pleased with the scapegoating move. Human sacrifice is the extreme expression of this mechanism, and that is why it was so widely practiced, especially in societies that felt most acutely threatened by enemies or by the capricious elements of nature. The great pyramids of Teotihuacan outside Mexico City are architectural masterpieces, but they were also the setting for thousands upon thousands of human sacrifices offered to the bloodthirsty gods of the Aztecs. As I have suggested, Girard feels that to one degree or another all human groups—from the coffee klatch, to the faculty lounge, to the nation-state—tend to organize themselves around scapegoating, blaming, and recrimination.

When she appeared to Juan Diego, Mary said that she was the Mother of the Most High God, the one who had brought the God-man into the world. When her child came of age, he conquered violence through the power of nonviolent love. He became, himself, the victim of scapegoating violence and thereby unmasked the usually hidden dynamic that drives and orders most human societies. The cross of Jesus undermined any claim that the true God is pleased with human sacrifice, and it showed the way toward a culture grounded in love, what Jesus called the Kingdom of God. Therefore it is not the least surprising that the announcement of Mary's Son to the New World was the death knell for a religion centered on human sacrifice. Mind you, I labor under no illusions about the atrocities perpetrated by the Spaniards of the sixteenth and seventeenth centuries. I fully realize that they were no angels. But by God, the Son of Our Lady of Guadalupe was introduced to Mexico, and human sacrifice ended. In the sixteenth century, as Christianity was moving into an entirely new world, Mary was on mission. It is the conviction of the church that she will "proceed in haste" in her work until the return of her Son.

CONCLUSION

In the first chapter of the Gospel of Luke, we find Mary's great hymn of praise to Yahweh. It commences with the simple declaration, "My soul proclaims the greatness of the Lord." Mary announces here that her whole being is ordered to the glorification of God. Her ego wants nothing for itself; it wants only to be an occasion for giving honor to God. But since, as we have seen, God needs nothing, whatever glory Mary gives to him returns to her benefit so that she is magnified in the very act of magnifying him. In giving herself away fully to God, Mary becomes a superabundant source of life; indeed, she becomes pregnant with God. This odd and wonderful rhythm of magnifying and being magnified is the key to understanding everything about Mary, from her divine motherhood, to her assumption and Immaculate Conception, to her mission in the life of the church.

The great nineteenth-century Jesuit poet Gerard Manley Hopkins caught this in his ballad "The May Magnificat." He wonders aloud in the first few stanzas why May should be a month dedicated to Mary, and he provides Mary's own answer:

The Madonna of the Pomegranate *by Botticelli*
(*Uffizi Museum, Florence*). WORD ON FIRE.

Ask of her, the mighty mother:
Her reply puts this other
Question: What is Spring?—
Growth in every thing—

Then, with typical verbal dexterity and spiritual enthusiasm, Hopkins
delineates the modes of growth in springtime:

Flesh and fleece, fur and feather,
Grass and greenworld all together;
Star-eyed strawberry-breasted
Throstle above her nested

Cluster of bugle blue eggs thin
Forms and warms the life within;
And bird and blossom swell
In sod or sheath or shell.

And he imagines Mary the Mother of God surveying all of this life with
limitless pleasure:

All things rising, all things sizing
Mary sees, sympathising
With that world of good,
Nature's motherhood.

Mary's utter willingness to magnify the Lord made of her a matrix of life.
The spring itself, in all of its wild fecundity, is but a hint at the vitality
that she unleashes.

Chapter 5

THE INDISPENSABLE MEN: PETER, PAUL, AND THE MISSIONARY ADVENTURE

T here are any number of crucial players in the life of the early Christian movement. One thinks of Timothy and Titus, of Matthew, Mark, and Mary Magdalene, of Barnabas, Silas, Luke, and James, of Philip and John. But the two indispensable people, the ones without whom the church never would have emerged and survived, are Peter and Paul. Why these two? Peter was the head of the apostles, the one appointed by Jesus to lead the new Israel; he was the unwavering witness to the resurrection, the rock. And Paul was the first Christian theologian, the one who grasped the full implication of the resurrection of Jesus from the dead and who therefore helped the Christian movement to become a worldwide phenomenon. Due to their centrality, Peter and Paul are not merely of historical interest; they live on as determining archetypes in the community of Jesus to the present day. Every five years each Catholic bishop in the world is required to make what is called an *ad limina* visit to Rome. In the course of that pilgrimage the

Saint Peter, Basilica of St. John Lateran, Rome. WORD ON FIRE

bishop visits with the pope, but the primary purpose of the visit is to pray at the tombs of the two great apostles Peter and Paul and to draw strength from them. The church has intuited that these two saints remain, two thousand years after their deaths, the indispensable men.

Saint Peter was born Shimeon Bar Johannon, Simon the son of John, in the town of Bethsaida on the northern shore of the Sea of Galilee. He was, like his father, a fisherman (indeed "Bethsaida" is Aramaic for "house of fishing"), and because of his trade though he certainly was not aristocratic he was not poor. We have records that show that Galilean fishermen shipped their product across the Roman world. Simon was not well educated, but he probably spoke some Greek for business purposes along with his native Aramaic and perhaps some Hebrew for liturgical prayer. We know that he was married, for the Gospels speak of his mother-in-law, and some traditions (probably legendary) even name his son and daughter. The Gospel of Mark tells us that Jesus of Nazareth was one day walking along the shore of the Sea of Galilee when he spotted Simon and his brother Andrew "casting their nets into the sea" (Mk 1:16). Jesus said to them, "Come after me, and I will make you fishers of men," and "Then they left their nets and followed him" (Mk 1:17–18). Mark is certainly communicating to us the compelling, even mesmerizing, charisma of Jesus—on display in a number of other Gospel narratives as well—but he is also telling us something about these two brothers. Though established in their careers, they were willing to abandon *everything* to follow an itinerant preacher whom they had just met.

We see this almost reckless readiness to respond to the divine summons in many of the stories of Simon, including one from chapter 5 of Luke's Gospel. Because of the press of the crowd, Jesus got into Simon's boat and put out a little from the shore and preached from there. When he had finished speaking, he said to Simon, "Put out, into deep water and lower your nets for a catch" (Lk 5:4). The experienced fisherman responded that they had been hard at it all night and had caught nothing, but something in the command of Jesus was irresistible, so Simon added, "but at your command I will lower the nets" (Lk 5:5). What followed was the miraculous catch of fishes, a catch so impressive that it threatened to sink two boats. Simon's immediate reaction was to fall to his knees before Jesus and to protest his own unworthiness: "Depart from me, Lord, for I am a sinful man!" (Lk 5:8). There are overtones of the call of Isaiah in this passage. The Old Testament prophet saw the glory of the Lord in the Temple but then admitted his profound imperfection: "I am a man of unclean lips, living among a people of unclean lips" (Is 6:5). The proximity of the divine light does not diminish our sense of sin; it enhances it, much as bright light on a window brings out the smudges and marks that are otherwise concealed. Once Isaiah admitted his sin, God cleansed him and then sent him on mission. In the very same way, the penitent Simon was forgiven and commissioned: "Do not be afraid; from now on you will be catching men" (Lk 5:10). Here, in Luke's rendition of the commissioning, Simon emerges as the archetype of the church, which will always be a community of forgiven and empowered sinners.

Simon, whom Jesus renamed Peter, did indeed leave his home and his livelihood in order to join the company of Jesus's intimate followers, and he was with the Lord at some of the key moments of his life. He was present on the mountain, along with James and John, when Jesus was transfigured and spoke with Elijah and Moses. It was Peter who said, "Rabbi, it is good that we are here! Let us make three tents: one for you, one for Moses, and one for Elijah" (Mk 9:5). Thomas Aquinas wondered why those three disciples in particular were privileged to witness this event, and he speculated that James was there because he would be the first of the apostles to be martyred, and that John was there because he was the disciple whom Jesus specially loved, and Peter was on the mountain because, of all the apostles, he loved Jesus the most. There is a most important spiritual lesson here: precisely because the person of Jesus, rather than a set of convictions or ideas, stands at the heart of Christianity, falling in love with him is a sine qua non. Peter was in the boat with the other disciples when Jesus came walking toward them over the stormy sea. Thinking they were seeing a ghost, the disciples cried out in terror, but Jesus calmed them: "Take courage, it is I; do not be afraid" (Mt 14:27). Peter said, "Lord, if it is you, command me to come to you on the water," and Jesus said, "Come" (Mt 14:28–29). As long as he kept his eyes fixed on the Lord and not on the danger, Peter walked successfully on the waves, but when he looked about at his precarious situation, he began to sink. Once again, Peter functions as a symbol of the church, which is obliged to make its way through the stormy waters of history, and which will find its courage precisely in the clarity of its focus on Christ.

After Jesus's arrest, when the dark powers were gathering round, Peter found himself in the courtyard of the high priest's house. While he warmed himself by a fire, a woman confronted him: "You too were with the Nazarene, Jesus" (Mk 14:67). But Peter denied it: "I neither know nor understand what you are talking about" (Mk 14:68). Then a cock crowed. Moving away from his accuser into the forecourt, Peter met a servant girl who recognized him and told the bystanders, "This man is one of them" (Mk 14:69), but again Peter denied it. Then another person joined the scapegoating crowd: "Surely you are one of them; for you too are a Galilean" (Mk 14:70). Swearing an oath, Peter cried out, "I do not know this man about whom you are talking" (Mk 14:71). At that moment, a cock crowed a second time, and Peter recalled Jesus's prediction: "Before the cock crows twice you will deny me three times" (Mk 14:72). The head of the apostles then broke down and wept. After the resurrection, Peter and the other disciples returned to Galilee to ply their fishermen's trade once again. While they were fishing, they spotted Jesus on the far shore. The Gospel, curiously enough, tells us that Peter was naked (*gymnos* in the Greek) and threw on some clothes before going to the Lord. This detail is meant to remind us of the story of Adam in the book of Genesis. Prior to the fall, Adam walked in easy and unself-conscious nakedness before God, but after the primal sin, he hid himself, ashamed of his nudity. So Peter, still deeply regretting his denial of Christ, covers up his nakedness in the presence of Jesus. Then we witness a beautiful act of spiritual direction, as Jesus draws Peter back into his circle of intimacy. Three times the Lord asks Peter whether he loves him, and three times Peter affirms it: "Lord, you know that I love you" (Jn 21:15, 16, 17). Saint Augustine was the first to comment that the threefold statement of love was meant to counteract the threefold denial. Perhaps most tellingly here, Peter emerges as the archetype of the forgiven and commissioned church, for after each of his reaffirmations, Peter hears the command to "tend my sheep." Once we are brought back into friendship with Jesus, we necessarily love those whom he loves.

In chapter 1 I put a special emphasis on the peculiarity of the question that Jesus posed in the vicinity of Caesarea-Philippi, "Who do people say that I am?" But I would like now to return to that place in order to examine the answers that Jesus received, especially the one proffered by Simon. In response to Jesus's extraordinary inquiry, the disciples said, "John the Baptist, others Elijah, still others one of the prophets." We can easily imagine that Jesus, like any celebrity, had excited a buzz of interest and that there must have been many such opinions and interpretations bandied about. But what all of those readings—reflecting the popular consensus—had in common was that they were wrong. Having heard the results of this popular opinion survey, Jesus turned to his inner circle, the twelve, and asked, "But who do you say that I am?" (Mk 8:29; Lk 9:20; Mt 16:15). It is most instructive that silence ensued. Not even the intimate company of the Lord knew the answer. Finally, Peter alone spoke: "You are the Messiah, the Son of the living God" (Mt 16:16). He would have said *Mashiach,* "the anointed," the one who would gather the tribes and cleanse the Temple and defeat Israel's enemies, but then he added that startling phrase, "the Son of the living God" (Mt 16:16). Somehow, even at this relatively early stage in Jesus's ministry, Peter intuited that Jesus was much more than a prophet or rabbi or seer, however significant. He knew that there was something qualitatively different about his master.

Jesus responded to this confession of Peter with some of the most extraordinary language in the New Testament: "Blessed are you, Simon son of Jonah. For flesh and blood has not revealed this to you, but my heavenly Father. And so I tell you, you are Peter, and upon this rock I will build my church, and the gates of the netherworld shall not prevail against it" (Mt 16:17–18). Neither the crowds nor the aristocratic circle around Jesus knew who he was—only Peter knew. And this knowledge did not come from Peter's native intelligence or from an extraordinary education (he didn't have one) or from his skill at assessing popular opinion. It came as a gift from God, a special charism of the Holy Spirit. Because of this gift, given only to the head of the twelve, Jesus called Simon by a new

Saint Peter, Chora Church, Istanbul. WORD ON FIRE

name, in Aramaic *kephas* (rock or rocky), rendered in Greek as Petros and in English as Peter. On the foundation of this rock, Jesus declared that he would build his *ekklesia*, his church. Though it was fashionable some years ago for scholars to deny that Jesus ever intended to found a church, most scholars now hold that it would be hard to imagine a Messiah without a messianic community, that is to say, without a renewed Israel. And Jesus insists that this society, grounded in Peter's confession, would constitute an army so powerful that not even the fortified capital of the dark kingdom itself could withstand it. It is fascinating to me how often we construe this saying of Jesus in precisely the opposite direction, as though the church is guaranteed safety against the onslaughts of hell. In point of fact, Jesus is suggesting a much more aggressive, even offensive, image: his church will lay successful siege upon the kingdom of evil, knocking down its gate and breaching its walls. And notice, too, how Jesus uses the future tense—"I *will* build my church" (Mt 16:18). Therefore he cannot be speaking simply of Peter personally but of all those who will participate in his charism throughout the centuries—a theme to which I will return in a later chapter. The integrity of this *ekklesia* will be guaranteed up and down the centuries, not through appeal to popular opinion (as instructive as that might be), nor through the ministrations of an institutional or theological elite (as necessary as those might be), but rather through the pope's charismatic knowledge of who Jesus is.

One of the most consistent claims of the New Testament is that Peter was the definitive witness to the risen Jesus. Again and again, we hear, "The Lord has truly been raised and has appeared to Simon!" (Lk 24:34). After Pentecost the often wavering apostle became a tower of strength and resolve, and his proclamations center consistently on the resurrection. His speech in Jerusalem on that first Pentecost is a masterpiece of persuasive evangelism and perhaps typical of his kerygmatic preaching. Speaking to the throngs from many nations who had come to Jerusalem for the Feast of Booths, Peter quoted the prophet Joel: "It will come to pass in the last days, God says, that I will pour out a portion of my Spirit upon all flesh. Your sons and your daughters shall prophesy, your young men shall see visions, your old men shall dream dreams" (Acts 2:17). Peter knew precisely where his generation stood in the great story of Israel: they were living at the time of fulfillment, the time when the promises of the prophets were being realized, precisely through the resurrection of Jesus from the dead. He goes on: "You who are Israelites, hear these words. Jesus the Nazorean was a man commended to you by God with mighty deeds, wonders, and signs . . . This man, delivered up by the set plan and foreknowledge of God, you killed . . . But God raised him up . . . Therefore let the whole house of Israel know for certain that God has made him both Lord and Messiah" (Acts 2:22–36). So powerful was this speech that the audience, Luke tells us, was "cut to the heart" (Acts 2:37). The successors of Peter have always had the fundamental task of witnessing in just this way to the resurrection of Jesus.

About two decades after Pentecost, sometime in the late fifties or early sixties of the first century, Peter went to Rome. His exact reasons for going are lost to us, but we can certainly speculate that he had journeyed to this center of world empire because it was the natural place to declare that the whole world had a new Lord. He settled probably in the Jewish quarter of Rome, today's Trastevere and the neighborhood just across the

Santa Maria, Trastevere, Rome. WORD ON FIRE

Tiber from there. Ancient sources tell us that Mark, the author of the first
Gospel, was Peter's secretary and translator—and indeed the Gospel of
Mark includes an extraordinary number of stories concerning the chief
of the apostles. Peter died around the year 65, the most prominent victim
of Nero's persecution of the Christians in Rome. Tradition tells us he was
crucified upside down—since he was unworthy to die in the same manner as his Lord—in the circus of Nero, which was situated between the
Vatican and the Janiculum hills outside the city proper. In the center of
spina, the spine that ran down the middle of the circus, there stood a
great obelisk that the emperor Augustus had brought back from Egypt.
It was likely one of the last things that Peter saw as he hung dying. After
Peter died, they cut down his body and buried him in a little cemetery
on the Vatican Hill. For the first three centuries of the church's life that
spot was remembered and reverenced by local Christians. In the fourth
century the first Christian emperor, Constantine, built on the site a magnificent basilica, which endured until the end of the fifteenth century,
when it was torn down and replaced by the present basilica of St. Peter's.
In the mid-twentieth century, Pope Pius XI ordered an excavation of the
area beneath the high altar of St. Peter's and archeologists unearthed the
first-century cemetery in a remarkably good state of preservation. Amid
the grave markers and monuments they found a stone that bore a fascinating graffito: *Petros eni* (Peter's inside). When they opened that grave
they found the bones of a sturdily built man between the ages of sixty
and seventy. What the bones of Peter impress upon us is a point I've
been stressing throughout this book—namely, that Christianity is not
a philosophy or an abstract set of convictions. It is about this Jesus, the
friend of Simon Peter and the other disciples, these first-century men
who knew the Lord. In his first letter Saint John says, "What was from
the beginning, what we have heard, what we have seen with our eyes,
what we looked upon and touched with our hands concerns the Word of
life—for the life was made visible; we have seen it and testify to it and
proclaim to you the eternal life that was with the Father" (1 Jn 1:1–2).
Simon Peter, whose bones lie beneath the basilica in Rome that bears

St. Peter's Basilica, Vatican City. WORD ON FIRE

his name, touched the risen Jesus. It is upon that witness, rock-like in its concreteness and surety, that the church is built.

THE APOSTLE TO THE GENTILES

The second of the indispensable players in the early church was Paul, born Shaul (Saul) in the town of Tarsus in the southeast quadrant of Asia Minor around the year 10, making him a younger contemporary of Jesus. A child of Diaspora Jews, Saul was born into a mixed culture, Jewish and Greek, and he became at some point in his early life a Roman citizen. Therefore he combined in his person the three great cultures of his time and place, and this made him, when the propitious moment arrived, a particularly apt bearer of the message of the God of Israel to the wider world. Young Saul probably received a fairly decent classical education, reading Plato, Aristotle, Aeschylus, Sophocles, and Homer. We can glean from his letters, for example, that he had a good knowledge of the norms of Greek rhetoric. But Saul's most significant intellectual formation came through his immersion in the world of the Hebrew Scriptures,

Saint Paul, Basilica of St. John Lateran, Rome. WORD ON FIRE

which began when he was very young and which intensified when he was sent, probably as a teenager, to Jerusalem in order to study at the feet of Gamaliel, one of the leading rabbis of the time. In Jerusalem with Gamaliel, Saul searched out the Scriptures and participated in the liturgies and rituals of the Temple. Though Gamaliel was known to be relatively broad-minded in his reading of classical Judaism, Saul moved in the opposite direction, becoming, as he would later put it, "a zealot for my ancestral traditions" (Gal 1:14).

As he grew into his twenties, what bothered this young Jewish zealot most was the emerging Christian movement, and, indeed, how could it not? The claim that a crucified carpenter was the Messiah of Israel ran counter to all of the expectations of pious Jews. There was no more compelling piece of counterevidence to a messianic pretention than execution at the hands of Israel's enemies. And thus Saul set out, with fanatic passion, to persecute the early Christian community, which he undoubtedly saw as a group of renegade and unfaithful Jews. There is a chilling passage in the Acts of the Apostles that describes Saul as "breathing murderous threats" (Acts 9:1) against Christians and entering their homes to drag them away in chains to prison. The very first reference to Saul in the

New Testament is in connection with the stoning of Stephen, the first Christian martyr. As a stone-throwing mob is putting Stephen to death, Saul is said to be looking on with approval.

Conversion and Mission

Saul received permission from his superiors to root out Christians in far-off Damascus, so he set out with firm purpose. On the way something happened that changed Saul and changed the world. What took place on the road to Damascus so fascinated the first Christians that we find five separate accounts of it in the New Testament. Here is Luke's laconic telling in chapter 9 of the Acts of the Apostles: "On his journey, as he [Saul] was nearing Damascus, a light from the sky suddenly flashed around him. He fell to the ground and heard a voice saying to him, 'Saul, Saul, why are you persecuting me?' He said, 'Who are you, sir?' The reply came, 'I am Jesus, whom you are persecuting'" (Acts 9:3–5).

In the Cerasi Chapel of the church of Santa Maria del Popolo in Rome, Caravaggio's masterpiece *The Conversion of Saint Paul* hangs in a side chapel. Due to the influence of thousands of pictures, we tend to imagine Saint Paul as an old, bearded man, but Caravaggio correctly depicts him in this painting as a man in his twenties. Saul's arms are lean and muscular; he wears the armor of a warrior, bears a menacing sword, and around his shoulders is a fine Roman-style red cape. We can easily picture him—armed and dangerous—galloping with a soldier's confidence into Damascus. How wonderfully Caravaggio captures the moment of transformation. The soldier lies on his back, disempowered, while his arms gesture helplessly upward and his eyes are closed. His confidence and directionality gone, he gropes, physically and intellectually, to find his way. Caravaggio shows us the moment when invisible grace knocked Saul to the ground, stripped him of his sword, and shut his eyes—and thus prepared him for a new journey, a new kind of fighting, and a new way of seeing.

Blind and helpless, Saul was led into Damascus, and after a few days

The Conversion of Saint Paul *by Caravaggio, Santa Maria del Popolo, Rome.*
WORD ON FIRE

he was baptized by a Christian disciple named Ananias. When Ananias laid hands on Saul, "things like scales" (Acts 9:18) fell from the former persecutor's eyes and he was able to see: it was a physical manifestation of an inner transformation. After this life-altering experience Saul—and here we pick up his own account in his letter to the Galatians—went away at once into Arabia and then back to Damascus. Only three years later did he venture to Jerusalem to visit with Peter and the other "pillars" of the church. What was he doing during this time? Some speculate that he was preaching and doing missionary work, but I think it is much more plausible that he was simply trying to figure out what in the world had happened to him and how he could reconcile his encounter with the living Jesus and the traditions of Israel that he loved. He was striving to rethink ancient Israel in relation to the figure of Jesus, or better, to understand Jesus as the climax of Israel's story. Out of these meditations the first Christian theology emerged.

At some point at the culmination of those three years, Paul realized that his mission was to declare to everybody—Jew and Gentile alike—that they had a new king. Through the power of the resurrection, Jesus had been revealed as the fulfillment of all of the promises that God had made to Israel and therefore he was the light to the nations, and Paul felt commissioned by Christ himself to be the bearer of this message. The second half of the Acts of the Apostles tells the story of Saul (now called Paul) scurrying furiously around Asia Minor, Palestine, Greece, and Italy for around twenty years proclaiming this Lordship of Jesus. Perusing these breathless pages, one is struck by the boundless energy and unremitting focus of the man. On his first missionary journey he preached his way through the island of Cyprus, coming finally to Sergius Paulus, the Roman proconsul, whom he converted to the faith. Next he lighted in Antioch in Pisidia, where he preached in the synagogue, delivering a magnificent speech in which he summed up Israelite history and identified the risen Jesus as the culmination of God's dealing with his chosen people: "We ourselves are proclaiming this good news to you that what God promised our ancestors he has brought to fulfillment for us, [their] children, by raising up Jesus" (Acts 13:32–33). And then he made the theological move that he would repeat continually throughout his ministry. He reached deep within the Jewish tradition to find the promise that the revelation given to Israel was meant, in the last days, to become a message of liberation for all the world: "I have made you a light to the Gentiles, that you may be an instrument of salvation to the ends of the earth" (Acts 13:47).

Next he traveled to Lystra, another town in Asia Minor, and he cured a man who had been unable to walk from birth, demonstrating thereby that Christ was now at work in the church, remaking his creation. In the wake of this miracle, the people of the town were convinced that Paul and his companion Barnabas were gods and they endeavored to offer sacrifices to them. Upon hearing this, the two Christians tore their clothes and confronted the crowd, shouting, "Men . . . we are of the same nature as you, human beings. We proclaim to you good news that you should turn from these idols to the living God, 'who made heaven and earth and sea and all that is in them'" (Acts 14:15). This rejoinder shows clearly that the whole purpose of Paul's preaching and healing was to proclaim the

true God, the story of whose dealing with human beings had reached its
climax in the death and resurrection of Jesus. I think it is fair to say that
Paul was only mildly successful in this effort since, just days later, certain
Jews arrived in Lystra and turned the people against the Christian evangelists. The crowd, which had wanted to declare Paul a god, now stoned
him and "dragged him out of the city, supposing that he was dead" (Acts
14:19). When some of Paul's Christian disciples surrounded his prostrate
body, Paul calmly got up and, undaunted, went back into the town.

One of the most decisive events in the history of Christianity took
place not long after this. Paul, Barnabas, and a number of the other leaders of the early Christian movement gathered in Jerusalem to discuss a
potentially explosive issue, namely, whether the new converts to the faith
that Paul and others were attracting from among the Gentiles should be
required to follow all the demands of the Mosaic law, including circumcision, abstaining from unclean foods, and so on. The question was a vexa-
tious one, because Christianity was at one and the same time deeply
Jewish yet also something altogether new. Apart from the story of creation, the fall, the formation of a people Israel, and the promises made
through the patriarchs and prophets, the proclamation of Jesus and his

Saint Paul, Chora Church, Istanbul. WORD ON FIRE

resurrection made little sense. Still, in the brilliant light of the resurrection Paul and others saw that certain forms of Jewish life, though signposts of the truth to come, were now obsolete and no longer strictly necessary.

After "much debate" and after having heard the stories that Paul and Barnabas told of their Gentile conversions, Peter spoke: "My brothers, you are well aware that from early days God made his choice among you that through my mouth the Gentiles would hear the word of the gospel and believe. And God . . . bore witness by granting them the holy Spirit just as he did us" (Acts 15:7–8). What is clear from this intervention is that Peter had come to understand things along Paul's lines: as long as the Gentiles have received the spirit of the risen Christ, why should they be burdened with all of the regulations and directives that Jews themselves had never been able to keep? It was then decided that the new converts should not be "troubled" with the Mosaic law, except for the prohibition against idolatry (which was essential to the Christian proclamation of the Lordship of Jesus) and fornication (which disrespected the dignity of the body). The Gentiles would be, to use Paul's own language, "grafted" on to Israel (Rom 11:17), but they would not be compelled to follow all of the practices that set Jews off ethnically from the rest of the world. With that, Paul found his commission from the risen Christ to be an apostle to the nations now formally ratified by the church. And from that moment on the ambition of Christian evangelism knew no bounds.

After this first "council" of Jerusalem, Paul and Barnabas returned to Asia Minor in order to encourage the churches they had established. While in Troas, a coastal town, Paul had a dream of a man from Macedonia, the land of Alexander the Great, beckoning him to come and preach the word. This prompted Paul to take the short journey from Asia to Greece. The Catholic historian Christopher Dawson observed that the entry of Paul into Macedonia, certainly unnoticed by any of the bien-pensant commentators of the time, was in fact one of the most momentous happenings of the past two thousand years, since it represented the beginning of European Christianity and hence of a revolution in culture that would eventually affect all the world.

Paul's first important stop in Europe was in the Roman colony of Philippi, named for Alexander the Great's father, Philip of Macedonia, and the site of the decisive battle between Antony and Octavian and their nemeses Brutus and Cassius, the murderers of Julius Caesar. Outside Philippi, Paul met a woman named Lydia, who was a dealer in purple goods (we would say a buyer and seller of upscale garments), and, we are told, "the Lord opened her heart to pay attention to what Paul was saying" (Acts 16:14). Lydia was a "worshipper of God," which meant a Gentile who was nevertheless affiliated with the synagogue and cognizant of the story of Israel. In the course of his ministry Paul dealt sometimes with Jews, sometimes with Gentiles, and often with people like Lydia, using different means of persuasion and argument with each group, demonstrating the flexibility of an effective evangelist. After he baptized Lydia and her family, Paul was making his way to prayer when he was accosted by a young slave girl who had a "spirit of divination" and hence made her owners a good deal of money. Paul drove the demon out of her, which presumably benefited the young woman but infuriated her owners, who had just lost their principal source of income. They hauled Paul before the local magistrate and accused him of "advocating customs that are not lawful for us Romans to adopt or practice" (Acts 16:21). The apostle was stripped, beaten, and shackled in the innermost cell of the prison. That night, while he was singing hymns with his companion Silas (a wonderful thing for a beaten and imprisoned man to be doing!), an earthquake struck and the doors of the prison were thrown open. Supposing the prisoners had escaped, the jailer drew his sword in order to impale himself on it, but Paul stopped him: "Do no harm to yourself; we are all here" (Acts 16:28). The shaken man then asked what he must do to be saved. The simple and magnificent answer of Paul and Silas was: "Believe in the Lord Jesus and you and your household will be saved" (Acts 16:31).

There, *in nuce*, is the whole Gospel that Paul preached: submit to the Lordship of a new king, Christ crucified and risen. The letter that Paul would later write back to the community of Philippi—one of the gems of the Christian tradition—contains a hymn that Paul adapted to

Philippi, Greece. WORD ON FIRE

his purposes and that also provides a pithy encapsulation of his teaching: "Christ Jesus, Who, though he was in the form of God, did not regard equality with God as something to be grasped. Rather he emptied himself, taking the form of a slave . . . Because of this, God greatly exalted him and bestowed on him the name that is above every name, that at the name of Jesus every knee should bend, of those in heaven and on earth and under the earth, and every tongue confess that Jesus Christ is Lord" (Phil 2:5–7, 9–11). First, we notice that the divinity of Jesus is clearly affirmed: he is in the form of God and he has the name above any other name. And second, we see the consequence of this affirmation: Jesus is the *kyrios* (the Lord) to whom final allegiance is due within the political and cultural sphere and indeed throughout the cosmos and the invisible order as well.

Having left Philippi, Paul journeyed to Thessalonica and immediately went to the Jewish synagogue to proclaim the good news. As he laid out his story, some were persuaded, but others were enraged and managed to stir up a mob that "set the city in turmoil" (Acts 17:5). The formal charge brought against Paul and his Christian companions is fascinating: "These people who have been creating a disturbance all over the world have now come here . . . They all act in opposition to the decrees of Caesar and claim instead that there is another king, Jesus" (Acts 17:6–7). Quite right. Paul's message was indeed designed to turn the world upside down, precisely because it was the proclamation of a new king and therefore of an entirely new way of organizing things. The dark powers—at work, for example, in the girl with the "spirit of divination" in Philippi—have been overthrown, and both Jews and Gentiles have to look at the world afresh. I don't think it is the least bit accidental that when Paul wrote back to the community at Thessalonica (the earliest Christian document we have), his major motif was the end of the world as we know it and the longing for Christ to come to remake the cosmos. When Paul speaks in that text of Christ arriving on the clouds and of Christians going up to meet him in the air, he is not predicting a great escape from the world of matter; he is envisioning a welcome committee of believers moving out to escort into the world its new king. N. T. Wright relates the wonderful story of an Anglican bishop who said, "when Paul preached, there were riots; when I preach, they serve me tea." If our teaching of the faith is too often tepid and uninspiring, authentic Christian proclamation is as subversive and explosive as the earthquake that shook the prison walls in Philippi.

Resurrection

Paul's next stop on his missionary journey was Athens, and the speech that he gave there on the Hill of Mars (the Areopagus), the public forum just below the Acropolis and the Parthenon, provides an occasion for exploring the foundational theme of Paul's preaching: the resurrection of Jesus from the dead. After complimenting the Athenians for their religiosity, evident in their many shrines and altars, Paul drew their attention to a particular altar he had seen inscribed "To an Unknown God" (Acts 17:23). The nature of this God—unknown obviously to the philosophers of Athens—will be the subject, he says, of his proclamation. The true

God, he tells them, is the maker of the universe in its entirety and there-fore "does not dwell in sanctuaries made by human hands," nor is he "like an image fashioned from gold, silver, or stone by human art and imagina-tion" (Acts 17: 24, 29). Speaking those words within sight of the Parthe-non, in which a magnificent statue of the goddess Athena was worshiped, Paul was being typically provocative. This God has, furthermore, "estab-lished a day on which he will 'judge the world with justice' through a man he has appointed, and he has provided confirmation for all by raising him from the dead" (Acts 17:31). There is the heart of it. The resurrection of Jesus was the validation of his messianic claim and therefore the ground for Paul's declaration that Christ is *Kyrios* of the world. When the learned debaters on the Areopagus heard this, "some began to scoff, but others said, 'We should like to hear you on this some other time'" (Acts 17:32).

If those few interested people had listened further, what would they have heard? There were many viewpoints among thoughtful people of the time concerning what happens after we die. The Jewish Sadducee party, for example, held the view, which is on display in many ancient biblical texts, that the dead simply return to the earth and decay. Other Jews believed that the dead entered the shadowy realm of Sheol, a place

Parthenon, Athens, Greece. WORD ON FIRE

of sadness and boredom, not unlike the underworld of the Greek imagination. Still others—the author of the book of Daniel is an example—
thought that the righteous dead would exist somehow in fellowship with
God. By the time of Jesus, the Pharisees had come to believe in the
resurrection of the bodies of all the righteous at the end of time, at "the
close of the age." In Greek thought, of course, there was the mythic view
alluded to above as well as in the more sophisticated philosophical account of Plato, according to which the intellectual energy of the individual escaped at death from its bodily prison. Paul, a Jew with deep
roots in the Hellenistic world, would have been acquainted with all of
these perspectives, but his message of resurrection was something completely different. He did not say that Jesus had gone to Sheol or that he
was vaguely "with God"; nor did he express a mere hope that one day he
would rise along with the saints; and he most certainly did not claim that
Jesus's soul had escaped from his body. He declared that the crucified
Jesus of Nazareth rose bodily from the realm of the dead and exists now
in a transfigured physicality. The risen Christ presented himself as very
much an embodied person, and yet his bodiliness was not limited by the
ordinary constraints of space and time. He had flesh and bones, yet he
passed through walls and appeared and disappeared at will. His was a
physicality at a higher pitch of perfection and attainment.

In the fifteenth chapter of his first letter to the Corinthians, Paul
lays out this central teaching: "Now I am reminding you, brothers, of the
gospel I preached to you . . . For I handed to you as of first importance
what I also received: that Christ died for our sins . . . that he was buried;
that he was raised on the third day" (1 Cor 15:1, 3–4). But notice how
he specifies the claim by naming the very particular people to whom
Jesus appeared after his resurrection: "he appeared to Kephas [Peter],
then to the Twelve. After that, he appeared to more than five hundred
brothers at once, most of whom are still living . . . After that he appeared
to James, then to all the apostles" (1 Cor 15:5–7). This is not the way
someone who is trading in vague religious hopes, myths, or philosophical
speculation speaks. He mentions very real and specific persons to whom

Jesus appeared and who could, in principle, be interrogated on the matter. How important is the bodily resurrection for Paul? "[I]f Christ has not been raised, your faith is vain" (1 Cor 15:17), he said, and, "If for this life only we have hoped in Christ, we are the most pitiable people of all" (1 Cor 15:19). This is true because a dead man who stayed in his grave would be, necessarily, a false messiah, and his teaching, however inspiring, could never hold off the power of death.

Participation in Christ

Paul became convinced that the risen Jesus—the bearer of God's promises and the rightful king of the world—is like a force field, like an energy, or to use one of his favorite words, a power. If ancient Israel was taught to follow the law, Paul now says, "enter into Christ" who is himself the embodiment and fulfillment of the law. If the Jews were instructed to enter into the covenants made with Abraham, Moses, and David, Paul now says, "live in Christ" who is in person the fulfillment of the covenants. If the chosen people were commanded to offer sacrifice to Yahweh in the Temple, Paul now says "trust in Christ" who through his crucifixion became the new and definitive sacrifice. In the tenth chapter of his first letter to the Corinthians, Paul is discussing the Eucharist celebrations of the early Christian community, and he makes this crucial observation: "The cup of blessing that we bless, is it not a participation in the blood of Christ?" and "The bread that we break, is it not a participation in the body of Christ?" (1 Cor 10:16). The Greek word behind "sharing" is *koinonia*, which means, in ordinary usage, "communion," but which has, as Paul is using it, the overtone of mystical participation. The community of Christ is much more than a congregation of like-minded people; it is, as Paul's metaphor of the body suggests, an organism of interdependent cells, all of which derive their life from the primal energy of Jesus.

It is only against this background that we can approach the famously vexed question of justification in the writings of Paul. In the sixteenth century the Christian church in the West tore itself apart over this question, and those wounds are very far from being healed. At the feet of Gamaliel, Paul would have frequently heard the Hebrew term *Mispat,* which means "justice" or "right order." *Mispat* was, first, a quality of God and, by extension, a quality of those who were in proper relation to God. Paul uses the Greek rendering of this term—*dikaiosyne* (righteousness)— with great frequency in his letters, but what precisely does he mean by it? He saw that in Christ Jesus, faithful Yahweh has finally met faithful Israel. Though the Temple, the law, and the covenants were meant to bring God and his people together, the sin of Israel always rendered those means ineffective, and hence the *Mispat* of God was never successfully transferred to humanity. But now through the obedience of Christ, the divine righteousness is on full offer to Israel and through Israel to the world. And therefore participation in Jesus, *koinonia* with him, is the path to salvation, a path that is, in principle, open to everyone, Jew and Greek alike. How is this participation effected? Paul could not be clearer that the first step is faith. The Greek term he used here is *pistis,* which means much more than acquiescing to certain intellectual propositions. It carries the connotation of deep, personal trust. We trust in Jesus Christ, relying on the power of his cross and resurrection, and we thereby enter into his force field, the space of justification. But there is more, for Paul knows that once we've entered into the adventure of faith, we are invited to swim in the energy and power of Christ, to "put on the Lord Jesus Christ" (Rom 13:14), to become conformed in mind, will, and body to him. In a word, we are invited to embrace the love that follows upon faith.

One of the very best summaries of Paul's spiritual and theological thought on this score is verse 13 of his first letter to the Corinthians, a text that also ranks as one of the most beautiful in the Western literary tradition. I'm speaking of the "hymn to love." Paul is addressing a Corinthian Christian community that was captivated by the more spectacular manifestations of the spiritual life: speaking in tongues, trading in words

Corinth, Greece. WORD ON FIRE

of knowledge, engaging in prophecy. He wanted to bring them back to what is fundamental, so he insisted on the superiority of love. "If I speak in human and angelic tongues but do not have love, I am a resounding gong or a clashing cymbal. And if I have the gift of prophecy and comprehend all mysteries and all knowledge; if I have all faith so as to move mountains but do not have love, I am nothing" (1 Cor 13:1–2). Paul himself spoke in tongues and confessed to having had an extraordinary mystical experience of the "third heaven," and he certainly sang the praises of faith, but he asserts here that these gifts count for *nothing* unless they are accompanied by, and give rise to, love. Why should this be true? It is true because love is what God *is*; love *is* the divine life—and the entire purpose of spirituality is to get that life in us. If I have the accompaniments of the divine life but not the thing itself, I am indeed nothing. And what is love? As I've said previously, love is not primarily a feeling or emotion (though love can be accompanied by feelings and emotions); it is willing the good of the other as other. When we love, we escape the black hole of our own clinging egotism and live for someone else; to love is to leap ecstatically out of the self.

And this is why, Paul explains, "Love is patient, love is kind" (1 Cor 13:4). Many of us are good or just to someone else so that he or she, in turn, might be good or just to us. This is not love, but rather indirect egotism. When we are caught in the rhythm of that sort of reciprocal exchange, we are very impatient with any negative response to a positive overture that we have made. If someone responds to our kindness with hostility or even indifference, we quickly withdraw our benevolence. But the person characterized by true love is not interested in reciprocation but simply in the good of the other, and therefore he is willing to wait out any resistance. He is long-suffering and kind. This is also why, as Paul insists, "[love] is not jealous, [it] is not pompous, it is not inflated" (1 Cor 13:4). Gore Vidal, the American novelist, described with admirable honesty the feeling of envy this way: "when a friend of mine succeeds, something in me dies." True love hasn't a thing to do with this sort of resentment, for it wants the success of the other. And the person who loves is not conceited, because she feels no need to raise herself above the other. Just the contrary: she wants the other to be elevated, and hence she takes the lower place with joy. Once we understand the nature of true love, we know why "It bears all things, believes all things, hopes all things, endures all things" (1 Cor 13:7). Because the one who loves is not focused on himself but on the object of his love, he is not preoccupied with his own weariness or disappointment or frustration. Instead he looks ahead, hoping against hope, attending to the needs of the one he loves.

Paul concludes his encomium with the observation that "Love never fails" (1 Cor 13:8). In heaven, when we are sharing the divine life, even faith will end, for we will see and no longer merely believe; hope will end, for our deepest longing will have been realized. But love will endure, because heaven *is* love. Heaven is the state of being in which everything that is not love has been burned away. And that is why "faith, hope, love remain, these three; but the greatest of these is love" (1 Cor 13:13). Paul here has named the essence not only of his own theology but of the Christian life itself. Everything else is commentary.

THE SPIRIT OF PETER AND PAUL

Hans Urs von Balthasar, one of the greatest theologians of the twentieth century, said that Peter and Paul are enduring archetypes in the life of the church. Peter, who led the original band of the twelve, stands for office, structure, hierarchy, and headship—all those ways that the church is ordered to achieve its purpose. Every priest, bishop, pastor, and pope is, in this sense, a descendant of Peter. And Paul, who went out to the nations as an evangelist to the Gentiles, stands, Balthasar says, for mission, the engagement of the culture, and proclamation. Every missionary, teacher, preacher, and theologian is, in this sense, a son or daughter of Paul. Without the Petrine discipline, the Pauline work would be unfocused and continually in danger of dissolution. Without the Pauline energy, the Petrine work would devolve into cold management and ecclesiastical bureaucracy. The two together, in tensive harmony, have propelled the church through the centuries and around the world.

The spirit of Peter and Paul led Saint Francis Xavier to journey from Portugal to India, Goa, and Japan—indeed to the very doorstep of China; it compelled Matteo Ricci, the great Jesuit missionary, to carry the faith to the court of the Chinese emperor; it brought missionaries to the Philippines in the sixteenth century; Paraguay and Brazil in the seventeenth century; Hawaii, Australia, New Zealand, and sub-Saharan Africa in the nineteenth century. One of the most extraordinary fruits of the African mission was the witness of the vibrant and youthful church of Uganda in the face of terrible persecution. In 1885 a particularly wicked Ugandan king sought sexual favors from certain young Christians in his court. When the young men refused, they were brutally put to death and joined thereby the great company of martyrs. One of the most festive liturgies on the African continent today takes place on the feast day of these courageous and faithful witnesses.

In 1933, on the nineteen-hundredth anniversary of the redemption, Pope Pius XI invited Christian missionaries to take the Gospel literally to the ends of the world, to ensure that the message was heard everywhere. The Missionary Oblates of Mary Immaculate took up the challenge. A small group was sent to the northern reaches of Canada, where they proclaimed Jesus Christ risen from the dead. Then they asked, "Are there any people further north?" When the answer came back in the affirmative, they set out, found the more distant community, and proclaimed Jesus to them. This process continued until they came, finally, to a tiny gathering of people who said, "No, we're the last ones." When the Oblates had preached to this little band, they went back to Rome with the message: "We've announced Jesus Christ to the ends of the world." That kind of evangelical panache, that playful spiritual adventurousness, would have been unthinkable apart from Peter and Paul.

Chapter 6

A BODY BOTH SUFFERING AND GLORIOUS: THE MYSTICAL UNION OF CHRIST AND THE CHURCH

How strange that we believe in the church. In the Nicene Creed, Catholics profess their faith in the Father, the Son, and the Holy Spirit, the three divine persons, and that seems reasonable enough. But then they proceed to declare their *belief* in "one holy catholic and apostolic church." Does this not amount to the conflation of Creator and creature? Is it not effectively blasphemous to announce one's faith in a human institution? To answer these questions is to come to the heart of the Catholic understanding of the church, for Catholics hold that the church is not merely a human organization, simply a coming together of like-minded people, a community of purely worldly provenance and purpose. Rather, the church is a sacrament of Jesus and, as such, shares in the very being, life, and energy of Christ. According to the inexhaustibly rich metaphor proposed by Saint Paul, the church is the body of Jesus, an organism composed of interdependent cells, molecules, and organs. Christ is the head of a mystical body made up of everyone

Chartres Cathedral, detail, France. WORD ON FIRE

across space and time who has ever been grafted onto him through baptism. And lest we think that this organic understanding was a peculiar invention of Paul, call to mind the vivid language that Jesus himself used in order to express the relationship that obtains between himself and his followers: "I am the vine, you are branches (Jn 15:5); "remain in me" (Jn 15:4); "unless you eat the flesh of the Son of Man and drink his blood, you do not have life within you" (Jn 6:53). I could be such an admirer of Abraham Lincoln that I would be inspired to join the Abraham Lincoln society and regularly attend its meetings, but I would never be tempted to speak of eating Lincoln's body and drinking his blood. I could admire the life and work of Mahatma Gandhi so enthusiastically that I might be moved to found a Gandhi society, but it would never occur to me to speak of being grafted onto Gandhi. But we Catholics say such radical things when we describe our relationship with Jesus.

Two great New Testament passages, which we have already considered in other contexts, come to mind here. The first is Jesus's statement in chapter 25 of Matthew: "whatever you did for one of these least brothers of mine, you did for me." The Lord does not say simply that if we feed the hungry and clothe the naked and visit the imprisoned we are doing ethically praiseworthy things or that God is pleased with us. We might imagine any number of religious teachers saying as much. He states instead that these acts are performed *for him* personally, but this can make sense only on the condition that the poor, the hungry, and the imprisoned belong to Jesus, that they are incorporate with him. The second passage is from chapter 9 of Acts. Knocked to the ground and blinded by the supernatural light, the sworn enemy of the Christian community hears the words, "Saul, Saul, why are persecuting *me*?" (my italics; Acts 9:4). Saul was intent on persecuting Jesus's followers, whom he saw as deeply misguided Jews. He had never met Jesus and was confident that the leader of this rebellious band was safely in his grave. Yet this mysterious Christ insisted that Saul was harassing him personally—"I am Jesus, whom you are persecuting"—a claim that makes sense only on the condition that Jesus has identified himself with his followers in a manner so vivid and incarnate that when they suffer, he suffers.

In the apse of the Basilica of San Clemente in Rome, there is a gorgeous twelfth-century mosaic that gives visual expression to the idea we have been exploring. At the center of the composition is the crucified Jesus, the source of the church's sacramental life. Surrounding the cross of the Lord are twelve doves, symbolizing the apostles who would fly around the world with the message of salvation. Growing from the cross and swirling around it in ordered patterns are a congeries of vines, leaves, branches, and tendrils, suggesting the mysterious organicity of the mystical body of Jesus, all the people joined to Christ and hence to one another down through the ages. And if I might press the nature symbolism a bit further, the mosaic indicates how the body of Christ includes not only the human order but in a sense the whole of creation, both seen and unseen. In his letter to the Colossians, Paul speaks of Christ as the lynchpin of the entire universe: "He is the image of the invisible God, the firstborn of all creation. For in him were created all things in heaven and on earth, the visible and the invisible . . . He is before all things, and in him all things hold together" (Col 1:15–17). And just after this lyrical description of Christ's cosmic power, Paul adds, "He is the head of the

Basilica of San Clemente, interior, Rome. WORD ON FIRE

body, the church" (Col 1:18). From its earliest days the Christian community saw itself as nothing less than the means by which Jesus would bind the universe back together.

At her trial on trumped-up charges, Saint Joan of Arc was asked for her understanding of the relationship between Christ and his church. This is how she responded: "About Jesus Christ and the church, I know only this: they're simply one thing, and we shouldn't complicate the matter." As an articulation of the peculiarly Catholic sense of the church, it would be hard to improve on that.

EKKLESIA

As we have seen, the biblical God is a great gathering force. In his own nature he is a community of love, a unity in difference. This infinitely intense divine love gives rise to a universe of interconnected things, all joined to one another through their common center in God. God's preoccupation, from the beginning, is the coming together of the many as one, gathering in. That which stands opposed to God, therefore, is always a power of separation. The early church father Origen of Alexandria commented "*ubi divisio ibi peccatum*" (where there is division, there is sin), and the English word "sin" is rooted in the German *Sunde*, which means "sundering" or "separating." In the wake of sin, God conceived a rescue operation in the form of a people Israel. He gathered in the family of Abraham and shaped them according to his own heart, giving them the laws, covenants, and rituals that would unite them in love and hence make them pleasing to God and attractive to all the nations. As is argued throughout the Bible, the distinctiveness of Israel was, therefore, not *against the world* but *precisely for the world*. Jesus is none other than the fulfillment of Israel—the true covenant, the embodiment of the law, the authentic temple—and therefore he is the supreme gatherer: "when I am lifted up from the earth, I will draw everyone to myself" (Jn 12:32). His body the church is the instrument by which he continues this work up and down the centuries.

In order to understand this more fully, let us return once more to that conversation Jesus had with his disciples outside of Caesarea-Philippi. To Jesus's peculiar question "Who do people say that I am?" Simon responded, "You are the Messiah, the Son of the living God," and the Lord

Crucifix, Orvieto Cathedral, Italy. WORD ON FIRE

said in reply, "Blessed are you, Simon son of Jonah! . . . I say to you, you are Peter, and upon this rock I will build my church, and the gates of the netherworld shall not prevail against it" (Mt 16:16–18). The term behind "church" here is the Greek word *ekklesia*, which is derived from *ek-kalein*, "to call out from." When examining the *ekklesia*, therefore, we should ask three questions: Who does the calling? What is one being called from? And what is one being called to?

In the contemporary Western view of things, people join organizations and decide on their own terms and for their own purposes of which communities they wish to be part. But this cannot be true of the church, for members of Christ's body have been summoned by someone else, incorporated by a higher power. Greeting the Corinthians, Paul says that he was "called to be an apostle of Christ Jesus by the will of God" (1 Cor 1:1). We notice how he uses the passive voice, "was called," and how he characterizes himself as someone who has been sent ("apostle" comes from the Greek *apostelein*, "to send"). This supreme churchman, writing to a church that he helped to form, relativizes his own will and places whatever desires he has within the context of the desire of a greater will. One might join a voluntary organization, but one is called into the church of Christ. In his classic text *Habits of the Heart*, the sociologist Robert Bellah relates the musings of a young nurse called Sheila. When asked about her religious convictions Sheila said that she adhered to no particular faith or set of dogmas but had instead pieced together her own religion from a number of different sources and according to her whim. She had, she said, "my own little religion, which I call 'Sheila-ism.'" Bellah remarked that he had stumbled here upon the distinctively American form of religion: eclectic, superficial, and above all, willful. Paul's self-presentation in 1 Corinthians is the antithesis of Sheila-ism and the prototype of the properly ecclesial attitude: humble, alert to God's grace, waiting to be surprised.

Now to the second question: what have church people been called from? They have been summoned out of what the Bible calls "the world," the whole network of institutions, beliefs, behaviors, and practices that

Ecstasy of St. Teresa. BRIDGEMAN ART LIBRARY

Chora Church (apse). WORD ON FIRE

Hagia Sophia (interior). AYSE TOPBAS

Cologne Cathedral. ROBERT HARDING

St. Peter's Square and Basilica. WORD ON FIRE

La Pietà by Michelangelo. Nino H. Photography

The Last Judgment (Sistine Chapel, Vatican City). Word on Fire

Our Lady of Guadalupe. THE BASILICA OF GUADALUPE, MEXICO CITY

Annunciation (Leonardo da Vinci). Word on Fire

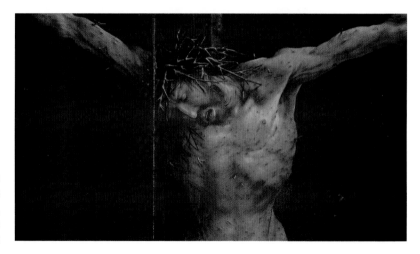

Isenheim Altarpiece (detail). Word on Fire

Santa Maria in
Trastevere.
WORD ON FIRE

Church of the Holy Sepulchre, Chapel of Calvary. MEDIOIMAGES/PHOTODISC

fosters division. Karl Barth referred to this as *das Nichtige*, the nonbeing; the Bible sees it as the *tohu-va-bohu*, the primal chaos out of which God brought creation; and Saint Augustine calls it "the region of unlikeness," which is to say, that place where we lose our similitude to God. It is the realm of hatred, racism, sexism, violence, oppression, imperialism, what Augustine termed the *libido dominandi* (the lust to dominate). Members of the church have been pulled by the power of Christ out from all of that and branded as belonging to him. When the Israelites returned from exile, they endeavored, under the leadership of Nehemiah, to rebuild the walls of Jerusalem, left breached and burned years before by the Babylonians. And when the walls were restored, Ezra the priest read to the people from the Torah and compelled them, over the course of an entire day, to listen. Nehemiah and Ezra knew that in order to realize its purpose, Israel had to maintain its distinctiveness. It had to remember that it had been called out from the ordinary run of things.

Most of the medieval Christian cathedrals were oriented, which is to say, built, so as to face the east. The front of a cathedral is the apse, the place where the altar is situated, and this means that the façade, which faces the west, or the setting of the sun, is actually the back. This

Notre Dame, Paris. WORD ON FIRE

explains the fierce, imposing, battering-ram quality of the great cathedral façades: they stand like a wall or a shield against the powers of darkness. They signal what the church is against.

Another biblical type for the church is Noah's ark, a place of safety when the *tohu-va-bohu* of the flood waters wiped out life on earth. The ark was interpreted, by both the rabbis and the church fathers, as a microcosm of God's good order maintained during a time of chaos, as a place where life was preserved behind carefully constructed walls during a season of death. And this is why the medieval architects endeavored to make the cathedrals look like great ships. The nave (from the Latin *navis* meaning "boat") is surrounded by high walls, which in turn are supported by flying buttresses, which look, for all the world, like oars coming out the side of a ship. The naval suggestion is especially strong at Notre Dame Cathedral in Paris, which is situated on the Ile de la Cité, an island in the middle of the Seine. The idea is that the church is Noah's ark, moving through the stormy waters of sin, the place of safety into which sinners have been called. So the church is shelter from the storm, a boat tossing on the waves of a dysfunctional world. If we follow the church fathers in their development of this image, we will understand that this defensiveness, this over-and-against quality, serves finally a positive purpose. According to the narrative in the book of Genesis, once the flood waters receded, Noah eagerly and immediately let out the life that he had so carefully preserved. That microcosm of God's good order was not meant to hunker down permanently aboard the ark, but rather to flood out into the world and remake it. So the church gathers in a faithful remnant and shapes them according to God's mind, but then it purposely scatters them abroad like seeds on fertile ground.

The documents of the Second Vatican Council speak of the universal call to holiness, that is, the summons of all the baptized to be a transforming leaven in the wider society. The Vatican II fathers wanted to inspire a generation of great Catholic lawyers, great Catholic business leaders, great Catholic nurses and physicians, great Catholic teachers and writers, in the hopes that such people would carry the holiness they learned in the church out to their areas of specialization in the secular world. This biblically based vision runs counter, of course, to our modern preference for the privatization of religion, the sequestering of the faith within the interiority of the individual conscience. In terms of the Noah story, the contemporary approach is tantamount to keeping the animals on the ark! But the life of the church is not meant to hunker down permanently behind the walls of the ship; it is meant to invade the world.

A particularly apt illustration of these principles is the extraordinary career of Karol Wojtyla, Pope John Paul II. Young Wojtyla arrived at the Jagiellonian University in Kraków in September of 1939 to commence his advanced studies. This was, sadly, the same moment when the Nazi armies poured into Poland. Once the Germans were in control, they effectively decapitated Polish society, rounding up writers, commentators, intellectuals, and priests. Almost immediately after the Nazi takeover the faculty of the Jagiellonian was either killed outright or shipped off to concentration camps. In biblical terms, this was a season of the flood, of the *tohu-va-bohu*. Wojtyla, all of nineteen, was forced underground, both literally and figuratively. He left his shuttered university and became a day laborer in a great quarry outside Kraków. And he also, along with a small group of friends, formed a society called the Rhapsodic Theatre, which would meet, usually at night, behind locked doors and shaded windows, to recite together, clandestinely, by candlelight or flashlight, the great works of Polish poetry and drama. Since the Nazis wanted to stamp out Polish culture, the group of young people knew that if they were caught they would be imprisoned or killed. By reading these literary works, the Rhapsodic Theatre was doing much more than preserving the Polish language and culture, because an inescapable ingredient in the plays and poems they loved was Catholicism. To read Polish literature was to remember God, creation, the fall, the prophets of Israel, the Incarnation, the redemption, the cross, eternal life, and the irreducible dignity of the human being. As a particularly intense darkness descended, Wojtyla and his friends cupped their hands around a flickering light and kept it glowing. During those terrible years, Wojtyla, having resolved to

Karol Wojtyla.
EAST NEWS/
WOJTEK LASKI

become a priest, commenced attending classes held secretly at the palace of Adam Sapieha, the archbishop of Kraków. There he studied the classical Catholic intellectual and spiritual tradition, especially the works of Thomas Aquinas and John of the Cross. Again, since the Nazis would most likely have imprisoned or murdered any of these hidden seminarians if they had discovered them, Wojtyla and his brothers were putting themselves at enormous risk as they sequestered themselves behind the walls of Sapieha's residence. This was the time when young Karol Wojtyla entered the ark.

In 1945 the Nazis were finally expelled from Poland, but they were succeeded by the perhaps only slightly less oppressive Communists. Father Wojtyla was ordained November 1, 1946. During the Communist period he continued to keep a low profile. He gathered around him small groups of young people whom he formed in Catholic thought, culture,

Cardinal Karol Wojtyla (John Paul II).
EAST NEWS/WOJTEK LASKI

and practice. These sessions took place at church, in private homes, and sometimes on kayaking trips through the mountains of southern Poland. Wojtyla also became a professor of ethics at the Catholic University of Lublin, and in that more formal setting he immersed his students in the principles of Christian morality, the chief of which is that a human being, made in the image of God, should never be treated as a means to an end. He began to see that the central problem of both Nazism and Communism was faulty anthropology, a fundamental misconception of the nature of the human being. While the Communist apparatus relentlessly inculcated false humanism all around him, Wojtyla worked to preserve the authentic humanism of the Bible and the Catholic tradition. In a word, as a churchman he knew that he had been called out of a particularly dysfunctional form of life into an infinitely richer and more satisfying one, but for many years he had to remain satisfied with pursuing that life within rather cramped confines.

Many years passed, and then came the propitious moment. That young student of Polish theater, that young priest, became, through God's always strange providence, the bishop of Rome, the successor of Peter. Armed with the full authority of his office and the sheer strength of his personality, John Paul II visited Poland in 1979. Despite the enormous opposition of the Communist government, despite misinformation campaigns, roadblocks, and threats, millions of Poles ventured out to hear him. And John Paul spoke of those values that he had learned from Polish literature and from the treasures of the Catholic tradition; he spoke of God and creation, of the human being made in the image of God, of Jesus Christ and his redeeming cross, of the promise of eternal life—and he thereby changed the country. At that moment, the life, long preserved during dark and dangerous years, came flooding out. And John Paul's words served as a clarion call to the armies of people—now writers, journalists, business leaders, and politicians—whom he had shaped. So it goes in the rhythm of life of the *ekklesia*: stowing away on the ark followed by a world-transforming explosion of life. At the close of the book of Revelation, the final text of Scripture, the author reports a vision of the heavenly Jerusalem coming down out of heaven like a bride adorned for her husband. This is an image of the perfected church, the eschatological *ekklesia*. But he makes the curious observation that in this perfected Jerusalem there is no temple. One would think that in such a place, the Temple, which was the entire raison d'être of the earthly Jerusalem, would be highlighted, not eliminated. But then we recall that the purpose of the church is the transfiguration of the world, the invasion of the secular by the sacred. This is why, in its final state, the church coincides with the city, disappearing into the now sanctified arenas of business, politics, sports, commerce, and the arts. We will return to this idea when we speak, in our closing chapter, of heaven.

ONE

We have seen what the *ekklesia* is called out of (the region of unlikeness) and who does the calling (the sovereign voice of Christ), but what precisely is the church called to? In chapter 10 of Mark's Gospel, we find the story of the blind man Bartimaeus. Sitting helplessly by the walls of Jericho and hearing that Jesus is passing by, Bartimaeus cries out, "Jesus, son of David, have pity on me" (Mk 10:47). Then, Mark tells us, Jesus called (*kalein*) him, and the people encouraged Bartimaeus, "Take courage; get up, he is calling [*kalein* again] you" (Mk 10:49). The Lord asks what he can do for the blind man, and Bartimaeus responds, "My teacher, let me see again." And after Jesus cured him, Bartimaeus "followed him on the way" (Mk 10:52). This vignette, rooted in a real encounter, is also a beautiful icon of the church. For a first-century Jew, Jericho would carry with it the connotation of sin and corruption, since it was the city whose walls came down so that the conquering Israelites could enter. Therefore Bartimaeus, sitting in blindness by the walls of Jericho, evokes all of us in the region of unlikeness, lost in our sin and unable to see the world aright. Jesus calls Bartimaeus, gathering him into the community of the *ekklesia*, thereby giving him sight and enabling him to walk the right path. The church is that community in which we learn, through Christ, how to see and how to walk. In the ancient world when a young man joined a philosophical school, say Plato's academy, he was not simply enrolling in a series of classes or course lectures in Platonic philosophy. He was signing on for an entire style of life, involving practices and bodily disciplines, as well as new patterns of thought. We find something very similar in the Acts of the Apostles, where the early Christian church is referred to as "the Way," a term that catches this practical, embodied dimension of Catholic life. The church is that society, that mystical body, in which people learn to see with the eyes of Christ and to walk the path that Christ walked.

Traditional ecclesiology specifies this by speaking of the community of Jesus as "one holy catholic and apostolic," and I would like, in the

Chora Church, interior, Istanbul. WORD ON FIRE

remaining pages of this chapter, to explore, however briefly, each of these dimensions.

The church is one because its founder is one. As we have seen earlier, Jesus compels a choice precisely because he claims to speak and act in the very person of God. Jesus simply cannot be one teacher among many, and therefore those who walk in his way must be exclusively with him. Moreover, the God whom Jesus incarnates is one. As we have seen, the Israelite conception of God is fiercely monotheistic and hence it excludes any diversity or syncretism at the level of basic belief: "The Lord your God is a jealous God." Joseph Ratzinger commented that the opening line of the Nicene Creed, *Credo in unum Deum* (I believe in one God), is a subversive statement because it automatically rules out any rival claimant to ultimate concern. To say that one accepts only the God of Israel and Jesus Christ is to say that one rejects as ultimate any human being, any culture, any political party, any artistic form, or any set of ideas. Søren

Kierkegaard said that the saint is someone whose life is about one thing; a Christian, I would argue, is someone who, at the most fundamental level of his or her being, is centered on the one God of Jesus Christ. This helps to explain why, on the last night of his life on earth, while sitting at supper with his disciples, the core of the church, Jesus prayed, "I pray not only for them, but also for those who will believe in me through their word, so that they may all be one" (Jn 17:20–21).

What precisely are the bonds of unity within the body of Christ? What are the elements that foster Christian unity? I would first mention the creeds, which voice the one faith of the apostles. At every Sunday Mass, Catholics stand to profess together the Nicene Creed, in all of its verbal and conceptual complexity, recapitulating thereby the victories won in the early church by the advocates of the apostolic faith over those who would have compromised it. I would mention as well the Liturgy and the sacraments and devotional practices. We are one in that we participate together in common worship and in common means of accessing the divine life. We are united, too, in our commitment to our brothers and sisters through the corporal and spiritual works of mercy. And finally, we are one through our shared structure of order, which comes from the apostles, about which we will have more to say later in the chapter. Through these various means, we become saints, people whose lives are about one thing. None of this, of course, is to gainsay that there is ample room for multiplicity in the life of the church. There are a variety of liturgical rites, styles of sanctity, schools of theology, paths of spirituality, and so forth, but these diversities do not compromise the integrity of the church's unity. Rather the play between the one and the many in church life is within the tensive harmony of the three divine persons of God.

I realize that, especially today, many are uneasy with any sort of claim to unity. In our time we put a great stress on variety, diversity, and tolerance of the other, for we have seen far too much violence and oppression visited upon the weak in the name of unity. For many in our culture the valorization of the one seems tantamount to tolerating totalitarianism. To be sure, the church does not have an altogether unblemished historical record in this regard. There are far too many examples of church people up and down the centuries who imposed unity either violently or disrespectfully and thereby undermined the very body of Christ they were attempting to build up. But the church at its best has found a creative way to deal with this problem of unity and diversity, a way grounded in the uniqueness of Jesus himself. As we have argued throughout this book, Jesus should not be construed as one religious teacher among many but as the Logos of God, the very pattern of the divine mind, the incarnation of the reason by which the entire universe was fashioned. This implies that whatever is true, whatever is good, and whatever is beautiful in nature or in human culture participates in him, reflects him, and finally leads back to him. Therefore, the church of Jesus Christ can and should embrace the positive dimensions of whatever cultural environment surrounds it.

In the third century, Origen of Alexandria, who was the head of the catechetical school in his native city, coordinated his massive knowledge of the Bible with his equally impressive expertise in Neoplatonic philosophy and produced one of the earliest and most powerful Christian theologies. He did not set the Bible over and against philosophy, but rather found echoes of the Logos in the "words" of the philosophers, and he used the latter to communicate the former to the academic audience of his time. By this intellectual tour de force, Origen set the tone for much of the theologizing done within the Catholic tradition. Saint Augustine followed Origen in the use of Platonic thought, commenting that what he learned in the books of the Platonists helped him enormously on his journey toward Christianity. Indeed, almost all of the church fathers delighted in finding what they called *logoi spermatikoi* (seeds of the Word) in the pagan religion and philosophy that surrounded them. In the thirteenth century, Saint Thomas Aquinas, under the tutelage of Saint Albert the Great, took in what was, at the time, the highly suspect Aristotelian philosophy and science and used it in his architectonic presentation of the Christian faith, which is, even today, stunning in its depth and complexity. In the course of his work, Aquinas also relied on the Jewish philosopher Moses Maimonides, as well as the Islamic thinkers Averroes and Avicenna and a whole congeries of classical philosophers from Epicurus and Epictetus to Plato and Cicero. In the nineteenth century, John Henry Newman, faced with the onslaught of a fierce rationalist critique of Christianity, blithely utilized the work of David Hume and John Locke in his own articulation of religious epistemology; and in the twentieth century, the German Jesuit Karl Rahner made extensive use of both Kant and Heidegger in his presentation of Catholic theology. And in its document on the church and the non-Christian religions of the world, *Nostra Aetatae*, the Second Vatican Council argued that there are "rays of light," echoes of the fullness of truth, in all of the non-Christian religions.

Newman spoke of the church's power of assimilation, by which he meant its capacity to take into itself elements from the cultural environment and adapt them to its purposes. To press the analogy, just as a healthy animal is able to take in what it can from the world around it, as well as to resist what it must, so the church uses *logoi spermatikoi* even as it holds off elements that are incompatible with its identity and proper functioning. Two clear indications of disease within an organism are precisely the incapacity to assimilate and the incapacity to resist, and therefore the church remains healthy in the measure that it is organic and assimilating in its unity.

One of the very best visual illustrations of the principle I've been describing is the church of Santa Maria Rotonda in Rome, better known as the Pantheon. The emperor Hadrian constructed the Pantheon in the early second century as a shrine to all the gods, and to my mind it sums up, better than any other building, the best of the pagan consciousness. For the more sophisticated of the pagans, the gods and goddesses disclosed in symbolic form the necessities inherent within nature and the dynamics of human life. Hence Zeus—fierce, powerful, capricious—represented the heavens; Apollo—handsome, wise, creative—stood for reason; and Venus—sensual, unpredictable, beautiful, dangerous—symbolized love. The Pantheon, with a dome so like the heavens, with its ordered harmonies mimicking the intelligibilities within nature, with its

Pantheon, detail, Rome. WORD ON FIRE

oculus that lets in the natural elements themselves, is a beautiful built form of the pagan mind. The genius of the church was that it assimilated this building to its purposes, transforming it, almost unchanged, into a place of Christian worship. At its best, the unity of the church is not totalitarian but assimilating.

HOLY

We say next that the church of Jesus Christ is holy. It is holy because Christ is holy and the church is Christ's mystical body. Holiness is deeply related to unity, since holiness is a kind of wholeness or integrity, a cohering around a center. It is fascinating how across the languages the terms for health and holiness are similar: "holy" and "whole" in English, *saint* and *sain* in French, *Heil* and *Heiligkeit* in German, *santo* and *sano* in

Procession, Feast of St. Charles Lwanga Namugongo and Companions, Uganda.
WORD ON FIRE

Spanish. Holiness is the integration that results from placing God unambiguously at the center of one's concern; it is the coming together of all of one's faculties—mind, will, imagination, energy, body, sexuality—around the single organizing power of God. Or, to shift the metaphor, it is the suffusing of the entire self with the love of Christ. The church is a bearer of this holiness in its authentic traditions, in its Scriptures, in its sacraments (especially the Eucharist), in its Liturgy, in its doctrinal teaching, in its apostolic governance, and in its saints. In all of these expressions the church is the spotless bride of Christ, the fountain of living water, the new Jerusalem, the recovery of Eden. And by its holiness the church makes people holy. Indeed, that is its sole purpose, its raison d'être. In a wonderful text composed toward the end of her life, Thérèse of Lisieux, whom we will consider in detail later in this book, identified the holiness that animates the church as love: "If the Church was a body composed of different members, it couldn't lack the noblest of all; it must have a Heart, and a Heart BURNING WITH LOVE. And I realized that this love alone was the true motive force which enabled the other members of the church to act; if it ceased to function, the Apostles would forget to preach the Gospel, the martyrs would refuse to shed their blood." That love of Christ—embodied in the saints, sacraments, and structures of the church—*is* the holiness of which we are speaking.

Now here again, I realize, many people balk. How could one possibly declare as holy a church that has been implicated in so many atrocities and outrages over the centuries? How could a holy church have supported the Crusades, the Inquisition and its attendant tortures, slavery, the persecution of Galileo and Giordano Bruno, and the burning of innocent women as witches? How could a holy church have given in to so much institutional corruption? How could it have countenanced the accumulation of so much wealth? And to bring this litany of crimes up to date, how could a holy church have permitted the sexual abuse of children by some priests and the covering up of that outrage by some bishops? The resolution of this problem hangs on a key distinction between the church in its mystical integrity and all of those sinners who are members of the church. To say that the body of Christ is holy is not to deny for a moment that that body is composed of sinful people—sometimes of the highest ecclesiastical rank—who have done cruel, stupid, and wicked things. Was the great Saint Bernard wrong, even sinful, to preach the Second Crusade? Probably. Was the Spanish church, in collusion with the Spanish government, wrong, even sinful, to launch the Inquisition? Yes. Were a number of popes mistaken, even sinful, in their implicit support of slavery? Undoubtedly. Was Cardinal Robert Bellarmine ham-handed, even cruel, in his handling of the Giordano Bruno and Galileo cases? Of course.

But none of this gainsays that the church is holy and a bearer of holiness. In the fourth century Saint Augustine did battle with the Donatists, a Christian sect that argued that those priests and bishops who had abandoned the faith during times of persecution had forfeited the grace of

Saint Matthew, Basilica of St. John Lateran, Rome. WORD ON FIRE

their ordination and were no longer worthy to preside at the Liturgy and distribute the sacraments. The holy church, the Donatists maintained, should be served exclusively by holy ministers, and only the righteous could be conduits of grace. Donatism, in a somewhat modified form, is still a lively force today, evident in the many critics who say that the bad behavior of so many churchmen and churchwomen over the centuries effectively undermines any holiness or credibility that the church might claim for itself. Very much in the Donatist spirit, these commentators hold that only sinless people can serve a holy church. Thank God Augustine held off this challenge, arguing that the grace of Christ can work even through entirely unworthy instruments. Otherwise sin would overwhelm grace—and this would be repugnant to God's sovereignty. And Augustine was merely amplifying a statement of Saint Paul's in his second letter to the Corinthians: "we hold this treasure in earthen vessels, that the surpassing power may be of God and not from us" (2 Cor 4:7). So the holiness of the church comes from Christ and therefore endures despite the weakness of those who are charged with bearing it to the world.

CATHOLIC

The *ekklesia* into which Jesus calls us is also "catholic." The word "catholic" comes from the Greek terms *kata holos* (according to the whole) and thus designates both the internal integrity of the church and its universal outreach. The Catholic Church has all of the gifts that Christ wants his people to have: Scripture, Liturgy, theological tradition, sacraments, the Eucharist, Mary and the saints, apostolic succession, and papal authority. From the Roman Catholic point of view, all of the non-Catholic Christian churches have sacrificed one or more of these qualities and therefore fall short of completeness or catholicity. This does not mean for a moment that Protestant and Orthodox churches might not exercise one or more of the gifts better than Catholics do. One might argue, for example, that many Protestant churches have a more developed sense of the centrality of the Bible or that the Orthodox church has a more mystical sensibility in regard to the Liturgy. But the church of Jesus Christ "subsists" in the Catholic Church, because that communion possesses full integrity; it operates "according to the whole." A wise teacher of mine once commented

St. Peter's Basilica, interior, Vatican City. WORD ON FIRE

on the "grandma's attic" quality of Catholicism, by which he meant our wonderfully stubborn refusal ever to throw anything out.

The other dimension of catholicity is more outward looking. It indicates the dynamism of Jesus's church toward the evangelization of *all* peoples, the gathering in of the *entire* human race. The author of John's Gospel was a master of irony, and one of his most delicious twists involves the sign that Pontius Pilate placed over the cross of the dying Jesus: "Iesus Nazarenus Rex Iudaeorum" (Jesus of Nazareth, King of the Jews). The Roman governor meant it as a taunt, but the sign—written out in the three major languages of that time and place, Hebrew, Latin, and Greek—in fact made Pilate, unwittingly, the first great evangelist. As we have discussed in the first chapter, the king of the Jews, on the Old Testament reading, was destined to be the king of the world—and that kingship is precisely what Pilate effectively announced. Paul's declaration of Jesus as *kyrios* was simply a reiteration of Pilate's message. Even at Calvary, where Jesus's church had dwindled to three members, his little community was catholic for it was destined to embrace everyone. At Pentecost the disciples, gathered in the Upper Room, were filled with the Holy Spirit and, we are told, they began to preach the good news and were heard, miraculously, in the many languages of those who had gathered in Jerusalem for the Feast of Tabernacles. As the church fathers clearly saw, this phenomenon was the reversal of the curse of Babel, when the one language of the human race was divided and the people, accordingly, set against one another. Through the announcement of the Lordship of Jesus, the many languages again become one, for this message is the one that every person, across space and time, was born to hear.

The Catholic Church, at its best, has always exulted in this culture and language transcending universality. In the Middle Ages, Saint Anselm, born in Italy, could become a monk and abbot in France and finally end his life as the archbishop of Canterbury in England. And Thomas Aquinas, another Italian, could be educated in Germany and become a world-renowned professor in Paris. John Paul II embodied this spirit when he inaugurated the World Youth Days in the 1980s. The pope summoned young people from all over the world to gather together for several days of prayer and celebration, and he never wanted them to deny their national identities: the flags and songs of particular countries are a staple at World Youth Days. But he wanted to convince them that they belonged to a family that transcends their particular nationalities. He wanted them to feel in their bones their shared identity as members of Christ's mystical body. It strikes me as altogether appropriate that the largest crowd ever gathered in human history came together around John Paul at World Youth Day in Manila in 1995 to celebrate precisely this catholicity of the church of Jesus.

This church's catholicity has a good deal in common with its unity, and it therefore raises some of the same objections regarding totalitarianism and intolerance. Won't a church that is convinced of its universality run roughshod over any religious group that stands in its way? Many commentators complained bitterly, for example, when John Paul II published the declaration entitled *Dominus Iesus*, which presented the traditional Catholic teaching that Jesus Christ is the sole source of salvation. The best way to respond to such concerns is to show how the many faiths, religions, and philosophies do, in fact, to varying degrees, already participate in the fullness of Christ's gifts and are hence implicitly related to the Catholic Church. We have already gestured toward the significant points of contact with other Christian faiths, but there are many analogies with the non-Christian religions as well. With Jews, Catholics share a belief in the one Creator God who called Israel to be a light to the world. With Muslims, Catholics hold to the faith in the one providential God of mercy who speaks through a variety of prophets. Buddhists and Catholics come together in a keen sense of the finally ineffable quality of ultimate reality, and in their commitment to definite forms of mystical contemplation. Catholics and Hindus share a profound sense of the immanence of God to the world. All of these points of contact, all of these "rays of light," are not only *semina verbi* (seeds of the word) but also *semina catholicitatis* (seeds of catholicity).

APOSTOLIC

Finally, the church of Jesus Christ is apostolic. This means something very simple: that the community of the church is grounded in the twelve people who were privileged to be in Jesus's intimate company. In the first chapter of his Gospel, Saint John relates the story of two disciples of John the Baptist who were told by the Baptist himself to follow Jesus. When the Lord turns to them and asks what they want, the disciples respond with a question, "Rabbi, where are you staying?" Jesus said in reply, "Come, and you will see" (John 1:38–39). And then we hear that they stayed with him that day. The apostles were those who stayed with Jesus, who heard how he spoke and saw how he moved and reacted, who took in at close quarters his manner of being.

As I have mentioned many times throughout this book, Christianity is not a philosophy or a universal mysticism; it is, first, a relationship with Jesus of Nazareth, this particular first-century Jew from Galilee. And that is why it is a religion that is rooted in the faith of those apostles who knew him best and who apprenticed to his way. And that is why, furthermore, in the early church, apostolic pedigree, that is to say, the ability of a particular Christian community to trace its origins back to one of the apostles, was so important. Jerusalem was central because it was the church of James, and Antioch because it was the church of Peter, and Alexandria because it was associated with Mark, and so forth. The reason that Rome emerged in time as the central see of Christianity was not primarily because it was the capital of the empire, but because it was the burial place of *two* apostles, Peter and Paul. The Basilica of St. John Lateran in Rome is the pope's cathedral church, which is to say, the place that contains the chair from which the bishop of Rome definitively teaches. Placed throughout the nave of the basilica are imposing statues of the twelve apostles of Jesus, forming, as it were, the structuring elements, the ribs, of the building itself—and we find this motif repeated in church architecture throughout the world, usually in the form of twelve columns that support the roof. We are being reminded

Basilica of St. John Lateran, interior, Rome. WORD ON FIRE

of those twelve apprentices to the Master who have bequeathed their faith to us.

The apostles are not simply a distant memory; they live on through what we call the apostolic succession. The New Testament witnesses to the practice in the early church of the apostles placing their hands on the heads of those to whom they wished to communicate authority. These chosen few, formed by the apostles themselves, were entrusted to preserve the faith, and, in time, these successors passed on their apostolic authority to another generation, and so on, the Catholic Church holds, to the present day. Therefore the apostolicity of the church is our guarantee that we are, despite many developments and changes across the centuries, still preserving the faith that was first kindled in that company of Jesus's friends. When I was ordained a priest, a successor of the apostles laid hands on me and thus gave me a share in his authority. Whatever capacity I have to govern, sanctify, or teach in the church comes from my participation in that apostolic charism. I realize that this talk of apostolic authority runs counter to many of our cherished assumptions, at least in the West, about democracy, the free play of ideas, freedom of expression, and so on. Why doesn't the church democratize itself and accept the authority of the majority of its people? Again, it is most important to note that the apostolic church is not a debating society that endlessly bats around ideas or a democratic polity whose direction is simply a function of popular choice. The church is grounded in the revelation personally granted to a chosen few, who in turn passed it on to others and so forth. The church of Jesus Christ would not be itself if it denied the divinity of Jesus, the facticity of the resurrection, the existence of the Triune God, the activity of the Holy Spirit, the efficacy of the sacraments, the real presence of Jesus in the Eucharist, and so on. Mind you, every one of these tenets has been denied by church people up and down the centuries, and I frankly wonder how many would pass muster if they were voted on today.

This brings us to what is perhaps the most controversial and misunderstood dimension of the church's apostolicity, namely, the charism of infallibility enjoyed by the pope, the successor of the prince of the apostles. It would be helpful first, I think, to state as clearly as possible what papal infallibility is not. It does not mean that the pope is omniscient; it does not mean that he can predict the future; it does not mean that he is immune from making bad practical judgments; and it certainly doesn't mean that he is above criticism or incapable of sin. In fact, some of the saints were sharp critics of popes, and Dante places some wicked popes in the lower circles of hell. The concept of infallibility means that the pope, by a special gift of the Holy Spirit, knows who Jesus is and therefore is able to articulate correctly those doctrinal and moral teachings that flow from that knowledge. At Caesarea-Philippi, Peter, under the influence of God's spirit, correctly confessed the identity of Jesus, and because of that confession Jesus declared him the rock upon whom the church would be built. The infallibility of Peter's successor, when he teaches on matters of faith and morals, is grounded in that same charismatic guarantee.

I fully realize that this claim raises the hackles of contemporary people. Even with the clarifications that we have made in mind, one might still wonder whether it is healthy for anyone to claim infallible authority.

Once again, John Henry Newman might prove helpful. Newman said that if it pleased God to reveal himself to his church, it should also please him to give that church a living voice of authority that could interpret the revelation down through the ages. In Newman's time, as today, many would say that the Bible is all the authority the church needs. But Newman saw that the Bible is subject to a wide variety of interpretations and hence cannot, on its own, resolve disputes. Some argued—and still argue today—that the consensus of the church fathers and the great theologians is sufficient authority, but Newman held that those figures, as wise as they were, do not constitute a living voice that can intervene here and now to determine right and wrong. What is required is precisely what the Catholic Church claims to have: the voice of the infallible pope, which can in a magisterial and definitive way adjudicate questions regarding the interpretation of revelation.

The point of Newman's insight is brought home if we make a comparison to a game. A game of baseball, for instance, would devolve, in very short order, into chaos were it not for the presence of an umpire who was on the field and able to make a call: safe or out, ball or strike, good or foul. Without that living voice, the flow of the game would stop and be replaced by bickering. Appeals to the rule book of baseball or to past examples of similar situations would be hopeless, for they would never serve to resolve the present and pressing question. Because of, and not despite, the umpire's authoritative voice, the play is able to resume. The infallible pope has a similar umpiring role in the play and flow of the church's life: in its teaching, its care for the poor, its liturgy, its art, and so forth. His voice is not meant to shut down that liveliness, just the contrary. It is meant to enhance it and to cause it to resume when it has been interrupted.

Just before entering the train that would carry him to Rome and the conclave that would elect him pope, Cardinal Angelo Roncalli commented, in regard to himself and his fellow cardinals, "we are not here to guard a museum, but to cultivate a flourishing garden of life." The church of Jesus Christ is not a collection of cultural objets d'art, not a stuffy institutional holdover from another age; it is, as the mosaic at San Clemente suggests, a living thing, an organism, a body. Its head is Jesus himself and its lifeblood is the Holy Spirit. Its purpose is to be a conduit of the divine life to the world, a light to the nations, a new Eden.

As any serious gardener will tell you, the tending of flowers and plants is anything but a passive business. It involves cutting, pruning, weeding, and constant attention. Similarly, those who tend the life of the church must sometimes make difficult decisions, chastise those who have wandered from the straight path, and articulate unpleasant but necessary truths. The image proposed by Cardinal Roncalli is not romantic or idealistic. But it speaks beautifully of the living, evolving, unfolding quality of the mystical body.

St. Peter's Square, Vatican City. WORD ON FIRE

WORD MADE FLESH, TRUE BREAD OF HEAVEN: THE MYSTERY OF THE CHURCH'S SACRAMENT AND WORSHIP

Aristotle said that the best activities are the most useless. This is because such things are not simply means to a further end but are done entirely for their own sake. Thus watching a baseball game is more important than getting a haircut, and cultivating a friendship is more valuable than making money. The game and the friendship are goods that are excellent in themselves, while getting a haircut and making money are in service of something beyond themselves. This is also why the most important parts of the newspaper are the sports section and the comics, and not, as we would customarily think, the business and political reports. In this sense, the most useless activity of all is the celebration of the Liturgy, which is another way of saying that it is the most important thing we could possibly do. There is no higher good than to rest in God, to honor him for his kindness, to savor his sweetness—in a word, to praise him. As we have seen in chapter three, every good comes from God, reflects God, and leads back to God, and, therefore, all value is summed up in the celebration of the Liturgy, the supreme act by which we commune with God.

This is why the great liturgical theologian Romano Guardini said that the liturgy is a consummate form of play. We play football and we play musical instruments because it is simply delightful to do so, and we play in the presence of the Lord for the same reason. In chapter one I spoke of Adam in the garden as being the first priest, which is another way of saying that his life, prior to the fall, was entirely liturgical. At play in the field of the Lord, Adam, with every move and thought, effortlessly gave praise to God. As Dietrich von Hildebrand indicated, this play of liturgy is what rightly orders the personality, since we find interior order in the measure that we surrender everything in us to God. We might say that the Liturgy bookends the entire Scripture, for the priesthood of Adam stands at the beginning of the sacred text and the heavenly Liturgy of the book of Revelation stands at the end. In the closing book of the Bible, John the visionary gives us a glimpse into the heavenly court, and he sees priests, candles, incense, the reading of a sacred text, the gathering of thousands in prayer, prostrations and other gestures of praise, and the appearance of the Lamb of God. He sees, in short, the liturgy of heaven,

Basílica de San Francisco el Grande, interior, Madrid. WORD ON FIRE

the play that preoccupies the angels and saints for all eternity. For these reasons—and others besides—Vatican II referred to the Liturgy as "the source and summit of the Christian life," that from which the whole of Christianity flows and toward which it returns. What I should like to do in the course of this chapter is to move through the Mass, the supreme expression of Catholic liturgical life, exploring the dimensions and aspects of this supremely serious form of play.

THE GATHERING

In a certain sense, the Mass commences with a gathering of people. They come from all walks of life, from different social and educational backgrounds, from a variety of economic strata, with differing levels of moral excellence, and from both genders—and they all form the community gathered around the altar of Christ. In this diversity, they form an eschatological icon of God's holy people. The fallen world is marked by division, separation, stratification; we sinners are intensely interested in questions of priority and exclusivity: Who is in and who is out? Who is up and who is down? But, as Paul told us, in Christ "there is neither Jew nor Greek, there is neither slave nor free person, there is not male and female" (Gal 3:28); all are members of the mystical body. As we gather for Mass, we become a great anticipatory realization of this vision. When Dorothy Day was considering her conversion to Catholicism, she would attend Sunday Mass. Though the Liturgy was in a language she didn't know, and though its central action was surrounded by much baroque decoration, she was deeply impressed by the fact that both the rich and the poor, both the educated and the uneducated, both the housekeeper and the grande dame attended, kneeling side by side. The Catholic historian Christopher Dawson upon telling his mother that he was converting to the Catholic faith from his native Anglicanism was met with this response: "It's not so much the doctrines that concern me; it's that now you'll be worshipping with the help!" Both Dorothy Day and Mrs. Dawson intuited the properly subversive nature of the way Catholics gather for prayer.

Once gathered, we sing. Singing at the Mass should not be construed as merely decorative or incidental, for the harmonizing of the many voices as one is an embodied expression of how we, as children of God, ought to live. The ritual of the Liturgy properly begins with the sign of the cross and the priest's intonation of the words "In the name of the Father, and of the Son, and of the Holy Spirit." By this gesture and this simple phrase we announce that we belong to the Triune God. Modern secularism is predicated on the assumption that we essentially belong to no one, that we are self-determining and self-directing, pursuers of happiness according to our own rights. But Paul told Christians long ago, "None of us lives for oneself, and no one dies for oneself. If we live, we live for the Lord, and if we die, we die for the Lord; so then, whether we live or die, we are the Lord's" (Rom 14:7–8). In contradistinction to modernity, Catholics say "your life is not about you," and the Liturgy signals this at the very beginning of the Mass with the sign of the cross. But there is more. To speak of the cross is to reference the great act by which the Father sent the Son into godforsakenness in order to gather us, through the Holy Spirit, into the divine life. Because the Son went all the way down, he was able to bring even the most recalcitrant sinner back into fellowship with God. Thus when we invoke the cross at the beginning of the Liturgy, we signify that we are praying *in* God and not merely *to* God.

Just after the sign of the cross, the priest greets the people, not in his own name but in Christ's: "The Lord be with you" or "Grace to you and peace from God our Father and the Lord Jesus Christ." Garbed in vestments that cover his ordinary clothes and hence, symbolically, his ordinary identity, the priest at the Liturgy is operating *in persona Christi* and not in his own person, and therefore his gestures, words, and movements are expressive not of his own perspectives and convictions but of Christ's. This is why the people respond, "And with your spirit," for they are addressing not the individual man but Jesus in whose person the priest is operating. Immediately after the greeting, the priest invites everyone in attendance to call to mind his or her sins. This simple routine is of extraordinary importance. G. K. Chesterton once remarked, "There are saints in my religion, but that just means men who know they are sinners." For the great English apologist, the relevant distinction is not between sinners and non-sinners, but between those sinners who know their sin and those who, for whatever reason, don't. The heroes of the faith—the saints—are precisely those who are ordered toward God and who therefore have a keener appreciation of how far they fall short of the ideal. Saint John of the Cross compared the soul to a pane of glass. When it is facing away from the light, its smudges and imperfections are barely noticeable, but when it is directed at the light, every mark, even the smallest, becomes visible. This explains the paradox that the saints are most keenly aware of their sins, even to the point of describing themselves as the worst of sinners. We might mistake this for false modesty, but it is in fact simply a function of a truly saintly psychology. Therefore as the Liturgy commences and we stand within the embrace of the Trinitarian love, we mimic the saints and become, perforce, not less but more aware of our sin.

In doing so we offer a corrective to the pervasive cultural tendency toward exculpation. "I'm okay and you're okay," we tell ourselves. But to subscribe to such a naïve sentiment is, *ipso facto,* to prove that one is not facing into the clarifying light of God. The calling to mind of sins is but a preparation for the *Kyrie,* the cry of "Lord have mercy, Christ have mercy, Lord have mercy." In saying those words we echo the cri de coeur of the blind beggar Bartimaeus who called out to Jesus, *Eleison me* (have pity on me). In the presence of the true God, there is no room for self-aggrandizement and self-deception; we know that we are incapable of saving ourselves, that we are beggars before the Lord. The Liturgy places us in this correct and finally liberating attitude, and then we hear the words of the priest: "May Almighty God have mercy on us, forgive us our sins, and bring us to everlasting life." God has no interest whatsoever in making us grovel before him in self-reproach. He *wants* to forgive, but it is imperative that we realize that there is something in us that *needs forgiving.*

After the *Kyrie* there is the *Gloria,* which is one of the most magnifi-

Altar Mayor, Toledo Cathedral, Spain. WORD ON FIRE

cent prayers in our liturgical tradition. One can read out of the *Gloria* practically the whole of Catholic theology, but I will focus only on the first line: "Glory to God in the highest, and on earth peace to people of good will." As we have seen in some detail in chapter two, giving God the glory is a kind of formula for a happy life. When he is clearly the supreme value for us, then our lives become harmoniously ordered on that central love. Peace, as it were, breaks out among us when God—and not pleasure, money, or power—is given glory in the highest. Our term "worship" comes from an older English word "worthship," designating what we hold dear. The Liturgy is the place where we act out our worship, where we demonstrate, by word and gesture, what is of greatest worth to us—and this is why the Mass is essential to peace. It would be helpful in this context once again to invoke Aristotle. In his *Nicomachean Ethics* the great philosopher comments that a friendship will endure only in the measure that the two friends fall in love, not so much with each other, but together with a transcendent third. If together they both look with love toward the truth or toward the beautiful or toward their country or their city, then their companionship with each other will deepen. If they look only with affection to each other, their relationship will devolve, eventually, into a kind of shared egotism. In saying (or singing) the *Gloria*, the gathered community is expressing their shared love of God's glory—and if Aristotle is right, joining in this prayer will deepen their friendship with one another ("peace to people of good will").

THE TELLING OF THE STORIES

After these extremely significant opening liturgical elements, everyone sits in order to listen to the Word of God, usually on Sunday a reading from the Old Testament, followed by a responsorial psalm, then a New Testament epistle, and finally a Gospel reading that is thematically coordinated to the first reading. The posture of sitting is not to be overlooked. In the ancient world, one would sit at the feet of a master in order to listen and learn. Sitting was therefore universally recognized, from the earliest days of the church, as the proper attitude of the apprentice or student. Seated in silence, prepared to hear the voice of the Lord, Catholics at Mass signal that they are humble learners, apprentices to the Word. Much of modern theology assumes that religion wells up naturally from the depths of human consciousness and experience. Without denying the validity of this perspective altogether, I would insist with Saint Paul that "faith comes from hearing." A message, a word, a voice comes from outside of our minds and our ordinary experience and tells us something that we would never otherwise know. Whereas both classical and modern philosophers celebrate the confident person, blithely in control of his thoughts and actions, the Bible holds up those figures—Abraham, Moses, Isaiah, Jeremiah, Peter, Paul—who listened to a puzzling word that came from outside their range of expectation.

Liturgical people listen to biblical texts so that they might be drawn into the peculiar power of the biblical world. J. R. R. Tolkien's great trilogy *Lord of the Rings* commences with a lengthy description of Bilbo Bagginss's birthday party. Someone who had been told that this was a roaring adventure story might legitimately wonder when the action will start.

But in order to orient his reader to the entirely new world that he was creating—a world of orcs, elves, wizards, humans, and hobbits, a place with distinctive topography, weather, customs, language, and modes of behavior—Tolkien had to take his time. Melville, of course, was doing much the same thing in his long and sometimes tedious examinations of the minutiae of the whale-boating culture in *Moby-Dick.* Moving into the world of Scripture, cutting through the thick undergrowth of this jungle, we learn to speak, react, and think in a different way. In this sense, the hearing of the Word is something like learning baseball, golf, or theater—or better, like becoming acclimated to a new language or culture. If people listen attentively to the Scriptures at Mass, they are, perhaps despite themselves, leaving the confines of their familiar world and entering a new psychological and spiritual space.

After the readings are proclaimed, the priest rises to preach. I mentioned earlier that the priest at the Liturgy is acting in the person of Christ and not in his own person. This opening up of a deeper identity

Church of the Dormition, interior, Jerusalem. DENIS R. MCNAMARA

becomes especially clear (at least in principle) during the homily, for the preacher is not meant to share his private convictions about politics or culture or even religion. He is supposed to speak the mind of Christ. To be sure, he ought to use all of the resources of the church's theology, spirituality, and biblical interpretation, and he ought certainly to apply the Scriptures to the present cultural situation, but he is not speaking in his own voice or out of his private convictions. Keeping in mind the noncompetitiveness of God, on which we've been insisting throughout this book, it might be better to say that the preacher, in surrendering to the divine voice, actually finds his own most authentic voice, and in conforming himself to the attitude of Christ he discovers his own most authentic attitude. The great Protestant theologian Karl Barth said that the Christian preacher or theologian is a sort of mystagogue, drawing his readers into the strangeness and dense texture of the biblical jungle, introducing them to characters such as Isaiah, Abraham, Jeremiah, David, and Jesus himself, figures whose motivations and moves are often inscrutable to us. And through it all, he is speaking of the supremely distinctive character of God himself, this transcendent power who nevertheless speaks and acts in history.

When the homily is complete, the people stand for the recitation of the creed. They can use the ancient and simple formula called The Apostles' Creed, but customarily they pray the great statement of faith that emerged from the Council of Nicaea in 325. In speaking the lyrical phrases "God from God, Light from Light, true God from true God, begotten not made, consubstantial with the Father," they are reiterating the resolution of the battle over the Arian heresy, which arose when a fourth-century Alexandrian priest named Arius denied the divinity of Jesus. "One in being" is the English rendering of the Greek *homoousios*, a technical term that the fathers of the council coined in order articulately to express their faith that the man Jesus is also fully divine. What the Council of Nicaea intuited was that this issue was decisive for the identity and survival of the church, for if Jesus is not truly divine, then Christianity necessarily devolves into another mythology or another philosophy. Nearly seventeen hundred years later we stand to repeat this same formula in order to ward off the same danger, and in so doing we signal to ourselves who we are. As we have seen in chapter five, there is something properly subversive about the opening declaration of the creed, "I believe in one God," since it precludes any other pretender to ultimacy—be it country, culture, political party, or charismatic leader. Hence those who state their faith in the one God are standing resolutely athwart all forms of idolatry both ancient and contemporary. When the recitation of the creed is over, the community offers prayers for the living and the dead. These "prayers of the faithful," to give them their liturgical name, are expressive of the inescapable interdependence of the members of Christ's mystical body. We pray for one another precisely because we are implicated with one another, connected by the deepest bonds in Christ. One member of the body cannot coherently say to another, "Your concern is not mine," for, as I have stated in the chapter on the church, we are not a club but an organism. Just as a cancer raging in the stomach profoundly affects the other organs, so the suffering or anxiety of one member of the mystical communion impinges upon all members of that communion. As we act out our faith in reciting the creed, so we act out our mystical identity as we pray for one another.

THE OFFERING

With the prayers of the faithful, the first part of the Mass, called the Liturgy of the Word, comes to a close, and the second part, the Liturgy of the Eucharist, commences. It might be helpful at this juncture to reflect on the Mass as an intense form of encounter. In almost every culture—certainly in ours—a formal encounter with another person involves, typically, two basic things: conversing and eating. At a party, reception, or banquet we greet guests and spend a substantial amount of time talking with them, and then we usually sit down to share a meal. The Mass is an encounter with Jesus Christ, a formal and ritualized act of "staying with him." In the Liturgy of the Word, we listen to him (in the Scriptures) and we speak back to him (in the responses and prayers); then in the Liturgy of the Eucharist we eat a meal that he prepares for us. Another perspective on the two sections of the Mass is that the Liturgy of the Word corresponds to the Jewish synagogue service, which centered on the reading and explaining of the Torah, while the Liturgy of the Eucharist corresponds to the Temple service at which grain and animal sacrifices were performed. The parallelism I've just proposed is not precisely balanced, because I've compared the second half of the Mass to both a meal and a sacrifice. But this in fact gets to the heart of the matter, for the Catholic Liturgy of the Eucharist participates in both those dimensions.

At this point I must pause to say a word about this juxtaposition. A fundamental biblical principle is that in a world gone wrong there is no communion without sacrifice. This is true because sin has twisted us out of shape, and therefore intimacy with God will involve a twisting back into shape, a painful realignment, a sacrifice. And this is why, on a biblical reading, covenant is almost invariably associated with sacrifice. God

Tabernacle, Church of the Dormition, Jerusalem. DENIS R. MCNAMARA

chooses Abraham and establishes a covenant with him—and then he asks him to offer animals as a holocaust; he chooses Moses and through him sets up the Sinai covenant—and then he asks him to slaughter oxen and splash their blood on the altar and on the people; he cuts (the typical biblical word) a covenant with David and then sets up the Jerusalem Temple where hundreds of thousands of animals were, for many centuries, offered up. Mind you, God has no need of these sacrifices; he's no pagan deity somehow mollified by our liturgical rites. As we have seen in chapter three, the true God has no need of anything at all. The point is that *we* need sacrifice in order to reorder us and thereby restore communion with God. God is said to be pleased with our sacrifice precisely to the extent that it makes us more fully alive. In an animal sacrifice, a person took one small aspect of God's creation and returned it to its source in order to signal his gratitude for the gift of his own existence and indeed the existence of the world. This acknowledgment of God's primacy is not easy for a sinner, and therefore it is entirely appropriate that sacrifice involves blood and death. The one who performs the sacrifice sees acted out in the suffering of the animal his own suffering; he is vicariously being twisted back into right relation with the source of his existence. All of this corresponds to what John Paul II termed "the law of the gift," the spiritual principle that one's being increases in the measure that one gives it away. What is given back to God, sacrificed to him, breaks against the rock of the divine self-sufficiency and returns for the benefit of the one who has made the offering. Sacrifice produces communion. This is the distinctive logic that undergirds the Liturgy of the Eucharist.

At the commencement of the second part of the Mass, small offerings of bread, wine, and water are brought forward so that the priest can offer them to God. To say bread and wine is to imply wheat and vine; and to say wheat and vine is to imply earth, soil, water, wind, and sunshine; and to say earth, soil, water, wind, and sunshine is to imply the solar system and indeed the cosmos itself. The tiny gifts are therefore symbolically representative of the entire creation. Taking these gifts in hand, the priest speaks the "Berakah" prayer, "Blessed are you, Lord God of all creation, for through your goodness, we have received the bread and wine we offer you." In one and the same gesture, he blesses God and offers him a small portion of creation as a gift, thereby giving back to the Giver and establishing the "loop" of grace that I have described previously. The bread and wine, offered to the God who doesn't need them, will return to the offerers immeasurably elevated as the Body and Blood of Jesus.

After the Berakah prayer the priest moves into the climactic prayer of the Mass, the Eucharistic Prayer, in the course of which Christ becomes really, truly, and substantially present. Just before the commencement of the prayer proper, the priest invokes the song of the angels, "And so we join the angels and saints in proclaiming your glory, as we sing . . ." It is most important to see that this is not simply a bit of pious boilerplate. At the outset of this chapter I mentioned that the Mass on earth links us to the eternal Liturgy of heaven, the praise of the angels and saints. At this point in the Mass we explicitly join our community and our ritual action to that transcendent play. The song of the angels, which is to say, their harmonious interaction born of shared worship of God, is a model for our own harmonious interaction here below. Therefore, as the gathered people sing, "Holy, Holy, Holy, Lord God of hosts. Heaven and earth are full of your glory," they are, like the angels, giving glory to God in the highest and hence actually realizing the unity that God desires for them.

The prayer commences with a word of gratitude to the Trinitarian God for the sheer grace of his creation and redemption: "You are indeed holy, O Lord, and all you have created rightly gives you praise, for through your Son our Lord Jesus Christ, by the power and working of the Holy Spirit, you give life to all things and make them holy." Once again, as the priest utters this prayer he reminds us that we are enfolded in the embrace of the three divine persons. He then beckons the Father to send down the Holy Spirit for the sanctification and transformation of the bread and wine: "Let your Spirit come upon these gifts to make them holy, so that they may become the body and blood of our Lord Jesus Christ." He then continues with what is termed the "institution narrative," which is an abbreviated form of the Gospel account of what Jesus

The Last Supper *by Cosimo Rosselli, Sistine Chapel, Vatican City.* WORD ON FIRE

said and did at the Last Supper. He recalls how Jesus took bread and gave thanks, but then he moves from third person description to direct quotation, speaking the very words of Jesus: "Take this, all of you, and eat it: this is my body which will be given up for you." And the priest does just the same in regard to the cup of wine, first recounting how Jesus gave thanks and passed the chalice to his disciples, and then moving into first person he says: "Take this, all of you, and drink from it: this is the cup of my blood, the blood of the new and everlasting covenant. It will be shed for you and for all so that sins may be forgiven. Do this in memory of me." The faith of the church is that by the power of these words the bread and wine are transformed into the body and blood of Christ. Jesus becomes "really, truly, and substantially" present to his people under the appearance of the Eucharistic elements.

EXCURSUS ON THE REAL PRESENCE

The teaching concerning the real presence is so central to the Liturgy and to Catholicism that I will pause at this point and consider it with some care. Though, as I've suggested, the institution narratives in the

Gospels are key texts in regard to this teaching, I would like to focus on the distinctive Eucharistic theology implicit in chapter 6 of John's Gospel. That chapter commences with the account of Jesus's multiplication of the loaves and fishes and his feeding of the multitude, and it continues with a description of Jesus walking on the surface of the water to the other side of the Sea of Galilee. It begins, in a word, with a clear affirmation of the divine power of Jesus as well as the Lord's intention to feed his people, two powerfully Eucharistic motifs. The crowds, amazed at Jesus's miracle, follow him to the other side of the lake. Jesus tells them bluntly, "Do not work for food that perishes but for the food that endures for eternal life" (Jn 6:27). Then they ask for a "sign" so that they might believe in him, something akin to the manna that God the Father gave the people to eat during their sojourn in the desert. Jesus assures them, "I am the bread of life; whoever comes to me will never hunger, and whoever believes in me will never thirst . . . I am the bread that came down

St. Monica–St. George Church, detail, Cincinnati.
DENIS R. MCNAMARA

from heaven" (Jn 6:35, 41). They balk at this, wondering how this man whose parents they know could have come down from heaven, but Jesus persists: "I am the living bread that came down from heaven; whoever eats this bread will live forever; and the bread that I will give is my flesh for the life of the world" (Jn 6:51).

One can certainly understand the consternation of Jesus's followers at this stage of the conversation, for it would be hard to imagine anything more theologically objectionable, and frankly, more disgusting, for a first-century Jew than what Jesus was proposing. Throughout the Old Testament there are clear prohibitions against the eating of an animal's flesh with its blood. To give just a handful of examples among many, the book of Genesis stipulates, "Only flesh with its lifeblood still in it you shall not eat" (Gn 9:4); the book of Leviticus states, "This shall be a perpetual ordinance for your descendants wherever they may dwell. You shall not partake of any fat or any blood" (Lev 3:17); and the book of Deuteronomy insists, "But make sure that you do not partake of the blood; for blood is life, and you shall not consume this seat of life with the flesh" (Dt 12:23). Yet Jesus is urging pious Jews to eat not only the bloody flesh of an animal but his own flesh and blood. Naturally enough, they protest: "How can this man give us [his] flesh to eat?" (Jn 6:52). At this point, Jesus is being offered every opportunity to soften his teaching or to explain it in a more metaphorical manner, as he did, for example, when Nicodemus balked at the idea that being born again meant crawling back into his mother's womb. But instead, Jesus intensifies his instruction, saying to them, "Amen, amen, I say to you, unless you eat the flesh of the Son of Man and drink his blood, you do not have life within you . . . For my flesh is true food, and my blood is true drink" (Jn 6:53, 55). To grasp the full import of this statement we have to attend to the Greek of John's text. The term that Jesus uses for "eat" here is not the expected *phagein*, invariably employed to suggest the way human beings eat. Rather he uses *trogein*, which is customarily employed to describe an animal's manner of eating, something along the lines of "gnaw" or "munch." In short, Jesus purposely emphasizes the very physicality to which the crowd was objecting.

St. Maria sopra Minerva, detail, Rome. WORD ON FIRE

We hear that in the wake of this exchange there was a mass defection among Jesus's followers: "Then many of his disciples who were listening said, 'This saying is hard; who can accept it?'" (Jn 6:60) and "As a result of this, many [of] his disciples returned to their former way of life and no longer accompanied him" (Jn 6:66). It is fascinating to note how often in the history of Christianity the teaching concerning Jesus's presence in the Eucharist has been a church-dividing issue, a standing or falling point. Plaintively, Jesus asks his remaining circle of followers, the twelve: "Do you also want to leave?" (Jn 6:67). What follows is John's parallel to Peter's confession of faith at Caesarea-Philippi: "Master, to whom shall we go? You have the words of eternal life. We have come to believe and are convinced that you are the Holy One of God" (Jn 6:68–69). Speaking for the others, Peter confesses that what Jesus has said about the Eucharist is true, and he ties that confession to a declaration of Jesus's sacred identity. From a Catholic point of view, this coming together of faith in the Incarnation and faith in the real presence is of great significance, for the Eucharist is nothing other than a sacramental extension of the Incarnation across space and time, the manner in which Christ continues to abide, in an embodied way, with his church. At this crucial moment in Jesus's public ministry, Peter got this, and he spoke his conviction on behalf of the core group of Apostles. It is the Catholic faith that Peter, down through the ages, has continued to get it.

Inspired by this discourse in chapter 6 of John, and sustained by the teaching of the successors of Peter and the apostles, the Catholic Church has held for the past two millennia to the doctrine of the real presence. One of the most articulate defenders of the real presence was Thomas Aquinas. Thomas Aquinas loved the Eucharist. He celebrated Mass every morning, and immediately after his own Mass he would concelebrate at another. It is said that he rarely got through the Liturgy without weeping copious tears, so strongly did he identify with the Eucharistic mystery. It has also been reported that when he was struggling with a particularly thorny intellectual difficulty, he would go to the tabernacle, resting his head on it and begging for inspiration. Toward the end of his relatively short life (he died at forty-nine), Aquinas composed, as part of his *Summa theologiae,* a treatise on the Eucharist. When he had finished this remarkably thorough and complex text, he was still unconvinced that he had done justice to this great sacrament. Therefore he laid his treatise at the foot of the crucifix in the Dominican chapel in Naples and he prayed. A voice came from the cross: *"Bene scripsisti de me, Thoma"* (You have written well of me, Thomas), and then, "What would you have as a reward?" Aquinas said simply, *"Nil nisi te"* (nothing except you).

What do we find when we look at the treatise that Aquinas placed at the foot of the cross? We find that Aquinas analyzed the real presence under the technical rubric of "transubstantiation." He argued that at the consecration the substance of the bread is changed into the substance of the body of Jesus, and that the substance of the wine is changed into the substance of the blood of Jesus, even as the accidents of bread and wine remain unchanged. If the terms "substance" and "accident" seem odd to us, we can translate them simply and accurately as "reality" and "appearance." Aquinas taught that the deepest reality of the Eucharistic elements changes into the personal presence of Christ, even as their appearances remain the same. The distinction between reality and appearance is referenced in practically all of the great philosophies of the world. There are references to it in Hinduism, Buddhism, Platonism, and Kantianism, and it also corresponds to our commonsense take on things. We know that most of the time reality (what something is) and appearance (what something looks like) coincide, but we also know that there are exceptions to the rule. If you look up into the sky on a clear night you see what appear to be stars in their present configuration, but the astronomers tell us that you are actually seeing into the distant past, since it has taken thousands of years for the light of those stars to reach your eyes. You are not looking at the stars that are there, but rather at the stars that *were* there: appearance and reality, in this case, divide. Or suppose you meet a person who makes a very poor first impression and you conclude that he is just not a likable man. But someone who knows him much better, who has watched him under a variety of circumstances and across many years, corrects you: "I know he can seem that way, but he really isn't." Once again, appearance and reality do not coincide, and the noncoincidence is pointed out by someone who has more experience than you do. Something very similar is at play in regard to the Eucharist.

But still how does Aquinas *explain* the change? Like Ambrose of

Crucifix, Pantheon, Rome. WORD ON FIRE

Milan, Aquinas saw the change as a consequence of the power of Jesus's words: "this is my body" and "this is the cup of my blood." As the language philosophers of the twentieth century have helped us to see, not only are words descriptive; they can also be, under certain circumstances, transformative: they can *change* the way things are. If someone walked up to you at a party and said, "You're under arrest," you would assume that he was making a joke or was deluded. But if a properly deputized and uniformed officer of the law told you that you were under arrest, you would be, in point of fact, under arrest, his words having effected what they enunciated. Or suppose you are watching a game from third-base box seats at Wrigley Field. One of the Cubs comes around second base and slides into third. You shout, "Safe!" Your exclamation might express your conviction and might even be an accurate assessment of the play, but it wouldn't affect reality at all. But standing right in front of you is a properly certified umpire of the National League, and he gestures vigorously with his right arm and shouts, "Out!" Whether you or the player who slid into third like it or not, the unfortunate Cub is in fact out. The word of that umpire has changed the reality of the game.

But those are only puny human words. Consider the divine Word. In the Bible, God creates the whole of the universe through the power of his word: "Let there be light," says the Lord, "and there was light" (Gn 1:3). The prophet Isaiah speaks for Yahweh and says, "For just as from the heavens the rain and snow come down and do not return there until they have watered the earth, making it fertile and fruitful . . . So shall my word be that goes forth from my mouth; It shall not return to me void, but shall do my will, achieving the end for which I sent it" (Is 55:10–11). God's speech does not so much describe the world as create it and constitute it. In the first chapter I insisted that Jesus is not simply one spiritual teacher among many but the Son of God, the very Logos of God, the Word by which the universe was made. Therefore what Jesus says is "Lazarus, come out!" (Jn 11:43), and he came out; "Little girl, I say to you, arise!" (Mk 5:41), and she got up; "Child, your sins are forgiven" (Mk 2:5), and they are forgiven. The night before he died, Jesus

Notre Dame Cathedral, interior, Paris. WORD ON FIRE

took bread and said, "This is my body, which will be given for you" (Lk 22:19). In the same way, after the meal, he took the cup and said, "This cup is the new covenant in my blood, which will be shed for you" (Lk 22:20). Since Jesus's word is the divine Word, it is not merely descriptive but transformative. It creates, sustains, and changes reality at the most fundamental level. When at the consecration the priest moves into the mode of first-person quotation, he is not speaking in his own person but in the person of Jesus—and that's why those words *change* the elements.

At the very beginning of her career, Flannery O'Connor, who would develop into one of the greatest Catholic writers of fiction in the twentieth century, sat down to dinner with Mary McCarthy and a group of other New York intellectuals. The young Flannery, clearly the junior member of this sophisticated circle, was overwhelmed and barely said a word all evening. McCarthy, a former Catholic, trying to draw O'Connor out, made a few nice remarks about the Eucharist, commenting that it was a very powerful symbol. Flannery looked up and in a shaky voice said, "Well, if it's only a symbol, I say to hell with it." I can't imagine a better summary of the Catholic doctrine of the real presence.

COMMUNION AND SENDING FORTH

At the close of the Eucharistic prayer, Jesus, who is really present under the forms of bread and wine, is offered as a living sacrifice to the Father. Lifting up the elements, the priest prays, "Through him, and with him, and in him, O God almighty Father, in the unity of the Holy Spirit, all glory and honor is yours for ever and ever." At this moment the Catholic priest is in the true holy of holies, and what he does is analogous to what the high priest did in the Temple on the Day of Atonement. In ancient times the Jewish priest would enter the holy of holies, which was symbolic of the heavenly realm, and there he would sacrifice an animal to Yahweh on behalf of all the people. Then he would sprinkle some of the blood around the interior of the sanctuary, and the rest he would bring out in a bowl and sprinkle on the people, sealing thereby a kind of blood bond between God and the nation. The Catholic priest, at the climax of the Mass, offers to the Father not the blood of bulls and goats but the Blood of Christ beyond all price. Since the Father has no need of anything, that sacrifice redounds completely to our benefit.

The priest and the other Eucharistic ministers then come down out of the sanctuary, carrying Christ's Body in the Host and his Blood in chalices and offering it as food and drink for the people. By this act they establish a blood fellowship between God and his people that is, in its intensity, beyond anything dreamed of by the Temple priests of old. We recall Paul's words to the Corinthians: "The cup of blessing that we bless, is it not a participation [a *koinonia*, or a communion] in the blood of Christ?" (1 Cor 10:16). If our troubles began with a bad meal—seizing at the fruit of the tree of the knowledge of good and evil—our redemption is affected through a properly constituted meal, God feeding his people with his own Body and Blood.

After the congregation has received communion and given thanks, they are blessed and sent forth. The priest says, "Go forth, the Mass is ended." It has been said that after the words of consecration these are the most sacred words of the entire Mass. Now that the people have gathered as one family, heard the word of God, professed their faith, prayed for one another, offered sacrifice to the Father, and received the Body and Blood of Jesus, the faithful are, at least in principle, more properly formed and hence ready to go out to effect the transformation of the world. The imagery of Noah's ark that we explored in an earlier chapter is apposite here, for the Liturgy is the preservation of the form of life that God desires for his people. Just as Noah opened the windows and portal of the ark in order to let the life out, so the priest dismisses the people, scattering them like seed into the fallen world.

In his meditations on the story of the visit of the Magi, Archbishop Fulton Sheen indicated that the three kings, having traversed a great distance, having withstood opposition from King Herod, having found the baby, having opened their treasures for him, and finally, "having been warned in a dream not to return to Herod, they departed for their country by another way" (Mt 2:12). Of course they did, Sheen concluded, "for no one comes to Christ and goes back the same way he came!" The liturgy is the privileged communion with the Lord; it is the source and summit of the Christian life. And therefore those who participate in it never leave unchanged; they never go back the same way they came.

St. Patrick's Cathedral, interior, New York. WORD ON FIRE

Chapter 8

A VAST COMPANY
OF WITNESSES:
THE COMMUNION
OF SAINTS

ho is a saint? The Catholic Church says that a saint is someone who has demonstrated heroic virtue, someone who is a friend of God, someone who is in heaven—and these all finally amount to the same thing. Saints are those who have allowed Jesus thoroughly to transfigure them from within. Paul caught this when he observed, "yet I live, no longer I, but Christ lives in me" (Gal 2:20). In chapter 5 of Luke's Gospel we find an odd story about Jesus and Peter. As the eager crowd presses in on him, Jesus spies two boats moored by the shore of the lake. Without asking permission, he gets into the boat belonging to Peter and says, "Put out into deep water and lower your nets for a catch" (Lk 5:4). What followed, as we have seen earlier when analyzing Mark's version of this scene, is the miraculous catch of fishes. Read with spiritual eyes, this story reveals the essential feature of sainthood. For a Galilean fisherman his boat was everything; it was his livelihood, his work, the means by which he supported his family.

Peter's fishing vessel represents, therefore, his professional creativity, his link to the wider world, the key to his survival. Jesus simply gets into the boat and commences to give orders—and the result is the greatest catch Peter the fisherman had ever made. Jesus's uninvited boarding of the vessel represents the invasion of grace, the incoming of the divine love into someone's life. Precisely because God is noncompetitive with creation, precisely because he wants human beings to come fully to life, this inrushing of grace does not destroy or interrupt what it invades; it enhances it and raises it to a new pitch. Peter, one presumes, had been successful enough as a fisherman, but now, under Jesus's direction, he goes out into the deep and brings in more than he could ever have imagined possible. This is what happens when we cooperate with grace, when we allow Christ to live his life in us.

The saints are those who have allowed Jesus to get into their boats and who have thereby become not superhuman or angelic but fully human, as alive as God intended them to be. The entire purpose of the church, as we have seen, is to produce saints. Scripture, tradition, Liturgy, official

The Duomo, interior, Florence. WORD ON FIRE

teaching, moral instruction, and the sacraments are all means to the end of fostering friendship with God. And that is why knowing and loving the saints is so essential to the life of the church. We need the saints in order to come to a richer understanding of God, for each saint in his or her particular manner reflects something of God's perfection. We might think of God as an absolutely intense white light that, when refracted in creation, expresses itself in an infinite variety of colors. The saints reflect particular colors, and that is precisely why their variety is so important in the life of the church. Saint Francis of Assisi speaks a very definite truth about God, but he barely begins to represent the fullness of the divine reality. And that's why we require lots of other saints.

What I would like to do in this chapter is to explore briefly the lives of four relatively contemporary friends of God: Katharine Drexel, Thérèse of Lisieux, Edith Stein, and Mother Teresa of Calcutta.[1] I want to place special emphasis on the manner in which Jesus, uninvited, graciously invaded their lives and with their cooperation transfigured them from the inside out. I will tell the stories of these women, for it is crucially important that we *see* them in action so that we can apprentice to them, learn from them, and finally fall in love with them. My hope is that these four stories will give at least some indication of the splendid variety on display in the lives of the saints so that you might more readily discover the form of holiness that is specially suited to you. I chose these four women because each represents an elevated or transfigured form of one of the virtues. Katharine Drexel shows us what justice looks like when it is invaded by love; Thérèse of Lisieux demonstrates what ordinary prudence—knowing the right thing to do—looks like when radicalized by Christ; Edith Stein is an icon of evangelical courage; and Mother Teresa of Calcutta embodies the power of poverty and asceticism when placed in the service of Jesus. I could describe these virtues abstractly, but you will better learn about them if you have the opportunity to *watch*

---

1. For a more detailed analysis of the lives and witnesses of these saints, see Father Barron's book *The Priority of Christ* (Grand Rapids, Mich.: Brazos Press, 2007).

them. I want you to apprentice to these women, and that requires some
patience and time.

Katharine Drexel

Katharine Drexel was born in Philadelphia on November 26, 1858, the
same year as the apparitions at Lourdes. Her father was Francis Anthony
Drexel, an internationally known banker and one of the richest men in
the United States. Katharine's childhood was, by her own admission,
idyllic. Along with her siblings she was given a first-class education in languages, literature, philosophy, music, and painting. She lived in a sumptuous mansion in Philadelphia and summered with her family at a lovely
country estate outside the city. On several occasions during her youth
she made the grand tour of Europe, staying in the finest hotels and taking in the sights, especially those dear to Catholic pilgrims. Katharine's

St. Katharine Drexel as a young woman, 1879.
ARCHIVES OF THE SISTERS OF THE BLESSED SACRAMENT

father and stepmother (her natural mother had died just after giving birth to Katharine) were both devout Catholics, and they maintained a chapel in their home. Most nights, after returning from work and before sitting down to dinner, Mr. Drexel would repair to the chapel for a half hour of intense prayer. Also three afternoons a week the Drexels would open up their home to the poor and needy of Philadelphia. They drilled into their children the conviction, deeply rooted in the Catholic sensibility, that their wealth had been entrusted to them and was destined, therefore, to be used for the common good.

When she was fourteen, Katharine met a man who would exert a decisive influence on her life, Father James O'Connor, the parish priest of the region where the Drexels' summer home was located. Katharine was already exhibiting signs of spiritual seriousness, and under Father O'Connor's direction she laid out a careful program for growth in holiness—a fairly unusual resolve for a teenaged girl. In 1878, when she was twenty, Katharine's formal education ended, and in January of 1879 she was officially presented to Philadelphia high society. One would think that for a young woman of her social class this event would have been of utmost importance, but Katharine was, frankly, rather bored and nonplussed by it all. Soon afterward, and within a few months of each other, Katharine's beloved father and stepmother died, and Katharine found herself the heiress to a very large fortune. She and her sisters each received approximately four million dollars from their father's estate, closer to four hundred million in our terms. But Katharine was deeply unsettled, not knowing quite what to do with the money—or, for that matter, what to do with her life, for her religious longings were at odds with her growing sense of worldly responsibility. At this difficult moment two men came to see her: Bishop Martin Marty and Father Joseph Stephan. Both were working for the Catholic Indian Mission, the church's institutional outreach to Native Americans on the Great Plains. The two churchmen described their work so eloquently that Katharine was inspired to give a large portion of her inheritance to support their mission.

These first connections with the work of missioners to the Native

Americans did little to settle the turmoil that Katharine was feeling in regard to the direction of her life. Her inner strife was accompanied by (and perhaps was the cause of) a good deal of physical suffering as well. During this time she commented to Father O'Connor that she felt like a little girl who had ripped the face of a beautiful porcelain doll only to discover that it was stuffed with straw: a wonderful image for this daughter of privilege. In order to alleviate her physical and psychological suffering, she did what any number of wealthy Americans of the time did in such circumstances: she went to Europe in order to "take the baths," to go to a series of spas and soak in waters that were thought to have restorative powers. On this trip Katharine's life would indeed change, but the transformation would have nothing to do with the baths. At the end of her sojourn, still anxious and unsettled, still distraught over the death of her parents, still unsure of her vocation, she had an audience with Pope Leo XIII. Kneeling before the pope, she spoke of her great passion for the Indian mission and then she said, "Holy Father, what you must do is find an order of priests or an order of sisters who will catechize, teach, and care for these people." The pope fixed her with his gaze and said, simply, "You should be that missionary." Leo XIII's words cut her to the soul. Suddenly feeling sick, she couldn't get out of the Vatican fast enough, and when she had left the building, she sobbed and sobbed. The pope had obviously struck a nerve—and through Leo's words, Jesus had begun, rather decisively, to get into Katharine's boat.

Prior to the meeting with Pope Leo, Katharine had been considering the possibility of a religious vocation, but her spiritual director had consistently warned her away from the idea, convinced that someone of Katharine's privileged background would not be able to adjust to the austerities of religious life. But the pope's words had focused her desire and emboldened her spirit. In 1888 she wrote to Father O'Connor: "Are you afraid to give me to Jesus Christ? God knows how unworthy I am, and yet can he not supply my unworthiness if only he give me a vocation to the religious life? Then joyfully I shall run to him." This was perhaps just the sign of Katharine's independence that her spiritual mentor was waiting

St. Katharine Drexel after final profession (vows for life), 1895. ARCHIVES OF THE SISTERS OF THE BLESSED SACRAMENT

for, because his capitulation to the young woman's demand was swift and complete: "This letter of yours . . . makes me withdraw all opposition to your entering religion." What soon became clear to Katharine was that she was to become not only a nun but, as the pope had suggested, also the founder of an order dedicated to some of the poorest and most forgotten Americans. In a letter to her spiritual director she said bluntly, "I want a missionary order for Indians and Colored people," and she concluded that since such a society didn't exist she'd have to found it. Once this resolution was clear in her mind and heart, all of her anxiety and inner turmoil melted away. She knew what she wanted, and, like Mary, she proceeded in haste to get it.

She entered the novitiate of the Sisters of Mercy of Pittsburgh in

May of 1889. Her purpose was to learn the ways of the religious life
in preparation for the establishment of her own community. Two years
later she made her profession as the first member of the Sisters of the
Blessed Sacrament for Indians and Colored People. From the beginning
she wanted to associate her missionary work closely with the Liturgy and
the Eucharist. Like so many of the saints, Katharine quickly managed to
attract a large number of people to her mission. The many young women
who eagerly joined her were given three years of training in a motherhouse outside Philadelphia and then sent out to do missionary work. One
of the first outposts of the sisters was among the Pueblo Indians of New
Mexico; next they set up a school for African-American children along
the James River in Virginia. What followed was perhaps Mother Drexel's
most important foundation, Xavier University in New Orleans. This
center of learning, dedicated to advanced Catholic education for young

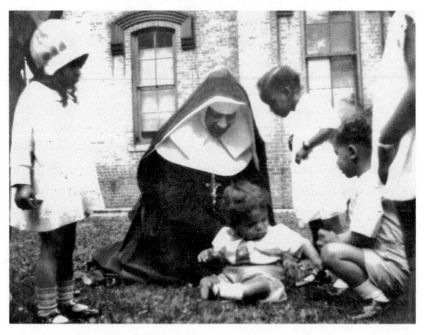

St. Katharine Drexel with children at Xavier University of Louisiana, early 1930s.
ARCHIVES OF THE SISTERS OF THE BLESSED SACRAMENT

blacks, was the first of its kind in the United States. In time Mother Drexel founded schools, hospitals, and institutes all across the country.

Where did the money come from for all of these works and undertakings? It came almost exclusively from Katharine Drexel's trust fund, the four million dollars bequeathed to her by her father. She gave and gave, until there was, literally, nothing left to give; she completely spent her considerable fortune in service of her mission. The ancient moral philosophers spoke of justice, the act of rendering to each his due. Inspired by this ethical ideal, many wealthy people across the ages have given of their surplus to help those who did not have enough and who were because of their innate dignity as human beings owed a better life. Was Mother Drexel's dedication born of justice? Yes, indeed—but it was so much more than mere justice. It was, if you will, elevated and transfigured justice, justice under the influence of grace, not simply a calculation of what was owed but a superabundant and excessive gift on behalf of the other. It was a going out into the deep—and a taking in of a miraculous catch of fish.

For many years Mother Drexel directed the work of her community from her headquarters near Philadelphia, but she was by no means a prisoner of the place. She traveled widely, all across the country, visiting her sisters at a time when travel, especially in the untamed West, was quite difficult. A trip that she undertook in 1935, when she was seventy-seven years old, is typical. After visiting her sisters in New Orleans, she journeyed to Port Arthur, Texas, and then by night train to Gallup, New Mexico. From there she went to San Francisco; Portland, Oregon; and Seattle, before making her way to the tiny outpost of Wenatchee, from which she set out on a four-hour trip to her sisters' mission. While on still another trip that same year, Mother Drexel suffered a heart attack, and her doctors told her that unless she curtailed her schedule, she wouldn't survive. Thus Katharine Drexel entered into what she came to consider the most spiritually productive period of her life. For the next twenty years, while sequestered in the motherhouse, she spent hours every day and night before the Blessed Sacrament, praying for the success of her order. Mother Drexel died on March 3, 1955, at the age of ninety-seven, but her work, born of transfigured justice, endures to this day.

THÉRÈSE OF LISIEUX

Outside the little French town of Lisieux there stands an enormous and elaborately decorated basilica dedicated to a very simple woman who is also one of the most extraordinary saints of the church. Thérèse was a cloistered Carmelite nun who died at the age of twenty-four and who at her death was known only to her family and her fellow sisters in the convent. One of her sisters, in fact, wondered what they could possibly write

St. Thérèse of Lisieux, 1881.

about her in the obituary that would circulate among the other French Carmelites. Yet within a few years of her death Thérèse had a worldwide reputation, and within a couple decades of her passing she was declared a saint and eventually a doctor of the church. When a reliquary carrying her bones was brought to the United States in the 1990s, millions of people responded, and when it was brought to Ireland, practically the entire country gathered to see it. How do we begin to explain this? We have to start with the spiritual autobiography, called *The Story of a Soul*, which Thérèse wrote at the prompting of her superior in the last years of her life.

I will confess that when I first read *The Story of a Soul* I was not particularly impressed. Like many others, I found it overly sentimental, and as a post-Freudian I was only too willing to see in its girlish spiritual enthusiasms evidence of neuroses and repressions. But then I noticed that a number of great intellectuals loved Thérèse. Among her cultivated admirers were Dorothy Day, Edith Stein, Thomas Merton, John Paul II, and Hans Urs von Balthasar. When I was a doctoral student in Paris, I attended a seminar conducted by my thesis director, Father Michel Corbin, a brilliant Jesuit specialist in medieval thought. Corbin commented that the French do not refer to Thérèse of Lisieux as "the little flower," as Anglophones do, but rather as *la petite Thérèse* (the little Thérèse), in order to distinguish her from *la grande Therese* (Teresa of Avila). But then he added, "After many years of reading both saints, I realize that Thérèse of Lisieux *est vraiement la grande Therese*" (she is really the great Thérèse). I knew then that I had to take a second look.

Thérèse was born on January 2, 1873, the youngest child of Louis and Zelie Martin, two extremely devout members of the French middle class. By her own admission, Thérèse's early childhood was arcadian. A beautiful girl, she was doted on by everyone, especially her father. He was her *petit roi* (little king) and she was his *petite reine* (little queen). She entered happily into the intensely religious rhythms and practices of the Martin household, and from a very early age she had the intuition that she would enter the Carmelite convent and become a nun. The idyll of her childhood came to an abrupt end with the death of her mother in 1877, when Thérèse was only four. In the wake of this trauma the little Thérèse became moody and withdrawn, "sensitive to an excessive degree." Her time at public school in Lisieux was unpleasant, for her sheltered and pampered background had not prepared her for the relative rough-and-tumble of the playground. Picked on mercilessly by her classmates, she felt for the first time in her life "weighed and found wanting."

The full effect of her mother's death on Thérèse would become clear when Pauline, her older sister and substitute mother, decided to enter religious life. After Pauline disappeared behind the walls of the convent, Thérèse experienced a strange malady, with both physical and psychological symptoms, some of them frightening. She would cry violently, suffer from severe headaches, and fall into fits of uncontrollable shivering. When Pauline "took the veil," Thérèse suffered a particularly violent episode: "she screamed and shrieked in extreme fear, contorted her face, rolled her eyes, saw monsters and nightmarish figures, was shaken by convulsions and had to be forcibly restrained." Here is Thérèse's own simple description of this awful period: "I was terrified of everything." It is easy enough to see this as a psychotic episode, but what matters is not so much the etiology of her malady as the way Thérèse assessed and handled it. She came in time to see this period of her life as a testing and a purging. What was being purged, she concluded, were precisely her narcissism and her fussy self-absorption.

What finally saved her from this suffering was a manifestation of grace. On May 13, 1883, Thérèse was bedridden, utterly debilitated physically and psychologically. She noticed a statue of the Blessed Mother, which had recently been placed in her room. She was struck by the ravishing beauty of Mary, especially by the Virgin's smile. Somehow, as she registered that smile and allowed it to permeate her being, all of her physical and psychological symptoms left her, and she was healed. How does one explain this extraordinary incident? I suppose it could be examined under any number of rubrics, but what matters is that Thérèse appreciated it as a manifestation of God's grace, which is to say, God's unmerited love. Without any prompting from us, not as a reward for our efforts, even while we are helpless, God breaks into our hearts and changes us. After she had come of age, Thérèse emerged as one of the great "doctors of grace" in the Catholic tradition, once comparing herself to a little child who, knowing her deep incapacity to please the Lord by her own exertions, stands before him and simply lifts up her arms, hoping to be raised up.

The next major step in Thérèse's spiritual journey was, again, a small, private affair, nothing to which a conventional biographer would think of drawing attention. It took place on Christmas Day 1886. There was a custom in the Martin household that just after Midnight Mass, on Christmas morning, the children would draw from their shoes little gifts that their father had placed in them. Thérèse loved this ritual and was especially delighted by her father's active participation in it. But on this particular Christmas morning, just before the commencement of the ritual, Thérèse went upstairs to fetch something, and when she was presumably thought to be out of earshot, her father said, "Well, fortunately, this is the last year." Normally, such a comment coming from her father would have broken Thérèse's heart, but something quietly miraculous happened: Thérèse calmly decided not to take offense and to respond in love. Suppressing her feelings of disappointment, she calmly descended the stairs and with unfeigned sincerity and enthusiasm entered into the family ritual. Certainly a simple scene, but when read through spiritual eyes, it was momentous precisely because it represented the breakthrough of God's love into Thérèse's heart. To love, as we have seen, is to will the good of the other as other, to break free of the preoccupations and needs of the ego. Deciding not to weep and not to indulge her hurt feelings and instead to bring joy to her father and sisters was an act of pure love, and this is why Thérèse felt it was so important that this birth of Christ in her heart took place on the feast day that celebrates Jesus's birth into the world. And it came suddenly, unbidden, changing her in an instant—the graceful entry of Jesus into her boat.

In the wake of this Christmas conversion, Thérèse resolved with re-

newed intensity to enter Carmel. Her desire to be a religious, which, as
we have seen, she had held on to since she was a very small child, now became a burning conviction, in her own words, "a divine call so strong that
had I been forced to pass through flames, I would have done it out of love
for Jesus." After some reluctance her father acquiesced to his daughter's
desire, though she was only fifteen, under the canonical age for entry into
the cloister. He agreed to be her advocate, and he accompanied her on
visits to a variety of ecclesiastics and bishops, all of whom initially told
her that she was too young and would be obliged to wait before entering
the convent. Through a combination of intelligence, charm, and sheer
moxie, Thérèse managed to wear all of them down. She came finally to
the bishop of Bayeux, and he adamantly refused to give the girl permission, at which point her father told her to give up. Undaunted, Thérèse
resolved to bring the case to the highest court. In the hopes of securing

St. Thérèse of Lisieux, 1895.

an audience with the pope, she joined a group of French pilgrims who were making their way to Rome. On November 20, 1887, Thérèse had her opportunity to speak to Leo XIII. Though she and the other pilgrims had been instructed not to say anything to the pope, Thérèse blurted out, "Holy Father, in honor of your jubilee, permit me to enter Carmel at the age of fifteen." The pope smiled and told her to do what her superiors ordered. But the girl persisted: "O Holy Father, if you say yes, everyone will agree." The pope responded, "Go . . . go . . . you will enter Carmel if God wills it." At that point, still begging and weeping, she was carried off bodily by two papal guards. How fascinating that both Thérèse of Lisieux and Katharine Drexel would, within a few years of each other, leave an audience with Leo XIII in tears. One month later the bishop of Bayeux relented and Thérèse was granted permission to enter the Carmel at Lisieux. For the next nine years, until her death at twenty-four, she never left the confines of that simple place and lived the austere life of a Carmelite religious.

In the course of those years she cultivated a spiritual path that she came to call "the little way." It was not the path of her great Carmelite forebears Teresa of Avila and John of the Cross, not the method suited for spiritual athletes, but a way that any simple believer could follow. It had a good deal to do with spiritual childhood, becoming little in the presence of God the Father: dependent, hopeful, waiting to receive gifts. Here is one of her own descriptions: "Jesus deigned to show me the road that leads to this Divine Furnace and this road is the surrender of the little child who sleeps without fear in its Father's arms." One cannot help but appreciate how Thérèse extrapolated from her own experience of tender intimacy with a father who offered unconditional love. Her approach also involved a willingness to do simple and ordinary things out of great love: little acts of kindness, small sacrifices graciously accepted, putting up with annoying people. One of the most entertaining and spiritually illuminating sections of *The Story of a Soul* is Thérèse's account of her infinitely patient dealings with a cranky old nun to whom she had been assigned as a helper. Every kindness of Thérèse was met with correction and signs of displeasure on the part of the old lady, but still the younger nun persisted in love.

I spoke of Katharine Drexel's sanctity as a sort of elevated justice. We might characterize Thérèse's holiness as a transfigured prudence, for at the heart of the little way is the capacity to know in any given situation the precise demand of love, how best in the here and now of the present moment to will the good of the other. Toward the end of her life Thérèse experienced the intense desire to do all the things that the great figures of church history had done. She wrote, "I wanted to be priest, martyr, missionary, evangelist, and doctor," but she wondered how she could possibly accomplish any of this tucked away in her little monastery in Lisieux. Then she read Paul's first letter to the Corinthians, and she was struck by the magnificent passage where Paul speaks of the more excellent way, the way of love. In a flash Thérèse grasped that love is the form of all the virtues, love is what makes the lives of the saints possible, love is what undergirds the efforts of priests, missionaries, evangelists, and doctors. She concluded, "Jesus, my love, I found my vocation. I will be love in the heart of the Church." That is the little way, which continues to beguile millions around the world.

I mentioned that I, like many others, first reacted negatively to the overly emotional, sentimental style of Thérèse of Lisieux, but even the most skeptical readers are usually won over by the account of her terrible struggle with unbelief at the very end of her life. This intense spiritual suffering coincided almost exactly with the onset of the tuberculosis that would eventually take her life. What began to plague Thérèse were terrible doubts concerning the existence of heaven. Like Hamlet she began to wonder whether anything followed "the sleep of death." And this was no passing bout of intellectual scrupulosity; it lasted up until the moment of her death: "The trial," she wrote just before she died, "was to last, not a few days or a few weeks, it was not to be extinguished until the hour set by God himself and that hour has not yet come." What is especially interesting is that Thérèse interpreted this struggle not as dumb suffering but as a participation in the pain experienced by many of her contemporaries who did not believe in God: "During those joyful days of the Easter season, Jesus made me feel that there were really souls who have no faith . . . he permitted my soul to be invaded by the thickest darkness." We will see how remarkably similar this language is to that of Mother Teresa of Calcutta. Thérèse of Lisieux died at age twenty-four on September 30, 1897.

EDITH STEIN

Edith Stein was born on October 12, 1891, the Jewish Day of Atonement, in Breslau, a town situated today within the borders of Poland but at that time part of the Prussian empire. She was the seventh and youngest child of pious Jewish parents, and like Thérèse she was doted on by her parents like, in her own words, "a cross between a fairy princess and a porcelain doll." One of Edith's earliest recollections is of herself standing in front of a "big white door, drumming on it with clenched fists because she wanted to get to the other side." That sort of fierce, even grim, determination would mark her all her life. Her father died suddenly when Edith was still quite young, and she bonded strongly with her mother. Frau Stein introduced her daughter to the disciplines and feasts of the Jewish religion, as well as the world of the Bible, and her elder brother Paul began to read to her regularly from the great works of German literature. During her teenage years Edith's passion for literature grew, even as her faith faded, and by the time she was ready for university study she considered herself an atheist.

As a university student she became fascinated by the work of Edmund Husserl, considered the founder of the famously complex system of philosophy called phenomenology. She longed to study with the master personally and so went in 1913 to Göttingen, where Husserl taught. Immediately she fell in love with the natural beauty and the deep intellectual culture of the place, and in short order she was introduced to Husserl and to the circle of brilliant students that had formed around him, including Dietrich von Hildebrand and Max Scheler, two thinkers who would deeply influence the development of Catholic thought in the twentieth century. She labored away at her doctoral studies, pursuing the typically phenomenological theme of empathy or fellow feeling, how one can enter into another's appropriation of experience. Like many doctoral students before and since, Edith felt tremendous strain while undertaking the project. She later wrote: "This excruciating struggle to attain clarity was waged unceasingly inside me, depriving me of rest day and night . . . Little by little, I worked myself into a state of veritable despair." Edith survived this period of struggle, finished her thesis, and earned her doctorate in 1915, barely two years after arriving in Göttingen. Upon reading her dissertation, the master himself commented approvingly if a tad condescendingly, "You are a very gifted little girl!" Soon after she finished her work, Husserl received an appointment to the University of Freiburg in Breisgau, and the master asked Edith to accompany him as an assistant. She went with him to Freiburg but found her work less than satisfying, because Husserl treated her, despite her enormous intellectual gifts, as a glorified secretary. In fact, many of Edith's friends were scandalized that someone with her great mind was being forced to perform such menial tasks.

In 1917, during the fiercest fighting of the First World War, Edith paid a courtesy call to the widow of Adolf Reinach, an old acquaintance from her Göttingen days who had been killed in battle. She expected to find the young woman devastated, but instead she found her sad but fundamentally at peace. Her serenity, Edith learned, was the product of the woman's Christian faith. Edith commented later, "It was my first encounter with the Cross and the divine power that it bestows on those who carry it." This insight was an extraordinary breakthrough for the intense, rational woman who long ago had given up on religious faith. What began to strike her, in the wake of this encounter, was that many of her colleagues in the Husserl circle—as well as the master himself—were devout Christians. This caused her to question her doctrinaire rejection of faith. Also phenomenology itself—which urged an openness to any and all phenomena—encouraged her to investigate religion more sympathetically and objectively. Jesus was preparing to enter the boat.

Another turning point occurred while Edith was strolling with a friend through the old section of Frankfurt. They chanced upon the cathedral, and the two women entered the building as tourists, intent on admiring the architecture. Edith spied a woman, fresh from her rounds of shopping, kneeling in the empty church, obviously lost in prayer. She had certainly seen people at prayer in the synagogue during services, but she had never seen anything like this communion with a presence personal and yet unseen. "I could never forget that," she wrote. Edith Stein's conversion was not like Paul's, sudden and dramatic. It was more like Augustine's or John Henry Newman's: gradual, interior, accompanied by a good deal of intellectual wrestling. One night, while staying with friends outside Freiburg, Edith searched through their library looking for something to divert her for the evening. She came upon

St. Edith Stein, c. 1916. PERMISSION OF JOSE-PHINE KOEPPEL, OCD

Saint Teresa of Avila's autobiography. She took the book off the shelf and stayed up all night reading it. The next morning she put down the text and declared simply, "That is the truth." What precisely impressed her about the book is impossible to say. When pressed on the matter later, Edith replied, "*secretum meum mihi*" (that is my secret). It seems fair to conclude that the reading of Teresa's *Life* was the galvanizing moment, the occasion for all of the strands to come together.

After a few weeks of reading and praying, Edith approached the local priest and asked to be received into the church. When he balked, due to her recent conversion, she said, "*Prufen-sie mich!*" (Test me!). She was baptized on January 1, 1922, in those days, the Feast of the Circumcision, the first shedding of Jesus's blood. Though she wanted, almost immediately after baptism, to join the order of Teresa, her spiritual director advised her to wait. Edith became an instructor in a teachers training academy run by a community of Dominican sisters. Among these daughters of Saint Dominic, Edith began to live what was essentially a religious life. She fell in love with the Eucharist, spending hours a day in silent adoration. So impressed were the Dominican sisters that they set up a special chair for her near the Blessed Sacrament. Edith was finding a new and vibrant center; Jesus was in the boat. During those years Edith deepened and broadened her scholarship, becoming a well-known lecturer throughout Germany. She made the reconciliation of the classical Catholic philosophy of Aquinas and the contemporary phenomenology of Husserl central to her intellectual work.

Her desire for Carmel continued to burn, and in June of 1933 Edith was accepted into the Carmelite convent in Cologne. Though she was far older than the other postulants and novices, she took readily to the discipline of Carmelite life, as though she was born for it. On April 15, 1934, she was formally received into the community and took the name Sister Teresa Benedicta a Cruce, literally, Teresa, blessed by the cross. She moved into the rhythm of prayer and work, but also at the prompting of her superiors she resumed her intellectual research, producing eventually the lengthy philosophical treatise *Eternal and Finite Being* as well as a thorough study of the thought of John of the Cross entitled *The Science of the Cross*. In 1938 Sister Teresa took her final vows as a Carmelite and was thus privileged to wear the black veil, evocative of her total consecration to Christ.

In November of that same year *Kristallnacht* (the Night of Broken Glass) took place, and suddenly Jews all over Germany were in acute danger. Concerned for her safety, Edith's superiors transferred her from the Carmel in Cologne to the Carmel of Echt in Holland. But just two years later the Nazis overran Holland, and Edith was once again threatened. Bravely the Dutch Catholic bishops raised their voices in protest over the ill treatment of Jews in their country. The archbishop of Utrecht went so far as to order that a condemnation of the Nazi policy be read publicly from every pulpit in the country. The Germans retaliated brutally, ordering a roundup of all Jews in Holland who had converted to Catholicism. On Sunday August 2, 1942, the Gestapo came for Edith and her sister, who had joined Edith in the convent. Amid the confusion, anxiety, and raised voices, Edith calmly said, "Come, Rosa, we're going for our people." The sisters were held briefly in a camp in Holland and then were packed onto what amounted to a cattle car for the trip to Auschwitz. A former student of Edith's reported an encounter with the nun when the train stopped briefly at a platform in Germany. After greeting her, Edith asked her to convey a message to the mother superior in Echt: "We are going to the East," a sentence with both a literal and a spiritual meaning. She was undoubtedly trying to communicate information about their geographical destination, but "the East" is also mystical language for heaven and eternal life. There is still another report from a German soldier who was making his way to the Russian front. On August 7 he was standing on the train platform in Breslau, Edith's hometown, when a train pulled up, filled with people packed together like animals. When the door slid open, the young man was practically overcome by the unbearable stench. Then a woman appeared in the characteristic habit of the Carmelites. She commented to the soldier on the terrible conditions

Site of St. Edith Stein's death, Auschwitz. WORD ON FIRE

on the train and then, looking about wistfully, said, "This is my beloved hometown. I will never see it again." Many years later this former soldier saw a photograph of Edith Stein and identified her as the nun he had met that day.

On August 9, 1942, Edith arrived at the death camp of Auschwitz-Birkenau. She was selected for immediate execution. The guards brought her to a crude barracks where she was forced to remove her clothes, and then to a small execution chamber where she was murdered by poison gas. Subsequently, her body was placed in a pit and burned—and the ashes strewn to the wind. The classical moral philosophers spoke of courage as the virtue that enables one to do the good despite external threats. What we see in a martyr such as Edith Stein is not ordinary courage but courage elevated and transfigured through love. We see a willingness to give away even one's life out of love for Christ and his people.

MOTHER TERESA OF CALCUTTA

Mother Teresa was born Agnes Gonxha Bojaxhiu on August 26, 1910, in Skopje, Serbia. When she was a girl of twelve Agnes felt called to the religious life, though she had up to that point never as much as laid eyes on a nun. A key player in the shaping of her vocation was a young Croatian Jesuit priest who introduced her to the spiritual exercises of Saint Ignatius and who shared with her inspiring stories of the missionary activity of Jesuits around the world, especially in India and Bengal. Moved by these accounts, Agnes applied at the age of eighteen to the Loreto Sisters, the Irish branch of the Institute of the Blessed Virgin Mary, which had a strong missionary presence in India. During her postulancy she took the name Sister Mary Teresa of the Child Jesus, after the recently canonized Little Flower. After spending a brief training period in Ireland (where she learned the English language, which she would use for the rest of her life), Sister Teresa set sail for India.

When she arrived in India she was dazzled by its luxuriant natural beauty and shocked beyond words by its grinding poverty. Though she had known poverty in Serbia, nothing had prepared her for what she saw in India. The conviction grew in her that service to such poor would involve a radical simplifying of her own life. After completing her novitiate Teresa began teaching at the convent school in Darjeeling, a tranquil city near the Himalayas, and working part-time as a nurse in the order's hospital. Then she was sent to Calcutta to teach in a school run by the Loreto Sisters. This city, marked by crushing poverty, would be her home for the rest of her life. At first Sister Teresa was relatively isolated from the worst of Calcutta's misery, teaching courses in geography and English behind the high walls of a boarding school. But in time she made her way to a primary school some distance away where she once again came face-to-face with dreadful destitution. For the next several years Teresa (called "Mother" after she had taken final vows) worked at a furious pace, teaching, administering a variety of institutions, and caring for the sick. So arduous was her work that she experienced a breakdown and was sent to recuperate at Darjeeling, the restful place where she had been a novice.

On the train to Darjeeling she had the experience that would change her life. On that dusty ride she heard the voice of Jesus calling her "to be a Missionary of Charity" and to serve "the poorest of the poor," to follow him with reckless abandon and utter trust. She called this vocation within her vocation "the hidden treasure for me," and it was the moment when Jesus most decisively got into her boat. When she returned to Calcutta she submitted herself to the spiritual direction of Father Celeste Van Exem, a Belgian Jesuit who would prove an extremely helpful and important figure in her life. After a year of prayer and discernment, Mother Teresa and Father Van Exem went to Ferdinand Périer, the archbishop of Calcutta, to present the idea of founding an order to serve the

Blessed Teresa of Calcutta, 1987. MICHAEL COLLOPY

poorest of the poor. A wise character, Périer tested the vocation of the little nun, throwing up all sorts of objections and roadblocks. Despite his opposition, she persisted, and the archbishop's admiration for her grew. Périer eventually consulted experts in canon law and devised a way to release Mother Teresa from her formal ties to the Loreto Sisters so she could found her own community. In April of 1948, after several years of testing and waiting, canonical approval came from Rome, and Mother Teresa said to the archbishop simply, "Can I go to the slums now?"

In the first weeks and months of her new life, Mother experienced terrible bouts of loneliness, depression, and discouragement—and an accompanying desire to return to the relative comfort and stability of the Loreto Sisters. But she persevered, for she knew that she had to become like the poor in every way—both physically and psychologically—in order to serve them effectively.

As we have come to expect from stories of the saints, people soon came to join Mother Teresa's mission, some of them her former students. These became the first Missionaries of Charity. Mother quickly formed them into a religious community, fashioning a rule that combined elements of the Jesuit and Franciscan spiritual traditions. Throughout she put special emphasis on the sisters' identification with the poorest of the poor. The first Missionaries of Charity were allowed to possess only a cotton sari, some coarse underwear, a pair of sandals, a crucifix, a rosary, a metal bucket for washing, and a very thin mattress that served as a bed. Also, like the early Franciscans and Dominicans, they were compelled to beg for their food. There was a kind of poverty built into the very rhythm of their day. During the week the sisters rose at 4:40 AM, brushed their teeth with ash from the kitchen stove, and scrubbed their bodies with a small bar of soap that had been divided into six pieces. Between 5:15 and 6:45 they meditated, prayed, and attended Mass. They then ate a small breakfast and were on the streets doing their work by 7:45. They returned at noon for prayers and a frugal midday meal and then rested and did spiritual reading before returning to their pastoral work in the slums.

Missionaries of Charity Final Professions, Washington, D.C., 1995.
MICHAEL COLLOPY

Mother called for a poverty that went beyond mere physical hardship. One newcomer to the order, a woman from a rather aristocratic background, found the toilet in the convent dirty one day and turned away in disgust. Mother Teresa passed by without seeing the sister and immediately rolled up her sleeves, took out a broom, and cleaned the toilet herself. Another time a young member of the order won a gold medal for her medical studies; Mother instructed the sister to give it to the student who had come in second, for she intuited that for that particular sister the hoarding of honors would be as detrimental to her work as the hoarding of wealth. Essential to the lives of the Missionaries of Charity was a complete and simple trust in God's providence. Once when the sisters were utterly without food they resolved to pray. Suddenly a knock came on the door and there stood a woman carrying some bags of rice, just enough, it turned out, to feed the community that night. The philosophers speak of temperance, the virtue by which we control our desires for food, drink, and sex so that we might achieve the demands of justice. What we see in Mother Teresa is elevated or transfigured temperance, a disciplining of the desires that goes far beyond the requirements of justice so as to serve the infinite demand of love.

At first the work of Mother's order was restricted to Calcutta, but beginning in the 1950s and 1960s the Missionaries of Charity spread throughout India and then around the world: Venezuela, Tanzania, Australia, the United States, England. By the end of the 1990s there were five hundred communities on six continents. Mother Teresa said, "If there are poor people on the moon, we shall go there too!" In time Mother became an internationally renowned figure, winning the Nobel Peace Prize in 1979. To the surprise of many outside the church, she used her Nobel speech as an occasion to decry abortion as the greatest enemy of peace in contemporary society. Mother never had any ambiguity in her mind about the different kinds of poverty and suffering that bedevil the human race.

No account of Mother Teresa's life would be complete without a reference to her terrible interior struggle, her unique participation in the anguish of Christ. Though she experienced extraordinary closeness to Jesus in her early religious life, including, as we have seen, a vivid encounter with him during the time of her call, once the order got under way she experienced just the opposite: an aching sense of the Lord's absence. And this darkness lasted, with one brief respite, for the rest of her life. Here is one particularly devastating account of what it felt like to endure this darkness: "In my soul, I feel just that terrible pain of loss—of God not wanting me—of God not being God—of God not really existing . . . my work holds no joy, no attraction, no zeal." It is important to note that this is not depression in the ordinary psychological meaning of the term. During the many years of abandonment, Mother functioned at a very high level, directing her community and traveling the world as a teacher and evangelist. She came to understand her suffering, as did Saint Thérèse, as a sharing in the passion of Jesus, his own feelings of abandonment by the Father. Feeling the absence of God, Mother Teresa entered even

Blessed Teresa of Calcutta, 1987. MICHAEL COLLOPY

more fully into the suffering of those she longed to serve, the poorest of the poor.

Mother Teresa died in Calcutta on September 5, 1997, at the age of eighty-seven. When her body was displayed for public viewing, it was, of course, clothed in the habit of the Missionaries of Charity, but it was left shoeless, revealing her remarkably misshapen feet. For many people, those gnarled feet bore the most eloquent witness to the hard years she had spent on behalf of the least of Jesus's brothers and sisters.

CONCLUSION

The holiness of God is like a white light: pure, simple, complete. But when that light shines, as it were, through the prisms of individual human lives, it breaks into an infinite variety of colors. The four women we've considered in this chapter couldn't be more different from one another—and that is why each one reveals a unique dimension of the divine holiness. God's grace shone through Edith Stein and gave us the clarity of her intellectual work and the beauty of her martyrdom; it shone through Thérèse of Lisieux and gave us the little way; it shone through Katharine Drexel, producing a miracle of transfigured justice; it shone through the unrepeatable identity of Mother Teresa and brought forth the Missionaries of Charity. The church revels in the variety of its saints because it needs such diversity in order to represent, with even relative adequacy, the infinite intensity of God's goodness.

Chapter 9

THE FIRE OF HIS LOVE: PRAYER AND THE LIFE OF THE SPIRIT

People pray all the time. Studies show that even those who describe themselves as nonbelievers pray. What precisely is this activity in which so many of us willingly engage? Prayer has taken on myriad forms over the centuries. Speaking, processing, singing, remaining silent, emptying the mind of all imagery and conceptuality, reading sacred texts, dancing, and petitioning from the bottom of one's heart have all been construed as modalities of prayer. But is there a common denominator, some fundamental characteristic? Saint John of Damascus, a monk and theologian from the eighth century, said, "Prayer is the raising of one's mind and heart to God," and Saint Thérèse of Lisieux said that prayer is "a surge of the heart, it is a simple look towards Heaven, it is a cry of recognition and of love, embracing both trial and joy." Prayer is born of that awareness, felt more than thought, that the transcendent realm impinges on our lowly world and hence can be contacted. A basic Christian conviction is that this reaching for God meets an even more passionate divine reaching for us. Perhaps we would put it best by saying that the mystical coming together of these two longings—our longing for God and God's longing for us—is prayer.

I don't know any other place on earth that evokes the power of prayer more than the magnificent Sainte-Chapelle in Paris. Built by King Louis IX (Saint Louis) in the thirteenth century as a grand repository for the relic of Jesus's crown of thorns, the Sainte-Chapelle is a jewel box of stained glass and gothic tracery. When you enter the building you have the distinct impression of having stepped across a threshold into another, higher world. Lord Kenneth Clark, the great twentieth-century art historian, said that when the light pours through the colored glass of the Sainte-Chapelle, it sets up a kind of vibration in the air, an electrical charge. It is, if you will, the artistic representation of the electric meeting of two spirits, human and divine. It is what a human heart, elevated to and by God, looks like: transfigured, luminous, radiantly beautiful.

In the Catholic tradition, prayer is learned through apprenticing to masters who are experienced in the way of prayer. Prayer seems to be one of those practices that, as the cliché has it, is caught rather than taught. In the course of this chapter we will sit at the feet of a series of masters and try to catch some of their wisdom in regard to this mysterious and alluring act of raising the mind and the heart to God. As we will see, one form of prayer is asking God for things; but in its more fundamental forms, prayer is being with God, becoming attuned to God, thinking his thoughts and feeling his feelings. We will understand this kind of communion only through careful attention to the lives of some of the people who have practiced it.

BEGINNING WITH THOMAS MERTON

I realize that speaking of prayer usually puts us in mind of rather alien figures: medieval monks in their choir stalls or perhaps hermits squirreled away in their desert huts. I believe that hermits and monks have a great deal to teach us, but I would like to begin with someone much closer to our own time and temperament, someone who tramped through Times Square and frequented the jazz clubs of Manhattan in the first half of the twentieth century, a spiritual teacher who emerged from the maelstrom of contemporary doubt and secularism. When Thomas Merton's autobiography, *The Seven Storey Mountain*, which chronicles his conversion, was published in 1948, it caused a sensation and contributed mightily to a spiritual revival across the United States and to an awakening of interest in the ancient traditions of mysticism of which most Americans were simply unaware. This very contemporary figure remains, therefore, a privileged portal through which twenty-first-century seekers can explore the meaning of prayer. I will provide a fairly detailed portrait of Merton, for I want to invite you to feel his need for God from the inside. I want you to know what motivated someone who experienced so many of the anxieties and opportunities of our time finally to dedicate his life to raising his mind and heart to God.

Thomas Merton was born in the south of France in 1915, the son of a New Zealander father and an American mother, his parents having met at art school in Paris just before the outbreak of the First World War. Merton's mother died when he was only a boy of six, and he subsequently lived a sort of vagabond life, wandering the world with his painter father, spending short periods in New York, Bermuda, France, and England. When Merton was sixteen and a boarding school student at Oakham in England, his father died, and the young man found himself more or less alone in the world. After a brief tour of the continent, he enrolled at Cambridge University in the fall of 1933 and commenced to conduct himself in a deeply irresponsible way: too much drinking, too much carousing, too much sex. Though this was kept secret for many decades, it has now been determined that Merton fathered a child during that chaotic year and that both mother and child were later killed in the London blitz of 1940. Merton's guardian, an old friend of his father's, was shocked by his young charge's reckless behavior, and after making certain legal and financial arrangements he sent Merton out of the country. Merton landed in New York and resumed his academic career at Columbia University.

Merton fell in love with Columbia, a place he referred to affectionately as "a great sooty factory." He became, in short order, something of a big man on campus, joining a variety of student organizations and delighting his contemporaries with accounts of his vivid experiences in a variety of countries. Merton was throughout his life and by all accounts great company: funny, musical, quick witted, and a gifted mimic. He was for a time the arts and humor editor of *The Jester*, the student literary publication at Columbia, and in connection with that magazine he met some of the intellectually liveliest and most creative students on the scene. Among his friends were Robert Lax, who would become a well-regarded avant-garde poet, and Robert Giroux, later a prominent publisher. Among his professors were the novelist Lionel Trilling and the great Shakespeare scholar Mark Van Doren. Van Doren especially would have a profound influence on Merton, eventually helping the young man with his writing and even planting some of the seeds of his vocation to the priesthood. Merton certainly flourished at the sooty academic factory of Columbia,

St. Patrick's Cathedral, New York. WORD ON FIRE

but it was the flourishing of a secular modern man seeking experience and, above all, pleasure.

In the spring of 1938 Thomas Merton was walking down Fifth Avenue in the vicinity of St. Patrick's Cathedral, and he paused at the display window of Scribner's Bookstore. He noticed a text called *The Spirit of Medieval Philosophy* by the French writer Etienne Gilson. Since he was taking a course at Columbia on medieval French poetry, Merton thought it might be helpful to know more about the intellectual assumptions of the time, so he bought the book. On the subway, making his way home, he eagerly opened the package and examined his purchase. Much to his surprise and chagrin, he noticed on the frontispiece of Gilson's text the Latin words *Imprimatur* (let it be printed) and *Imprimi potest* (it can be printed), signs that the book was officially approved by the Catholic Church. He said he was seriously tempted to throw the book out the window of the train. However, "by a special grace," he kept the book and actually read it.[1] It revolutionized his life. What he found in the pages of Gilson's study was a clear presentation of the subtle and sophisticated understanding of God that is characteristic of Catholic thought. Thoroughly modern Merton had assumed, like most of his peers, that God was a "noisy mythological figure," and religion the stuff of "neuroses and projections." He had never imagined that there was a disciplined academic tradition that spoke of God in such a compelling and intellectually satisfying manner. What he discovered, most specifically, was the idea of God's "aseity," that is, God's capacity to exist through the power of his own essence.[2] He found that God is not one being, however supreme, among many, but *ipsum esse subsistens*, the sheer act of being itself. It is not unimportant that around the time he was discovering Gilson's meditations on God as the ground of contingency both of Merton's grandparents, to whom he had been deeply devoted, passed away. More than any other experience, the death of loved ones typically convinces one that the world of ordinary

---

1. Thomas Merton, *The Seven Storey Mountain* (Orlando, Fla.: Harcourt Brace Jovanovich, 1948), 191.
2. Ibid.

experience is fleeting, evanescent, not self-sufficient and hence opens one to the properly transcendent. This visceral perception was for Merton at a propitious moment given substantive intellectual expression in the technical vocabulary of *The Spirit of Medieval Philosophy*.

In the wake of the encounter with Gilson's book, Merton's life began to change. The God described so persuasively by the Catholic tradition began to tug at him with great insistence, and Merton felt the desire to commune personally with the God he had discovered intellectually. His first move was to attend some Protestant services (his mother had been a Quaker, and some of his only childhood experiences of going to church involved the silent worship so characteristic of the Quakers), but he found himself unmoved. Then one Sunday morning Merton woke up with an intense desire to go to Mass, so he went to the Catholic parish associated with Columbia, the Church of Corpus Christi on 121st Street on the Upper West Side. He entered the place nervously, for he knew very little about the Mass or proper liturgical etiquette, and he slipped (unnoticed, he hoped) into a back pew. He made it through the ceremony, and though he understood very little of it, he was thrilled by the experience. Walking out of the church that morning, he said, was like entering a new world where "even the ugly buildings of Columbia were transfigured."[3] Then he sat down for breakfast at a dilapidated little diner on 111th Street and even in that simple place he felt as though he was "sitting in the Elysian Fields."[4] Having broken into Merton's life through the ministration of Gilson's book, God was now working his way deeper and deeper into the young man's heart.

Not long after this overwhelming Sunday morning experience, Merton presented himself to one of the priests at Corpus Christi for formal instruction in the Catholic faith. He drank in the catechetical lessons and was soon ready for baptism. The ceremony took place at Corpus Christi, and Merton's godfather was Edward Rice, the only Catholic in his largely Jewish circle of Columbia friends. Throughout his life Mer-

---

3. Ibid., 234.
4. Ibid.

ton would commemorate the anniversary of his baptismal day with great solemnity and gratitude. Not long after he became a Catholic, Merton was strolling down Sixth Avenue in midtown Manhattan with his best friend, Robert Lax, who was himself a deeply spiritual man. In the midst of their lively exchange, Lax suddenly asked, "Tom, what do you want out of life?" Merton replied, "Well, I suppose I want to be a good Catholic," and Lax countered, "No, no, that's not enough. You should want to be a saint."[5] Lax was, consciously or not, echoing a famous remark of Leon Bloy, the French spiritual master. Bloy commented that there is only one real sadness in life: not to be a saint. Whatever other sadnesses we might encounter—failure, poverty, dishonor, and so forth—are finally phantoms. Lax's observation unnerved Merton and convinced him that he had to think in a much more serious way about his spiritual life. He began to permit to resurface an intuition he had actually had for many years, and he began to explore the possibility of becoming a priest. He looked into a number of different religious orders, and after some deliberation he applied to the Franciscan order and was initially accepted. So confident was he in this choice that he fantasized about the kind of work he would do as a Franciscan and even about the religious name he would take: Frater John. He was devastated when upon learning more of the details of his past life the Franciscans subsequently rejected him. The account of his tearful breakdown in the presence of a rather cruel confessor, to whom he had poured out his frustration, is one of the most heartbreaking scenes in *The Seven Storey Mountain*.[6]

In time Merton got over the worst of his disappointment and took a job teaching English at the Franciscan college of St. Bonaventure in upstate New York. He resolved that there, as far as possible, he would live a quasi-religious life, praying the office of a priest and living under the same roof as the Blessed Sacrament. While he was in New York City on an academic break, he sat down with Daniel Walsh, an adjunct profes-

---

5. Ibid., 264.
6. Ibid., 330–32.

Photograph of Thomas Merton by Akers, 1959.
USED WITH PERMISSION OF THE MERTON LEGACY
TRUST AND THE THOMAS MERTON CENTER,
BELLARMINE UNIVERSITY

sor of medieval philosophy at Columbia with whom Merton had become friends. They spoke together of many different religious orders, and Walsh said that the one that impressed him the most was the Trappist order, the Cistercians of the Strict Observance, to give them their proper name, a community of men living the classic Benedictine rule in austerity and silence. Walsh urged Merton to make a Holy Week retreat at the Trappist Abbey of Our Lady of Gethsemani in Kentucky. What Merton found at Gethsemani took his breath away, for he later wrote that he discovered there "the still point around which the whole country revolves without knowing it."[7] Immersing himself for that week in a community radically dedicated to the praise of God, he encountered the power of *adoratio,* the right praise that rightly orders the soul and, ultimately, the entire society. He knew in his bones that he had to become part of Gethsemani.

Perhaps precisely because they saw themselves as a penitential order, the Trappists did not balk at Merton's checkered past. Several months after his retreat, on December 10, 1941, Merton entered the abbey as a postulant. He would stay there, almost continuously, for the remaining twenty-seven years of his life, confounding the predictions of some of his Columbia friends who had known him in his raucous days. There he gave himself entirely to prayer and matured as a monk, a writer, a poet, and a spiritual teacher. And through his writings—*The Seven Storey Mountain, The Sign of Jonas, Conjectures of a Guilty Bystander, The New Man,* and *New Seeds of Contemplation,* to name just a few—Merton conveyed the Christian spiritual tradition with special credibility to a contemporary age marked by the nihilism and superficiality from which he himself had managed, by God's grace, to escape. But what precisely did Merton teach? His writings are complex and multivalent and they are shaped by the thought of a bevy of philosophers, mystics, and poets. But Merton's greatest master, the figure who breathes through practically all of his writings, is a sixteenth-century Spaniard named Juan de Ypes Alvarez, better known by his Carmelite religious name, John of the Cross. Having walked through the Merton gate, I would like now to move, with you, into the spiritual world of John of the Cross.

JOHN OF THE CROSS AND CONTEMPLATIVE PRAYER

John of the Cross was born in 1542 and became a Carmelite friar in 1563. He was thoroughly trained in the high theology of his time, es-

---

7. Ibid., 363.

pecially the thought of Saint Thomas Aquinas. Under the influence of Teresa of Avila—about whom we will speak in detail later—John dedicated himself to the reform of his order, attempting to restore it to its Gospel simplicity and zeal. Like most reformers, John was unpopular among those he wished to reform. In December of 1577 a group of his Carmelite brothers arrested him and brought him to Toledo and effectively imprisoned him in a house of the order. They placed John in a stifling room, six feet by ten feet, letting him out only to make him kneel in the refectory, where he was subjected to beatings by his brothers. While holed up in what amounted to a tiny prison cell, John began to compose verses in his mind (he had neither pen nor paper), and these poems constitute not only some of the gems of Spanish literature but also some of the most eloquent articulations of the Catholic spiritual tradition. After nine months of imprisonment, John managed to escape, climbing through a tiny window and clambering down the wall of the

The Tomb of Saint John of the Cross, Segovia, Spain. WORD ON FIRE

Carmelite house and eventually over the wall of the city to safety. He then resumed his work of preaching, writing, and reforming.

What stands at the heart of John's teaching? In his poem "The Living Flame of Love," John offers a powerful image of the human soul. We human beings, he says, have within us "great caverns," which are infinitely deep, unfathomable. These are intellect, will, and feeling—and they are infinite, precisely because they are ordered to God. The mind eagerly comes to know particular things, individual truths, but none of these achievements finally settles the mind, just the contrary. The more the mind knows, the more it wants to know, each answer engendering a new question. The twentieth-century philosopher Bernard Lonergan said that the mind by an inner dynamism "wants to know everything about everything."[8] Thomas Aquinas spoke of the *intellectus agens* (the agent intellect), which restlessly asks the question *quid sit?* (what is that?) about whatever comes under its consideration. Both Lonergan and Aquinas knew that the mind won't rest until it comes to the fullness of truth, to what the theological tradition calls the "beatific vision," seeing God face-to-face.

The will reaches out to particular goods, but no limited good ever fully satisfies it. For example, you are reading these words because, presumably, you are seeking the particular good of learning more about Catholic thought and history. But that particular act of your will finds itself necessarily situated within the context of some higher or further desire. No matter how much satisfaction you might gain from reading and understanding my modest reflections, you will want something better, higher, more illuminating. A parent desires that her child successfully complete elementary school so that the child, in turn, might make it to high school and then university and then, perhaps, graduate school so that she might launch a successful and gratifying career, that she might make a contribution to society, and so forth. There is always a nesting of one desire in another, or, to shift the metaphor, always an opening toward newer horizons for the will.

---

8. Bernard Lonergan, *The Collected Works of Bernard Lonergan*, vol. 5, *Understanding and Being* (Toronto: University of Toronto Press, 1990), esp. 146–55.

Finally, our souls order us to beauty and justice. But no matter how much beauty we take in we always want more; in fact, the greater the beauty, the greater our appetite for beauty is whetted. We long for justice, and sometimes we achieve it to a degree, but no justice here below ever fulfills our desire for final, perfect justice. Martin Luther King Jr., who was personally responsible for some of the most remarkable social achievements in American history, could nevertheless speak of a "Promised Land" for which he still longed and which he knew would always elude him in this world.

This spiritual anthropology helps to explain why most of us are so unhappy most of the time. I don't mean that most of us are psychologically depressed; I mean that our infinite desire never meets in the world an object commensurate with it. And thus even as we experience great joy we still twist and reach with a restless dissatisfaction, like the figures on Michelangelo's Sistine Chapel ceiling. John of the Cross uses his image of the infinitely deep caverns to diagnose the fundamental spiritual disorder that we all share, namely, trying to fill those caverns with the petty goods of the finite world: pleasure, sex, power, and prestige. As we have seen in chapter two, this drive leads, inexorably, to addiction and hence to deeper dissatisfaction. Or maybe we cover the caverns over, pretending that they don't exist. This is the characteristic pathology of contemporary materialism and secularism: convincing ourselves, even as we are starving spiritually, that we're perfectly full. The good news, as far as John of the Cross is concerned, is that this subterfuge, this illusion created by the ego, cannot possibly endure, and the person must finally awaken to the insufficiency of the world. That is when he turns, perhaps in desperation, to the infinite. That is when he seeks, almost despite himself, to raise his mind and heart to God.

John of the Cross's dark night is often used as a metaphor for depression or loss of direction, but that is not at all how John meant it. If the soul is to order itself to God, it must rid itself of attachments to anything creaturely. That is, it must overcome its tendency to turn something less than God into God, and it must accordingly purge and let go of idols. It is most important to note that this purging hasn't a thing to do with a puritanical disdain for the body, or the cultivation of a *fuga mundi* (flight from the world) spirituality. John of the Cross fully shares the biblical and Catholic sense of the goodness of creation. The process of the dark night has to do with the proper ordering of desire: God first, everything else second and for the sake of God.

The purgative process unfolds in two steps, what John calls "the dark night of the senses" and "the dark night of the soul." During the first phase a person detaches himself from every sensual good or pleasure that has taken central position in his life. He lets go of food, drink, sex, and sensible delight in the measure that these have become soul-ordering values. In terms of the life of Jesus, the dark night of the senses would correspond to the Lord's long fast in the desert and his resistance to the tempter's suggestion that he turn stones into bread. Once the dark night of the senses is complete, one is ready to enter into the purgative discipline of the dark night of the soul. During this process the seeker learns to detach himself from those more rarified substitutes for God, which are the concepts, ideas, and images of the mind. There are spiritually alert people who have managed to free themselves from the more ordinary distractions but who are nevertheless beguiled by the products of their own religious consciousness, which are every bit as creaturely as food and drink and fame. These too have to be set aside, let go of. At this point, we can see why the image of the dark night has come to be associated with depression, for this purgative path is indeed painful, sometimes wrenchingly so. If one's life has been ordered around the love of some creaturely value, then the reordering process will cost dearly. There is, accordingly, indeed something austere about John's spiritual style. A story has been told about a younger Carmelite colleague of his who was a deeply spiritual man. One day he told John how much he loved a particular crucifix that had been given to him and that had proven a wonderful aid to prayer. John bluntly told him to surrender it, for it had become an object of attachment. Once again this is neither cruelty nor fussy puritanism; it is honesty and clarity in regard to the demands of the dark night.

I confess that I hesitated to share that anecdote, because I am loath to leave the impression that John of the Cross was nothing but a dyspeptic ascetic. He saw the dark night in both of its stages as merely preparatory, a conduit to a blissful experience of God. When the purgations are complete, the soul is ready for the journey into God, or, better, it is ready to receive the gift that God wants to give. Consider these gorgeous lines from John's poem on the dark night, composed during that awful sojourn in the prison cell in Toledo:

> One dark night,
> fired with love's urgent longings
> —ah, the sheer grace!—
> I went out unseen,
> my house being now all stilled.[9]

The stilled house symbolizes the soul that has passed through the dark night and has found rest from its addictive patterns of desire. But notice that the stillness is not an end in itself. Once the errant desires have been quieted, that deep, abiding, infinite desire can surface; "love's urgent longings" can at last be felt. And then the soul is ready for its journey toward God:

> On that glad night,
> in secret, for no one saw me,
> nor did I look at anything,
> with no other light or guide
> than the one that burned in my heart.[10]

Since it represents liberation, the night is "glad," and since the soul has rid itself of any need for approval or fame, it exults in the fact that no one sees it, and since it no longer relies on worldly goods, it doesn't "look at anything," and, finally, since the deepest desire of the heart has

---

9. John of the Cross, "The Dark Night," in *The Collected Works of St. John of the Cross,* trans. Kieran Kavanaugh and Otilio Rodriguez (Washington, DC: ICS Publications, 1991), 358.
10. Ibid., 359.

surfaced, the soul knows precisely where to go, needing "no other guide" than that very longing. This last idea finds an echo in "The Living Flame of Love," where John speaks of those infinite caverns being illumined by the light and heat of God.

Then come these lines, evocative of the high point of mystical union with God:

Upon my flowering breast
which I kept wholly for him alone,
there he lay sleeping,
and I caressing him . . .

I abandoned and forgot myself,
laying my face on my Beloved;
all things ceased; I went out from myself,
leaving my cares
forgotten among the lilies.[11]

Is there anywhere in the literature of the world a more compelling and beautiful description of union with God? In order to indicate what it is like to be, at last, in possession of the God who alone can satisfy the deepest aching of the heart, John reaches, naturally enough, for erotic language, the imagery of sexual intimacy. His heart (the "breast" in the imagery of the poem) has all along been ordered to God, though through much of his life he had allowed this truth to become obscured. Now, having gone through the dark night, he is ready to receive the one he was always destined to receive: "there he lay sleeping,/and I caressing him." Finally, he imagines himself face-to-face with God, literally in the attitude of *adoratio*. At the climax of the spiritual journey is the recovery of Eden, the restoration of the easy friendship that Adam enjoyed with God, the realization of the worship foreshadowed in the Temple.

---

11. Ibid.

TERESA OF AVILA AND THE
PRAYER OF THE CENTER

Perhaps the most important figure in the life of John of the Cross was Teresa of Avila, the Carmelite nun who inaugurated the reform movement in which John participated. A few decades older than John, Teresa was the daughter of nobility and enjoyed a fairly pampered childhood. When she was still a very young woman she entered the Carmelite monastery at Avila and lived a decent but unheroic spiritual life for many years. As Teresa entered her forties her spirituality became more intense and serious, and she began to receive a series of mystical visitations. She would see Christ, the Blessed Mother, and the saints, not so much with her bodily eyes as with the eyes of her mind and imagination. It would be wrong to dismiss these experiences as mere subjective fantasies, for they came to her unannounced and struck her with overwhelming and often disconcerting power. During these intense encounters she would typically pass into an ecstatic trance, sometimes lying motionless for up to half an hour. Other times she was known to levitate. There are even stories told of some of the stronger nuns being called upon to pull her back to the ground when she would take off! The most famous of these mystical encounters was what came to be called the "transverberation," which Teresa vividly describes in her autobiography. She relates that an angel repeatedly pierced her heart with a fire-tipped spear and that the experience was simultaneously painful and so pleasurable "that she wished it would never end." It was this scene that Gian Lorenzo Bernini so unforgettably immortalized in marble. In the writhing body, panting mouth, and contorted face of the saint, Bernini makes explicit the sexual overtone that is clearly implicit in Teresa's description, but which also vividly calls to mind John of the Cross's erotic analogies. I can only smile when post-Freudians announce that they have "discovered" the unconscious sexuality lurking behind Teresa's mystical experience. There was, I dare say, precious little unconscious about it, for the association of the intense union with God and sexuality is as old as the biblical Song of Songs.

The Ecstasy of Saint Teresa *by Gian Lorenzo Bernini, the Carnaro Chapel of Santa Maria della Vittoria, Rome.* WORD ON FIRE

What can we moderns, we inheritors of the skeptical scientific turn, make of all this? To be sure, such experiences are, even within the religious tradition, rare, and Teresa would be the first to insist that they don't constitute the heart of the matter, spiritually speaking. Her disciple John of the Cross, in fact, said that extraordinary visions should be taken in and then promptly let go of. Nevertheless, they do seem to play a role—from biblical times to the present day—in the divine economy. Might God not deign, occasionally, to signal his presence in a remarkable and vivid way? Might he not, at privileged times, allow the supernatural world to manifest itself in this ordinary world? Might he not, as Flannery O'Connor put it, "shout in the realm of the deaf," in order to remind us of his existence? In a word, we can make too much of Teresa's encounters, but at the same time, we can make too little of them.

At the prompting of her spiritual directors, Teresa began to write down her experiences in prayer for the benefit of her Carmelite sisters, and the books she composed—*The Interior Castle, The Book of Her Life, The Way of Perfection* among others—constitute some of the gems of the Catholic spiritual tradition. What stands at the heart of her teaching? To understand what she was trying essentially to communicate, it is best to look at the

Avila Cathedral, Spain. WORD ON FIRE

title of her most famous work. Teresa of Avila discovered, at the very depth of her soul, Christ dwelling in her, and this divine presence, she said, was like an interior castle. Consider what this image would have conveyed to a sixteenth-century Spaniard. A castle was a keep, a place of safety and power, shelter from the storm. To be grounded in Christ, Teresa realized, was to be rooted in the very power that is here and now creating the cosmos, in the God who is beyond the vagaries of space and time. As we have seen at different points in this book, most of us sinners seek to anchor our lives in some worldly good, but these earthly attachments are necessarily evanescent and therefore unsatisfying. They are vulnerable to corruption, criticism, wear and tear, the shifting moods of the crowd, and final dissolution. None of them—pleasure, money, power, honor—is, in a word, a castle. But Christ is—and that is why the wise person reorients his life toward him, seeks refuge in him, leans on him. Teresa essentially echoes Paul's "it is no longer I who live, but Christ who lives in me." The ego, with all of its preoccupations and false moves, all of its contradictory desires and flimsy defenses, is unreliable; but the inner Christ—eternal, omnipotent, commanding, clear—is like a rock, a redoubt, a castle.

In so many of the spiritual masters we find the theme of the center, which is to say, the divine still point around which the entirety of the self properly revolves. We have already analyzed the gothic rose windows along these lines and we have suggested that worship involves turning the entire self toward God. Meister Eckhart, a fourteenth-century Dominican spiritual writer, speaks of the *Seelengrund* (the ground of the soul) as the point where God and the creature meet in friendship, and John of the Cross described the "inner wine cellar," the place where, at the depth of the soul, the "spirits" are kept, a place of intoxication and elevation. Ignatius of Loyola, the founder of the Jesuit order and a contemporary of both Teresa and John, made detachment, or what he called "indifference," the organizing principle of his spirituality. He famously prayed, "Lord whether I have a long life or a short life, whether I am healthy or sick, whether I am rich or poor, is a matter of indifference to me, as long as I am following your will." That kind of insouciance can come only from having made contact with the center. Teresa's interior castle is still another evocation of this "place" where the soul rests confidently in Christ and where a mystical marriage unfolds.

In light of these considerations, we recall Teresa's most famous prayer, one that can only be uttered from the center:

Let nothing disturb you;
Let nothing frighten you.
All things are passing.
God never changes.
Patience obtains all things.
Nothing is wanting to him who possesses God.
God alone suffices.

All of this takes on a new resonance when one visits Teresa's hometown and sees the miles of castellated walls that surround and protect it. Teresa came of age as a nun and mystic within the confines of a great castle, and she came to realize that those exterior walls were but a fleeting and creaturely sign of the ramparts and castle within.

Segovia Cathedral, cloisters, Spain. WORD ON FIRE

PRAYER OF PETITION

We commenced with Thomas Merton, and Merton led us to John of the Cross, who brought us in turn to Teresa, and through these figures we've been exploring the meaning of John of Damascus's lyrical phrase "raising the mind and the heart to God." In Merton's ecstatic retreat at Gethsemani, in John's celebration of the mystical marriage, in Teresa's resting in the interior castle, we have caught a glimpse of what the church calls contemplative prayer, that rare and rarefied encounter with God beyond speech and words and concepts. But I imagine that when most people hear the word "prayer" they don't think immediately of such a thing; they probably think of asking God for something. And, indeed, petitionary prayer is one of the most fundamental ways that we raise our minds and hearts to God. It is also the commonest form of prayer in the Bible. Every major scriptural character—Abraham, Isaac, Jacob, Joseph, Moses, Joshua, Samuel, David, Solomon, Ezra, Nehemiah, Peter, James, Paul, and John—all pray in this way; they all ask God for things. There is something, of course, primal and elemental about this kind of prayer: "O God, please help me! O Lord, save my child!" If we could place a net capable of catching prayers as they waft their way to heaven from hospitals and churches, we would corral millions upon millions of them. Finally, the paradigmatic prayer that Jesus taught us—the Our Father—is nothing but a series of petitions, and Jesus urged his followers, again and again, to persevere in prayer: "Ask and it will be given to you; seek and you will find; knock and the door will be opened to you" (Mt 7:7).

Even though this form of prayer seems simpler and more basic than contemplation, in fact petitionary prayer is more difficult to make sense of theologically than contemplative prayer. When we speak of petitionary prayer, dilemmas and anomalies emerge that have puzzled religious thinkers for centuries. If God cannot change, what is the point of asking him for anything? And if God is omniscient, what is the point of telling him what you need? Keep in mind that the same Jesus who told us to ask

Woman at prayer. WORD ON FIRE

and ask again also informed us that God "knows what we need before we ask." One way to shed light on this problem is to refer to the biblical master metaphor for God, namely, the parent. Throughout the Bible, God is referred to as a father and even in some texts as a mother: "could a mother forget her baby?" and "let us nurse with delight at her abundant breasts." Parents hear petitions from their children constantly, persistent requests for things, some good and some quite bad—and decent parents know what their child needs long before she asks for it. But none of this conduces a parent toward stifling those requests or pronouncing them useless—even if he is obliged frequently to respond negatively. God indeed knows everything about everything, so he is aware of what we need before we ask; yet still like a good parent he delights in hearing our requests—and like a good parent, he does not always respond the way we would like him to.

Saint Augustine offers another perspective on our dilemma. God wants us to ask, seek, and petition persistently not in order that he might be changed but that we might be changed. Through the initial refusal to give us what we want, God compels our hearts to expand in order to receive adequately what he wants to give us. In the very process of hungering and thirsting for certain goods, we make ourselves worthy vessels. It is not as though in petitioning God we are approaching a stubborn pasha or big city boss whom we hope might be persuaded by our persistence. Rather it is God who works a sort of spiritual alchemy in us by forcing us to wait. In his treatment of the Lord's Prayer Thomas Aquinas tells us, very much in the spirit of Augustine, that the initial petition of the Our Father, "hallowed be thy name," is not asking for something to change in God, for God's name is always holy; it is asking that God might work a change in us so that we hallow God above all things.

Aquinas provides what I take to be the richest theological framework for petitionary prayer when he speaks of God praying through us. Aquinas is convinced that God, as the unmoved mover, can never be changed by our prayer; nevertheless, God can arrange his providential governance of the universe in such a way that what he wants to give will be coordinated with our asking for it. On this reading, whatever is good and right and true in our prayer is God already praying in us, adjusting our desire to his desire. Do not forget the attribute of God that I have been insisting upon throughout this book, namely, God's noncompetitiveness. Since he is not the supreme being but the very ground of being, God's "invasion" enhances us, makes us more authentically free. A very good example of this dynamic is the prayer for the liturgy of Augustine's mother, Saint Monica. The text begins as follows: "Lord, you graciously received the tears of Monica for the conversion of her son Augustine." Mind you, it does not say that the tears of Monica moved God to act or compelled him somehow to change the structure of his providence; it says that God accepted those tears in coordination with granting the grace of conversion to her son, implying that God himself was effectively crying through the tears of Monica.

BACK TO MERTON

During his years at Gethsemani Abbey, Thomas Merton was remarkably productive. Besides the dozens of books he authored, he wrote hundreds of poems and articles as well as private journals that have been published in eight volumes. He also maintained an impressive correspondence with writers, cultural figures, and religious leaders all over the world, including, among many others, the poet Czeslaw Milosz, the theologians Hans Urs von Balthasar and Jean Leclerq, the singer Joan Baez, and Pope John XXIII. He also almost single-handedly caused a revival of monastic life in America. Inspired by *The Seven Storey Mountain*, hundreds of candidates applied to Trappist and Benedictine houses all over the country. Gethsemani itself became filled beyond capacity. During the 1950s, as he emerged into national prominence, Merton wanted more and more to withdraw into solitude and contemplation. His abbot gave him permission to spend time alone in an old toolshed near the edge of the monastery property and, at Merton's prompting, came close to allowing his most famous monk to live atop a fire observatory post overlooking the forest. Eventually he gave Merton leave to live alone in a hermitage on the monastery grounds but off the beaten path. In that simple, humble, and isolated place, Merton lived and worked the last years of his life.

The pivotal theme of his writings, throughout the 1940s, '50s, and '60s was contemplation, the form of prayer that he learned from John of the Cross. Merton insisted, over and over again, that contemplation ought not to be seen as an arcane practice of certain spiritual athletes, but as something that stands at the heart of the Christian thing, since it is nothing other than the organization of a person's life around the divine center. In language redolent of Teresa, John of the Cross, and Meister Eckhart, Merton spoke of *le point vierge* (the virginal point), which is the place of

Photograph of Merton at Hermitage. USED WITH PERMISSION OF THE MERTON LEGACY TRUST AND THE THOMAS MERTON CENTER, BELLARMINE UNIVERSITY

contact between the soul and Christ. He characterized contemplative prayer as "finding that place in you where you are here and now being created by God." That magnificent description was born of Merton's discovery, many years before, of Gilson's notion of the divine aseity. If God is that which exists through the power of his own essence, then, as we have seen in chapter three, whatever else exists must come forth in its totality from the creative power of God. Creation, then, is not only an event "at the beginning of time"; it is something happening right now. To pray contemplatively is to find the place at the very bottom of one's being—the *point vierge*, the interior castle, the inner wine cellar—where God's life and love are sustaining you in existence. Once that center is found, everything else changes. When we find that place, we necessarily find that which connects us to everyone else and everything else in the cosmos.

This helps to explain why Merton wrote so energetically about nonviolence in the 1960s. Some see this as a surrender to trendiness on Merton's part and an abandonment of the more classically Catholic spirituality he espoused earlier in his life, but I believe that this is a superficial reading. In speaking incisively against atomic weapons and against the war in Vietnam, Merton was drawing practical moral conclusions from creation metaphysics and from the contemplative prayer that gave him access to the divine center. Merton consistently denied that he was a strict pacifist in the manner of Francis of Assisi or Dorothy Day; he insisted that practitioners of the Catholic spiritual tradition, adepts of contemplation, should always exercise a fundamental option for nonviolence, for their prayer must teach them that all people, despite whatever political or cultural conflicts might divide them, always remain, at the deepest level, siblings.

On March 18, 1958, Merton was in Louisville for some practical business and found himself at the corner of Fourth and Walnut Streets in the heart of the shopping district. In that ordinary place he had an experience in some ways as extraordinary as Teresa of Avila's encounter with the angel: "I was suddenly overwhelmed with the realization that I loved all those people, that they were mine and I theirs, that we could not be alien to one another even though we were total strangers. It was like

waking from a dream of separateness."[12] Merton had come to Gethsemani to escape the world, in the negative sense of that term, and to do
penance for his sins. In the course of his long retreat (at the time of the
Louisville experience, he had been seventeen years in the monastery),
he had moved, through contemplative prayer, deep into the center. And
it was from that place that this mystical perception of union was born.
"This sense of liberation from an illusory difference was such a relief
and such a joy to me that I almost laughed out loud. And I suppose my
happiness could have taken form in the words, 'Thank God, thank God
that I am like other men.'"[13] Merton clearly sees the paradox that it was
precisely his contemplative isolation that made this experience possible:
"This changes nothing in the sense and value of my solitude, for it is in
fact the function of solitude to make one realize such things."[14] He also
sees the Christological dimension of this moment: "I have the immense
joy of being man, a member of a race in which God himself became incarnate."[15] We are linked to one another not only through our common
creation but also by the universality of the mystical body of Jesus. Here is
how Merton summed up this ecstatic experience: "And if only everybody
could realize this! But it cannot be explained. There is no way of telling
people that they are all walking around shining like the sun."[16]

Somehow in that humdrum place in downtown Louisville it all came
together for Merton: metaphysics, creation, incarnation, contemplation,
nonviolence, and universal love. And this grandeur of vision, this unifica-
tion of thought and action, this sense of getting what it is all about is the
effect of real prayer, of raising the mind and heart to God.

---

12. Thomas Merton, *Conjectures of a Guilty Bystander* (New York: Doubleday, 1989), 156–57.
13. Ibid., 157.
14. Ibid., 158
15. Ibid., 157.
16. Ibid.

Chapter 10

WORLD WITHOUT END:
THE LAST THINGS

I would submit that the doctrines concerning the so-called Last Things—hell, purgatory, and heaven—are simultaneously the most fascinating and most objectionable of all of the beliefs of the Catholic Church. When people want to critique or dismiss Catholic doctrine they will often point to the supposed incompatibility of affirming the existence of an all-good God and the existence of an eternal hell, a place of unending torture. And at least from the time of Marx and Freud, many would point to the doctrine concerning heaven as an indication of, at best, the church's naïveté and, at worst, its duplicity. Is the belief in a place of perfect happiness after we die not a classic case of wishful thinking, childish fantasizing? And hasn't it been used as "opium for the masses," simply a way to mollify people while they endure the agonies of this life? John Lennon sang,

Imagine there's no heaven
It's easy if you try

Basílica de San Francisco el Grande, detail, Madrid. WORD ON FIRE

He was speaking for anyone with a fundamentally Marxist or Freudian orientation. And even many Christians who gladly accept the doctrines of heaven and hell find the Catholic teaching on purgatory bizarre and arbitrary, lacking in any biblical foundation.

At the same time, even nonbelievers often find themselves compelled by these teachings. Everyone—believer and nonbeliever alike—wonders and worries at some point about what will happen after we die. Hamlet spoke of death as "the undiscovered country, from whose bourn no traveller returns" (3.1. 78–79), and the entire "To be or not to be" speech reflects an uneasy, bewildered fascination with what awaits us once we've "shuffled off this mortal coil." Everyone loves a ghost story—in part because of its cathartic quality—but also because it seems to provide some hint of another world. More to it, the doctrines of heaven, hell, and purgatory beguile us precisely because of our sense of justice. Far too many good people die without receiving in this life a sufficient reward for their goodness, and many wicked people die without being compelled in this life to pay for their wickedness. If God is just, it seems there has to be some state of being, some place in which these injustices are set right. Here Marx seems wide of the mark indeed. For the vast

The Duomo, detail, Florence. WORD ON FIRE

majority of suffering people who believe in heaven and hell, these doctrines don't quiet their indignation at injustice in this world; rather they
arouse it.

In this final chapter we turn to the Last Things. What does the Catholic Church teach in regard to heaven, hell, and purgatory? What does it

Notre Dame, detail, Paris. WORD ON FIRE

hold concerning a dimension that we cannot directly see but that never-theless intrigues all of us who live on the near side of the sleep of death?

BEGINNING WITH DANTE AND HELL

T. S. Eliot said that Western literature is essentially divided between two great figures, Shakespeare and Dante, all the rest qualifying as second-ary. If Eliot is right, how fascinating that the principal work of one of the two greatest poets in the Western literary tradition is about our topic—about heaven, hell, and purgatory. Dante wrote his masterpiece, *The Divine Comedy*, while he was wandering in exile from his hometown of Florence, to which he would never return. Due to the machinations of his political enemies he had been condemned to permanent exile while he was on a trip to Rome. During those lonely and painful years, when he had lost his way both personally and politically, Dante composed his meditation on the next world. *The Divine Comedy* is a work of creative imagination, and therefore we shouldn't take it altogether literally; nev-ertheless it is filled with sound theology (we know that Dante studied theology for a time in Paris, not long after the death of Thomas Aquinas) and informed by the perceptiveness of a transcendently great poet who was also a believer. Therefore as we attempt to gaze through the veil into the world that lies beyond we can take Dante as a helpful guide.

The Divine Comedy commences with Dante's midlife crisis: "Midway on the journey of our life, I found myself alone and lost in a dark wood, having wandered from the straight path." He identifies the year as 1300, when he was thirty-five, precisely midlife for those who took the psalmist's statement seriously that the life span is "seventy years, or eighty for those who are strong." Having lost his direction (as many do at midlife), Dante cries out in despair, and his prayer is heard by Mary, the Mother of God, who sends for Lucy, the patroness of light, who in turn sends for Beatrice, whom Dante loved while she lived in this world. Finally, Beatrice sends for the Roman poet Virgil, who conducts Dante on a journey through hell. This opening shows us something of great importance, namely, that what we know about the next world affects profoundly our experience of this one, that, in a real way, heaven, hell, and purgatory affect the manner in which our present lives unfold. Sometimes, Dante is telling us, crises here below can be solved only by situating our suffering within the wider context of the transcendent order.

Virgil arrives on the scene and informs Dante that his suffering will end, but only after he has seen the dimensions of the next world, beginning with hell. Chilled by the famous sign ABANDON HOPE ALL YE WHO ENTER HERE, Dante nevertheless follows his guide into the underworld, where he is compelled to see a variety of sinners as they undergo punishment. Dante does not construe what he sees as arbitrary divine cruelty, but rather as an expression of justice, each sinner being allowed to experience the negativity that flows logically and naturally from his dysfunctional behavior. Hell, we learn, is a place created not by God but by errant human freedom. Down and down they go into an increasingly narrow space (hell, in Dante's imagination, is shaped something like an inverted cone). In his presentation of the topography of hell, the poet has intuited the narrowing of the soul that follows from sin, the turning inward characteristic of self-preoccupation.

At the very bottom of the pit Virgil and Dante confront Satan, the prince of darkness. There is certainly a tendency within the literature of the West to romanticize Satan as a powerful and clever figure: think, for example, of Milton's devil in *Paradise Lost*. But there is nothing of that in Dante. The medieval poet imagines the devil not as a hero but as a sad, even pathetic, figure. He is enormous—Virgil and Dante think they are seeing a giant windmill as they approach him—but he is powerless, stuck in ice that rises to his waist. He flaps his enormous wings, but they take him nowhere and only succeed in making the world around him colder. Ice, by the way, is a much better symbol of hell than the traditional fire, for it signals the stuck, immobile quality of sin, which effectively freezes one within the confines of the ego. Saint Augustine famously defined sin as the state of being "*incurvatus in se*" (caved in on oneself), and Dante's

Satan, the sovereign of a kingdom precisely the size of his own self, splen-
didly exemplifies the Augustinian definition. The spirit is meant to fly out
beyond itself—hence angels have wings—but sin traps us and weighs us
down. Chesterton commented that the angels can fly, because they take
themselves so lightly! Dante's Satan takes himself with utter seriousness.

As they get closer, Virgil and Dante notice that the devil has three
faces on his one head, a sort of gross mockery of the three persons of
the Trinity. The image subtly suggests a spiritual point of some moment,
namely, that each sinner, to the degree that he considers himself the
center of the universe, makes himself divine. Part of the intense joy of
heaven, as we shall see, is to know that one is *not* God and hence to
stand ready for an infinitely fascinating journey *into* God. Thinking that
he *is* God, Satan has precisely nowhere to go. Next Dante specifies that
Satan weeps from all six of his eyes. Again, there is nothing glamorous
about evil: sin is just a sad, depressing, soul-shrinking business. God has
made his creatures for joy, and this is why turning away from God invariably results in sadness. As Virgil and Dante approach the great beast we
expect some sort of confrontation: surely the devil will stop them or at-

The Last Judgment, *detail, by Michelangelo, Sistine Chapel, Vatican City.*
WORD ON FIRE

tack them. But he doesn't even notice them. Virgil tells Dante to hop onto the shaggy sides of Satan (he has haunches like a goat's) and to make his way down to the center of the earth. Though I suppose this scene is a tad anticlimactic, it speaks the spiritual truth that sin produces something like the fog of depression, which renders someone unresponsive, turgid, and dull-witted. The faculties of mind and will and sensuality and imagination light up precisely when they are directed to goods outside the self and finally toward the One who is supremely interesting. Dante's journey through hell gives us a vivid picture of what the rejection of God looks like, even a visceral sense of what it feels like.

Within the thematic context of *The Divine Comedy*, Dante is learning, by his exploration of hell, how he has managed to find himself, at midlife, in a hellish place. By examining the suffering of the damned and the deep sadness of Satan, he has come to appreciate how his own violence, self-absorption, indifference, pride, and cruelty have compromised his happiness. Hell—like heaven—can be anticipated even now. And this can help us to make sense not only of the existence of hell but also of the compatibility of hell with the infinity of the divine love. The existence of hell—at least as a possibility—is a corollary of two more fundamental convictions: that we are free and that God is love. As we have seen in chapter three, love is not one of God's attributes or an emotional state that God falls into from time to time; love is the very nature and essence of God. Love is what God *is*. Therefore God is like the sun that shines on the good and bad alike and the rain that falls on the just and unjust alike. God doesn't love in response to our goodness; instead, whatever goodness we have is a consequence of God's love.

Therefore the interesting question is this: how is that never-changing divine love experienced by human beings? And the answer is: it depends on the freedom of the one who does the experiencing. God surely delights in the simplicity and beauty of his nonrational creatures, but he especially delights in those who are capable of serving him "wittily in the tangle of the mind" and freely in the dramatic choice of the will. Endowed with mind and will, we human beings can respond to the divine love or we can reject it. We can bask in its light or we can turn from it. The choice is ours. God wants all people to be saved, which is just another way of saying that he wants them all to share in his life. But his life *is* love freely given, and therefore it can be *had* only in the measure that it is freely returned. "Hell" is a spatial metaphor for the state of having freely refused this love, having chosen to live outside of its ambit. Perhaps here we can see the applicability of the traditional symbol of fire. C. S. Lewis said that it is none other than the love of God that lights up the fires of hell. He means that when we resist the divine love it burns us in the same way that the bright light of day would torture the eyes of someone who had been trapped underground for an extended period, or in the way that a cheerful person would exquisitely annoy someone who is sunk in sadness. The sun is just being the sun, and the joyful person is just being joyful, but both can be received in a sharply negative way by someone who is ill disposed to take them in. It has even been proposed that heaven and hell are the same "place," but inhabited by people of entirely opposite dispositions. Picture a table piled high with food and surrounded by hungry diners, each of whom has a long fork attached to his or her wrist. Those who insist on feeding themselves will go hungry, while those who are willing to feed one another will be perfectly satisfied. What God holds out to everyone all the time is the banquet of his love, but some know how to eat at that table and others don't.

Many object that an infinitely good God could never send anyone to hell. What I've tried to show, with the help of Dante and Lewis, is that this manner of thinking is misleading. God "sends" no one to hell; rather people freely choose to go there. As Lewis pointed out, the door to hell is always locked from the inside. If there are any human beings in hell, they are there because they absolutely insist on it. The conditional clause with which the last sentence began honors the church's conviction that, though we must accept the possibility of hell (due to the play between divine love and human freedom), we are not committed doctrinally to saying that anyone is actually "in" such a place. We can't see fully to the depths of anyone's heart; only God can. Accordingly, we can't declare with utter certitude that anyone—even Judas, even Hitler—has chosen definitively to lock the door against the divine love. Indeed, since the liturgy compels us to pray for all of the dead, and since the law of prayer is the law of belief, we must hold out at least the hope that all people will be saved. Furthermore, since Christ went to the very limits of godforsakenness in order to establish solidarity even with those who are furthest from grace, we may, as Hans Urs von Balthasar insisted, *reasonably* hope that all will find salvation. Again, this has nothing to do with our perfectibility; it has to do with God's amazing grace.

PURGATORY

If the doctrine of hell is the most objectionable article of faith in the Catholic system, then the doctrine of purgatory is probably a close second. For many Christians—even for many Catholics—purgatory seems a holdover from the Middle Ages, a superstitious and unnecessary teaching with no clear biblical support. Especially in light of the way in which the doctrine was being used practically as a means of fund-raising (the buying and selling of indulgences), Martin Luther and the other Protestant reformers became sharp critics of the doctrine of purgatory. What precisely is the Catholic teaching in this regard? Here is the formulation found in the *Catechism of the Catholic Church*: "All who die in God's grace and friendship, but still imperfectly purified, are indeed assured of their eternal salvation; but after death they undergo purification, so as to achieve the holiness necessary to enter the joy of heaven. The church gives the name *Purgatory* to this final purification of the elect" (CCC 1030–1031). Traditional theology has distinguished between "mortal" and "venial" sins, that is, between those sins that involve a definitive rupture in one's relation to God and those that negatively affect but do not break one's friendship with God. As the name suggests, the first type of sin "kills" the divine life in the one who commits it. To get some sense of what this destruction of the relation to God means, imagine the effect that adultery has on a marriage. Venial sins, on the other hand, do not kill the divine life in a person; nevertheless they still compromise one's friendship with God and still affect the soul in a negative way, scarring it or warping it. Consider how a bad action, performed repeatedly, twists the will, predisposing it to choose along the same negative line in the future: cruelty begets more cruelty, and small acts of injustice usually conduce to greater injustice. This sort of sin, therefore, needs correction, the wounds that it leaves need healing, and the negative tendency it inculcates needs redirecting. We can see this happening in acts of penance, self-denial, fasting, and prayer that effectively bend the will back in the right direction.

L ough Derg is a rocky, uninviting island located in the middle of a forgotten lake in northwest Ireland. To this place, strangely, thousands of people come every year to make a penitential spiritual retreat. They are ferried to the island and then told to take off their shoes. They are to remain unshod for the duration of their spiritual exercise. They spend the first day praying the Rosary, walking on their knees over punishing beds of stone, and attending services. For that day and night they are not permitted to sleep. If they doze off at church, attendants rudely awaken them. A friend of mine who attends this retreat regularly said that the forced sleeplessness is by far the most trying feature of the retreat. After two and a half days of practically constant prayer and spiritual exertion, the retreatants are ferried back to the mainland. In the Middle Ages this island was known as St. Patrick's Purgatory, and popular legend said that the entrance to purgatory was nearby. We can dispense, of course, with the crude literalism, but we should still pay attention to the association of what took (and takes) place on Lough Derg and what the church means by purgatory in the supernatural sense. Those who come to the island love God. They wouldn't go through such punishment unless they did. But they recognize imperfections in themselves that need to be corrected so that their relationship to God can be set fully right, and therefore they willingly go through a crucible. Just as denizens of hell (if there are any) are there freely, so those who pass through purgatory do so because they want to. Once more, this has nothing to do with a supposed cruelty or capriciousness on God's part; it has to do with the sinner's perceived need to deal with the effects of his sin.

Imagine a worldly person—self-absorbed, superficial, spiritually un-developed—who suddenly experiences a conversion to God. He perceives the inadequacy of his life and he wants to change. And so, impulsively, he resolves to leave his job, travel to Calcutta, and help in the work of the Missionaries of Charity. As he shares the lives of the sisters and joins in their daily task of caring for the most wretched, he is, objectively speak-ing, in heaven, for he is fully surrendered to a life of love and self-denial. But his years of hedonism, materialism, and self-absorption have so poorly disposed him to such a life that he *experiences* his new situation as hellish suffering, and it awakens in him the deepest anxiety and resentment. If

Lough Derg, Ireland. WORD ON FIRE

he remains open to the new life, if he continues, despite his resistance, to give himself to it, he will find in time that his resistance weakens and his faults are purged away. He will discover, at last, that it is possible to walk the path of love effortlessly and freely. And at that moment the place of suffering will become a place of springs. This, I think, is an apt analogy for what the church means by purgatory. There are many people who leave this life as friends of God, but who are far from able to live the life of heaven effortlessly. They require, accordingly, a Lough Derg, a Calcutta, a necessarily painful training in the way of love—a purgatory.

In order to get an even fuller illustration of the meaning of this doctrine, it might be helpful to turn once again to *The Divine Comedy*. After Virgil and Dante finish their journey through hell, they pass through the middle of the earth and climb out the other side. There they spy the great mountain of purgatory, divided into seven levels or "stories." On each of the levels those who are saved but still imperfect are cleansed of the effects of one of the seven deadly sins: pride, envy, anger, sloth, avarice, gluttony, and lust. On the first story, the prideful are made to carry massive boulders, which weigh them down, pressing them to the earth. Pride is self-elevation, and therefore the effects of pride are purged away through a humbling of the ego, a reorientation to the earth (*humus* in Latin), to the simple truth of things. The envious spend their lives looking resentfully at the achievements of others and delightedly at the failures of others. Therefore on the second level they are punished by having their eyelids sewn shut. They are also compelled to hear the Gospel story of Mary, who at the wedding feast of Cana did not rejoice in the misfortune of the young couple but pressed Jesus to help them. On the third story the angry are inundated with smoke in order to make them feel how anger has blinded them and distorted their speech. The slothful, literally in the dead center of purgatory, are made to run, and they hear, over and again, the Gospel reminder that Mary "went in haste" to the hill country of Judea after the Annunciation. The avaricious, who in life were preoccupied with the goods that money can buy, are nailed to the ground, their faces quite literally rubbed in matter. On the sixth level, the gluttonous are, as we'd expect, starved; and on the seventh story the lustful are forced to pass through fire in order to feel the burning effect of their sexual dysfunction.

What I hope is clear is that none of this has a thing to do with divine cruelty. It is a function of what the church father Origen of Alexandria called the *schola animarum,* the school of souls. In his *Spiritual Exercises* Saint Ignatius of Loyola often recommended the *agere contra* (act against) principle: when a spiritual seeker discovers within herself a distortion, she ought to act, even in an exaggerated way, against it. If too much sensual pleasure is her problem, she ought to fast; if ambition is her difficulty, she ought purposely to take the lowest place; if envy bedevils her, she ought to praise those who awaken the feeling of resentment in her. Purgatory is a school of souls, where the *agere contra* principle is followed. And one is freed from this state precisely when one is ready.

Twice already I've referenced the classical Protestant objection that purgatory is an unbiblical doctrine, a medieval innovation. Is this true? To be sure, the word "purgatory" is nowhere to be found in Scripture,

Glendalough, Ireland. WORD ON FIRE

but, to be fair, "incarnation" and "Trinity" are equally absent. Yet one could argue that the seeds of the idea of purgatory are indeed in the Scriptures. One classic reference is in 2 Maccabees. After a battle the Israelite general Judas Maccabeus examines the corpses of fallen Jews and discovers idolatrous amulets on the persons of some of the dead, and he surmises that their apostasy was the reason for their demise. But then he urges that prayers and sacrifices be offered on their behalf. The author of 2 Maccabees comments: "[F]or if he were not expecting the fallen to rise again, it would have been useless and foolish to pray for them in death. But if he did this with a view to the splendid reward that awaits those who had gone to rest in godliness, it was a holy and pious thought. Thus he made atonement for the dead that they might be freed from this sin" (2 Mac 12:44–46). The assumption is that at least some of the dead are friends of God (asleep in godliness) but who can nevertheless benefit from prayer and who stand in need of deliverance from sin. They are, in short, in the condition of what Catholic theology calls purgatory.

EXCURSUS ON ANGELS AND DEVILS

We have been talking about hell and purgatory, states of being that transcend the world of ordinary experience. But is this kind of speech even coherent? Why should we imagine that there is anything beyond what we can see, touch, and measure? It might strike many today as surprising that in Europe prior to the scientific revolutions of the seventeenth and eighteenth centuries and in many cultures today where the scientific model isn't predominant a belief in a transcendent dimension inhabited by spiritual realities was and is taken utterly for granted. And I do not mean this as a critique of those cultures, but rather as a dig at a certain "scientism" that sharply reduces reality to the empirically verifiable. The Bible, for instance, is intensely interested in the full panoply of visible things: human beings, plants, animals, trees, the earth itself, even those insects that crawl on the ground. But it is equally interested

Isenheim Altarpiece *by Matthias Günewald, detail*
(*Unterlinden Museum, Colmar, France*). WORD ON FIRE

in the whole realm of God's invisible creation, the denizens of heaven. The Nicene Creed, which is conditioned by a deeply biblical consciousness, speaks of God who has created "the heavens and the earth . . . all that is seen and unseen." Can we inhabitants of the "disenchanted" post-Enlightenment universe make sense of this?

Thomas Aquinas in the thirteenth century and Teilhard de Chardin in the twentieth century mounted similar arguments for the existence of a transcendent spiritual order. Both drew attention to the explosive fecundity of God's creativity evident in our ordinary experience: the numberless insects, plants, cells, molecules, planets, and galaxies. And then both Aquinas and Teilhard wonder whether it is reasonable to suppose that between the stunning variety evident in the physical universe and God there yawns simply a great abyss. Wouldn't it be more rational, they conclude, to assume that mediating between the Creator and his material creation is an equally variegated and complex spiritual realm, an order of creatures who exist at a higher pitch of perfection and intensity than embodied things? And might this dimension be invisible to us not because it is merely fantastical but because we are not equipped to sense it? When considering Mary's Assumption in an earlier chapter, I spoke of the translation of her body into a higher level of existence, one that is not less real but more real, more complete, than ours. I meant that she entered the "space" of the angels and spirits. Again, when we picture these creatures we tend to see them in our mind's eye as diminished, wispy versions of ourselves, but this is to get it precisely backward. It would be much more correct to see ourselves as wispy versions of them. They exist more fully, more intensely, and more completely than we do.

Aquinas described an angel as a "separated intelligence," meaning a creature endowed with intelligence and will but independent of matter. This means that the angel can know in an immediate, intuitive way, not needing, like us, to go through the relatively messy process of sensing, imagining, and abstracting. It means that the angel transcends space and time, able to move effortlessly through both. Each angel, precisely as immaterial, Aquinas said, is its own species, for what accounts for individuation within a species is embodiedness. I am one instance of the species *Homo sapiens,* and you are another, because you and I are instantiated in different bodies, which give us unique features and enable us to occupy

The Last Judgment, *detail, by Michelangelo, Sistine Chapel, Vatican City.*
WORD ON FIRE

different spaces, and so forth. But angels, who have no bodies, cannot be differentiated that way. To make all of this abstract language a bit more accessible, picture, as far as you can, every human being who has ever lived, every human being currently alive, and every human being who will ever live up to the end of time. And now imagine all of them—with all of their powers and perfections—gathered into a single great entity. That might give you some idea of what one angel is like—and also why the typical reaction to an angel is fear.

In our tradition the angels are associated with the praise of God. In fact, the highest angels, the seraphim, derive their name from a Hebrew word that means "the burnt ones." They are on fire because their praise has brought them so close to the pure heat and light of God. We also speak in this context of the singing of the angels. Though we shouldn't literalize this language (spiritual realities don't exactly have voices), we shouldn't dismiss it as mere pious poetry. The harmonizing of the angels is meant to indicate the symphony of mind and will among these spiritual creatures as they praise God. In our exploration of the Liturgy we explained how the great Gloria ("Glory to God in the highest and peace to his people on earth") expresses the hope that when we together make God our highest concern that act will conduce to peace among us. We are praying for what the angels already have: a concord that comes from orthodoxy.

The word "angel" is derived from the Greek *angelos,* which means "messenger." As Saint Augustine indicated, angels are named based on their function, not their nature, for we come to know these pure spirits in the measure that they are sent by God on mission into our dimensional system. Thus the Bible speaks, for example, of Raphael's involvement with Tobit, the three angels who visit Abraham, and Gabriel's commission to announce the Incarnation to the Virgin Mary. Though they are at a higher pitch of existence, angels can, it seems, mix and mingle with us. How can we explain this? We shouldn't think of "spirit" and "matter" as mutually exclusive. Indeed, it would be very hard to account for God's creation of the material universe if spirit and matter were incompatible. I would suggest that we consider matter as a less intense expression of

Isenheim Altarpiece *by Matthias Grünewald, detail (Unterlinden Museum, Colmar, France).* WORD ON FIRE

being than spirit. This means that the spiritual order can stoop to the material, even if the reverse direction is not possible. An adult can condescend to enter into the thought world of a three-year-old, but the child could never, even in principle, rise up to understand the complexity of adult consciousness. In a similar way, angels can interface with our system—even to the point of assuming material form—though we cannot, on our own power, accommodate ourselves to their system.

I can easily enough imagine someone who has followed the argument to this point and has managed, perhaps with some reservation, to accept the existence of angels but who balks at affirming the existence of devils. Surely that conviction is a holdover from a superstitious and prescientific age. According to the mind of the church, a devil is a fallen or morally compromised angel. If we admit that human beings are capable of moral corruption (and it would be extremely difficult not to), I don't see why it would necessarily be difficult to grant that certain angels might have turned in on themselves and away from God and thereby fallen into corruption, and that they with malicious intent could involve themselves in the world of our ordinary experience. Saint Paul said that we do battle not with flesh and blood but with angels and principalities, that is to

Angel. WORD ON FIRE

say, with unseen powers that exert a malign influence on the affairs of human beings. Once again, we shouldn't think of the spiritual realm as "far away" in the ordinary sense, as though it were a distant corner of the cosmos. It is other indeed, but qualitatively, not quantitatively so, and this means that the spiritual realm can interact, both positively and negatively, with our realm. Before turning from this topic of the devil, I feel obliged to insist that all Gnostic and Manichaean fantasies concerning the devil as God's opposite or opponent have to be set aside. Satan is not the "dark side" that faces the light of God in a terrible cosmic struggle. He is a fallen creature whom God allows, for God's own inscrutable purposes, to work woe in the world. We should take the devil with requisite seriousness, but we shouldn't give this finally uninteresting and pathetic creature too much attention.

HEAVEN

In coming to the topic of heaven, we come to the end of these reflections and to the goal of the Catholic faith. Everything else that we have talked about—God, Jesus, the church, the sacraments, Mary, the Liturgy, the saints—is meant to conduce to heaven. What God finally desires for us human beings is participation in his own Trinitarian life, which is to say, the life of love. Heaven *is* love in the fullest sense, love completed. Paul said that there are three things that last—faith, hope, and love—and that the greatest of these is love. Love is the greatest because in heaven, faith and hope will fade away, but love will endure. Heaven is the "place" where everything that is not love has been burned away and hence heaven is the fulfillment of the deepest longing of the human heart.

There are many different images for heaven in the Bible and the great tradition: the banquet, the wedding feast, the wine of the Kingdom, life, light, peace, the Father's house, paradise, the heavenly Jerusalem, eternal rest, and refreshment, to name just a few (CCC 1027). Though each of these images speaks some truth concerning heaven, the reality itself lies

The Duomo, detail, Florence. WORD ON FIRE

beyond all our imagining, since it is equivalent to the very life of God, that which "no eye has seen, nor ear heard, nor the heart of man conceived." With this caution ever in mind, I should like to focus on three metaphors for heaven that have always struck me as particularly illuminating: the beatific vision, the city, and the new heavens and the new earth.

Thomas Aquinas said that the human mind is marked by a dynamism that propels it outward. The mind comes to know a particular thing by relentlessly asking the question "what is that?" This question leads to ever deeper insight into the object or event, opening up ever wider horizons of meaning. Thus I might say in regard to the machine on which I'm currently tapping, "That's a computer." But my mind is unsatisfied with that statement and asks, "What is a computer?" Through a series of perceptions, comparisons, insights, and judgments, my mind concludes that a computer is a type of machine. But what is a machine? It is an artificial contraption. But what is that? It is a cleverly designed coming together of physical objects. But what are those? Those are worldly things. What are worldly things? They are beings, existing things. But what is existence? At this point the mind has reached a sort of horizon or limit, for it is asking about the very nature of to be, the Truth Itself, if you will. It is looking, however inchoately, into the face of God. This is precisely why Aquinas says that in every particular act of knowledge, God is implicitly co-known; for God is the intended goal of the mind, whether the intellectual seeker explicitly knows it or not. Aquinas's analysis here is not far from John of the Cross's description of the inner caverns that can be filled only by God.

For Aquinas the will can be viewed in a similar way. Even in its simplest moves the will necessarily seeks the good, and it finds it, to a degree, in this world. But no matter how much good the will achieves, it is always unsatisfied, yearning for more. Even the greatest goods the world can offer—beauty, pleasure, power, esteem, adventure, success—leave the will restless, desiring a still greater good. Jean-Paul Sartre and his existentialist colleagues drew from this fact the conclusion that life is simply absurd. But Thomas Aquinas and the other masters of the Christian tradition have drawn a very different conclusion, arguing that the dissatisfaction of the will, even when it is in possession of the highest worldly goods, is a clear indication that the will is ordered to a transcendent value, one that is vaguely sensed but never attained in this life. This is why, as C. S. Lewis realized, the most exquisite experiences in life—aesthetic pleasure, sexual intimacy, deep friendship—are always accompanied by a certain aching sadness, a sense that there must still be something more. "Heaven" is what corresponds to that desire beyond desire and to that searching beyond searching. The mind and the will—despite (or because of) all of their achievements here below—still want definitively to *see*.

In his autobiographical novel *A Portrait of the Artist as a Young Man*, James Joyce told of the encounter between Stephen Daedalus (his literary alter ego) and a beautiful woman standing knee-deep in the water off the Dublin strand. Stephen sees the woman and is immediately entranced by her. He describes the harmonious balance of the various elements that constitute her figure and form. As he is completing the ecstatic appreciation of her beauty, she turns and for a moment looks at Stephen, "suffering" his gaze before turning back to contemplate the open sea. At this the young man exclaims, "Oh heavenly God!" Joyce, who was thoroughly trained in scholastic philosophy and who maintained a lifelong appreciation for Aquinas, has deftly caught the dynamic we've been describing. Precisely at the moment when Stephen possesses something radiantly true and beautiful he comes to an awareness of his longing for the heavenly God. The woman's glance out to the open sea is evocative of the transcendent ordering of the mind and will beyond what they can possibly attain here below. In his first letter to the Corinthians, at the end of the hymn to love in chapter 13, Saint Paul expresses in simple and poetic language that toward which I've been gesturing: "At present we see indistinctly, as in a mirror, but then face to face. At present I know partially; then I shall know fully, as I am fully known" (1 Cor 13:12). Seeing God in the face has accordingly become one of the principal metaphors for this heavenly fulfillment of the heart.

I first laid eyes on the north rose window at Notre Dame Cathedral

Rose window, Notre Dame, Paris. WORD ON FIRE

in Paris on June 12, 1989, the day I arrived in Paris to commence my doctoral studies. Though I was jet-lagged, anxious, and confused, though I barely knew where I was going, I made my way that day through the Latin Quarter to the Ile de la Cité so that I could see the building that I had for so many years loved and savored through photographs. I entered the cathedral, walked up the central aisle, turned left at the transept, and then stood fixed and mesmerized for twenty minutes by the sheer beauty of that window. Every single day that I was in Paris until I returned home for Christmas, I went to that spot and stared. What drew me there so compulsively? The north rose window is strikingly beautiful. Aquinas, who was working in Paris in the thirteenth century and would have known that window when it was brand-new, said that beauty occurs at the intersection of three elements: wholeness, harmony, and radiance. We say something is beautiful—a face, a painting, a golf swing—when it hangs together as one (it has wholeness), when all of its parts work together in consonance (it has harmony), and when it shines forth as an archetype of what such a thing should be (it has radiance).

The great wheel of the north rose window, with its myriad parts in harmonious interconnection and with the sunlight shining through it, certainly qualifies as a beautiful thing. But its beauty is in service of a higher good, for it is meant to be a foretaste of the beauty of the beatific vision. One is supposed, even while looking at it, to look beyond it and say, "Oh heavenly God." One of the clues of this transcendent purpose is in the window's numeric symbolism. Around the central figures of Christ and his mother are eight small circles. Then on the next major row we find sixteen circular images (*medaillons* in French), and on the next twice sixteen, or thirty-two, images, and then finally another row of thirty-two. If we add thirty-two, thirty-two, sixteen, and eight, we arrive at eighty-eight. In a word, the entire window is an artistic meditation on the number eight. Then we recall that eight is a symbol of eternity, since it stands immediately outside of seven, which evokes the seven days of the week, or the completed cycle of time.

Another clue is found in the very complexity and inexhaustibility of the window's composition. Why was I drawn for so many days to look at the rose window? Partly because there was just so much to take in. The vision of God is like that. Saint Bernard said that heaven will slake our thirst, but the very slaking will, paradoxically, make us thirsty for more. We will know all that we want to know, but that very satisfaction will convince us how much we don't know. Thomas Aquinas said that what the saints in heaven grasp for the first time is just *how* incomprehensible God is and therefore just what an adventure the life of heaven will be.

I realize that all of this talk about knowing and seeing can give the impression that the life of heaven is a rather lonely and passive business, like a solitary stroll through an art gallery. Wouldn't even the most fascinating and beautiful vision, we wonder, eventually become tiresome?

This is why it is most important to supplement the image of beatific vision with that of the city, the new Jerusalem. There is nothing passive or individualistic about a city—say, Paris, New York, Rome, San Francisco, or Rio de Janeiro—bustling with energy, life, and creativity. These are places where communal activities and entertainments of all varieties are on offer: business, sports, art, transportation, education, fine dining, and politics. Life in the heavenly Jerusalem is something like that. In union with the angels and saints, our minds, wills, and energies fully alive and properly focused, we will live in thrilling interdependent communion with one another. Because of our sins and the natural conflicts of finite existence, here on earth *communio* is so rare, so hard to achieve; but in the city on high, when we have been raised to a new pitch of perfection and when the self-absorption of sin has been burned away, we will rejoice in one another's accomplishments and delight in the harmony that we can achieve together.

Under this latter rubric, think of heaven as a kind of game, involving many participants gathered together around a common purpose, their powers and energies fully engaged. If you're a fan of football, imagine a beautifully executed touchdown pass; if you prefer basketball, think of a crisply turned fast break; if you like classical music, think of an orchestra working its way through an intricate section of Beethoven's "Emperor" Concerto with verve and panache. And now imagine those types of play being performed in front of a deeply appreciative audience who exult in the sheer beauty of what they are witnessing. And finally picture a city that is filled, night and day, with activities of such rare perfection. That might give you some idea of the heavenly Jerusalem, the house of Jesus's Father in which there are many mansions indeed.

A final image that I would like to consider is that of the new heavens and the new earth. The mere mention of "heaven" awakens, I'm afraid, the incipient Platonism that lies dormant in so many religious people. By Platonism I mean the conviction that there is, metaphysically speaking, a two-tiered universe, with the spiritual realm on top and the material realm very much on the bottom, and the accompanying conviction that the whole point is to escape from the lower into the higher as expeditiously as possible. Many Christians are more Platonist than biblical in that they see the goal of the spiritual life as getting out of this world and "going to heaven," or to put it more precisely, facilitating the soul's departure from the body and its subsequent journey to a purely immaterial realm. But this is not what Christian hope is really about.

The Apostles' Creed concludes with "I believe in . . . the resurrection of the body and life everlasting"; and the Nicene Creed closes with "We look for the resurrection of the dead, and the life of the world to come. Amen." Neither declaration of Christian faith speaks of the conviction that the soul will escape from the body and live forever in a disincarnate state; both speak of resurrection, which involves not the leaving behind of the body but the transfiguration of the body. The risen Jesus appeared very much in an embodied state to his disciples: "touch me and see that I have flesh and bones." The God revealed in the Bible made the physical universe and took infinite delight in it: "he found it all very good." At what a remove this stands from all forms of Gnosticism and Manichaeanism, which hold that the material world is something of a mistake, an offscouring of spirit. Presumably the biblical God who made the good earth has no intention of giving up on it, but rather wants to save it and redeem it. And this is precisely what the language of the resurrection of the body is all about: not an escape from matter but a renewal of it.

What will the resurrected body be like? Drawing inspiration from the Gospel descriptions of the risen Christ, Thomas Aquinas speaks of its *subtilitas* (subtlety), by which he means its capacity to transcend time and space; and of its *claritas* (radiance), by which he means its luminous brilliance; and of its *agilitas* (agility), by which he means its suppleness and athleticism. He imagines the glorified body as a body fully itself but exercising its power at a qualitatively higher degree of perfection. The contemporary theologian John Polkinghorne, who is also a particle physicist, has offered some fascinating speculations in regard to the resurrected body. Relying upon Aquinas's view that the soul is the "form" or patterning energy of the body, he speculates that at death that form is "remembered" by God, preserved in the divine mind, and then reconstituted with a new and immortalized materiality. We might imagine the way in which the "form" of a picture could be preserved in a computer and then downloaded in any number of new instantiations, bigger and more impressive than the original. Because it would be informed by the same pattern, this new body would be continuous with the old one yet be something altogether new, something more splendid and complete. And could this same manner of thinking help us to conceive what a "new heaven and a new earth" might be?

It has been said that the best way to prepare ourselves for life in the world to come is to cultivate our capacity for surprise.

IT'S ALL ABOUT GOD

There was a meeting of German theologians and bishops just prior to the opening of the Second Vatican Council. One of the attendees was the young Joseph Ratzinger, then a promising theologian, later, of course, Pope Benedict XVI. Ratzinger reported that the lively discussion centered on the question of which themes should be treated at the upcoming ecumenical council. In accord with the tenor of the times, many said that ecclesiological issues should be in the forefront: the nature of the church, the role of the laity, the church's engagement with the modern world, and so forth. At the close of an hours-long and sometimes heated conversation, Ratzinger reported, an elderly retired bishop rose unsteadily to his feet and said, "I have listened, brothers, with great interest to this debate, and I agree that issues concerning the church are important ones, but I'm convinced that the council should speak, first and foremost, of God." Then he sat down. In that simple exhortation, Ratzinger said, the participants felt they had heard the voice

of the Holy Spirit. Finally, what the church is about, what councils, theologies, pastoral programs, and liturgies are about, is God. Catholicism
speaks of God or it is a "resounding gong or a clashing cymbal."

My fondest hope is that this modest book has, in a small way, spoken
of God, or perhaps better, that it has shown how God uses Catholicism to
utter his Word. For I am certain that God speaks through the sinuous arguments of Aquinas, through the upward-thrusting lines of the Cologne
Cathedral, through the artfully crafted story of tortured Job, through the
tear-stained pages of Augustine's *Confessions,* through the letters that
Paul wrote from prison, through the profession of faith given by Simon
Bar-jona at Caesarea-Philippi, through a speech offered to puzzled philosophers on the Areopagus in Athens, and through the missionary jour-
neys of Matteo Ricci and Francis Xavier. I am sure that God whispers in
the apse mosaic in San Clemente, in that Noah's ark that is Notre Dame
Cathedral, in the statues of the apostles in the Basilica of St. John Lateran, in the infallible umpiring of the popes, in the Rhapsodic Theatre
of young Karol Wojtyla, and in the rhythmic "we want God" chant of the
Warsaw throng.

And I am convinced that God communicates himself in the angel's
"Ave" to a Galilean girl, in the torch-lit parade in Ephesus in honor of
Theotokos, in the heavenly lady who appeared to an Indian man on his
way to Mass, in what appears to the world to be the utter uselessness
of the sacred Liturgy, in transfigured signs of bread and wine, in the
troubled hearts of two women who left the presence of Pope Leo XIII
in tears, in the Birkenau gas chamber in which a brave and brilliant nun
died, and in a call heard on the way to Darjeeling: "help the poorest of the
poor." I am persuaded that God expresses himself in the electric intensity
of the Sainte-Chapelle, in the dingy coffee shop on 111th Street that became, for a young spiritual seeker fresh from Mass, the Elysian fields, in
the mystical poetry of a Spanish friar madly in love, in the pierced heart
of Teresa of Avila, in the epiphany at the corner of Fourth and Walnut,
in the severity of Lough Derg, in the chants and dances that honor the

young martyrs of Uganda, and in the singing of the fiery Seraphim, burnt by their proximity to the holy.

And I have based my life on the knowledge that God speaks with greatest clarity in the Bethlehem baby, too weak to raise his head but more powerful than Caesar Augustus, in the rabbi who, trumping the Torah itself, told all of us how to find beatitude, in the warrior who picked a fight in the Temple precincts, in the young man, tortured to death on a squalid hill outside Jerusalem, with the words, "Father, forgive them," on his lips, in the risen one who said "Shalom" to those who had abandoned and betrayed him, in Maschiach leshoua, Christ Jesus, the Lord of the nations.

To hear the echo of God's voice in all these things is to be a Catholic.

Index